The Reimagined PhD

The Reimagined PhD

· ·

Navigating Twenty-First Century Humanities Education

EDITED BY LEANNE M. HORINKO, JORDAN M. REED, AND JAMES M. VAN WYCK

Rutgers University Press

New Brunswick, Camden, and Newark, New Jersey, and London

Library of Congress Cataloging-in-Publication Data
Names: Horinko, Leanne M., editor. | Reed, Jordan M., editor. | Van Wyck, James M., editor.
Title: The reimagined PhD: navigating twenty-first century humanities education / Edited by
    Leanne M. Horinko, Jordan M. Reed, and James M. Van Wyck
Other titles: Reimagined Doctor of Philosophy
Description: New Brunswick, New Jersey: Rutgers University Press, [2021] |
    Includes bibliographical references and index.
Identifiers: LCCN 2020047038 | ISBN 9781978809116 (paperback: alk. paper) |
    ISBN 9781978809123 (hardcover: alk. paper) | ISBN 9781978809130 (ePub) |
    ISBN 9781978809147 (mobi) | ISBN 9781978809154 (PDF)
Subjects: LCSH: Doctor of philosophy degree. | Social sciences—Study and teaching
    (Graduate) | Humanities—Study and teaching (Graduate)
Classification: LCC LB2386 .R45 2021 | DDC 378.2—dc23
LC record available at https://lccn.loc.gov/2020047038

A British Cataloging-in-Publication record for this book is available from the British Library.

♾ The paper used in this publication meets the requirements of the American National
Standard for Information Sciences—Permanence of Paper for Printed Library Materials,
ANSI Z39.48-1992.

www.rutgersuniversitypress.org

Manufactured in the United States of America

For my family and friends, whose support made this a reality—LMH
For the mentors who made this book possible—JMR
For my parents, who always encouraged me to take up and read—JVW
For all the humanities PhDs who have and continue to reimagine
the PhD—eds.

Contents

Part II Beyond Plan B: Preparing for What's Next

Foreword

• •

Toward a Sustainable Future

LEONARD CASSUTO

Welcome to *The Reimagined PhD*. The book before you renders the academic workplace in terms at once both bracing and hopeful.

The "bracing" part may be easier to see at first. (Hang on for the "hopeful" part.) Disjunctions are rife throughout the academic profession. The academic job market, never in harmony with its surroundings, now appears more disconnected than ever. Professorships continue to disappear, as administrators convert many of them to full-time positions off the tenure track. Most PhDs enter graduate school hoping to become professors, but as Robert Townsend demonstrates in chapter 1, their chances of achieving that outcome have become statistically remote.

The traditional "publish or perish" dynamic that fueled university presses no longer pertains at a time when libraries purchase fewer books and presses look more eagerly for titles that can make money. As Michael McGandy explains in chapter 3, the prestige and influence economies that govern scholarly publishing decisions these days place different kinds of pressures on authors and publishers that influence them in new and different ways.

If you're a graduate student or recently minted PhD, you might ask, "Where does this leave me?" The answer: in charge. You're in charge of your own graduate education, and its sequel.

Although the chances of landing a tenure-track job are slim, navigating the academic job market is straightforward in ways that are easy to take for granted. All of the notifications of possible job openings are easy to locate in well-known locations, so the necessary information is all within reach. The conventions that govern the process of applying for those positions are, within each discipline, clearly and widely understood. (There are certain variations and nuances that require some insider's knowledge, but advisers usually know them, and in any case, books are out there to help too.)

Because the instructions are already out there, it's easy to give it your best shot—easier than in most other job markets. Yes, it can be maddening to jump through hoop after hoop, to craft multiple kinds of documents for different institutions. My point is simply that the instructions are out there to be followed. You don't have to wonder too much about what schools want, because they're usually telling you explicitly.

The problem, of course, is that there are lots of applicants and very few opportunities, so actually getting an academic job is brutally difficult. That means you have to look elsewhere, in other job markets that aren't as simply laid out as the academic one.

Outside of academia, you have to figure out what you want to do, and then look for a paying opportunity to do it. Most job markets work like that—the orderly presentation in academia is an anomaly. You may once have worked outside of the academy. If you did, you'll remember how much of the job search is up to you: you decide what you're looking for, and how to pursue it.

The simple and bounded search for an academic job causes too many graduate students to *un*learn how to look for other kinds of work. Maybe you haven't worked outside of academia since a summer job during your undergraduate years, or maybe all of your work experience has been as a teacher, tutor, or research assistant. Either way, give it a whirl. People who aren't as educated and talented as you are do it all the time. Even if you never leave academia, you'll have peace of mind when you feel that you can, if you want to. And as Joseph Vukov makes clear in chapter 7, academia is becoming an increasingly public-facing profession, so you need to know how to put yourself before the public whether you leave academia or not.

Maybe you'll look for a job as a stepping stone to another. Perhaps you'll even place that second stone yourself—as Will Fenton, a contributor to this volume, did when he collaborated with his supervisor and invented his own job. I've often noticed how unprepared many graduate students and recent PhDs are to do that. My advice to you: read this book.

The Reimagined PhD opens up the hopeful aspect of the academic workplace. From Augusta Rohrbach, for example, you'll learn that you already have some valuable and useful skills—and how you've been using them all through your graduate career. From Karen S. Wilson and Stephen Aron, you'll learn how to acquire those skills while you're in school. In fact, this book will help you become aware of what you already know—and what you can benefit from going out there to learn.

Here's the most important thing you need to know: You are the CEO of your own graduate education.

As the person at the helm, you have to plot your own course forward. Your advisers can help you steer, but you have to set the direction. The following chapters can help you do that.

To faculty and administrators: you sit on your graduate student's board of advisers, as it were. Your job is to use your experience and knowledge to help the person in charge. You should therefore educate yourself about what your students face so that you can help them design their graduate education and their diverse job search(es). This book will help you do that.

As I write this, the academic world has been turned upside down by the COVID-19 pandemic. The already-straitened academic job market has narrowed further, and pressure on the larger economy has brought forth comparisons to the Great Depression. Career diversity for graduate students has become more necessary than ever.

Call this an action memo. The action that this book calls for isn't specific: it's general forward motion. There's a scarcity of academic jobs, but many more professional—and scholarly—opportunities remain, and more are being created every day by people like you. Use your resources to help yourself figure out what you want to chase, and then go after it.

Fill your space. Do it with vitality and creativity. Take your energy and skills into the world, and do it soon, because society needs them—and you—urgently.

Preface

•••••••••••••••••••••

LEANNE M. HORINKO,

JORDAN M. REED, AND

JAMES M. VAN WYCK

This book is a positive call to action rooted in a grim moment for doctoral education in the humanities. A longitudinal view of the field reveals that this moment is nothing new: there have been long-standing fears over placement, completion rates, and just about every other marker by which we've judged success or failure for PhD programs. There are no satisfactory justifications for bloated time-to-degree numbers, or the circuit of postdoctoral fellowships ending in despair, or the adjunctification of faculty positions that erode higher education's mission from the classroom outward. As we write this preface, a global pandemic has disrupted every corner of higher education, and obliterated what was almost always optimistically described as the "market" for academic jobs. In response, we—editors and contributors alike—argue for and demonstrate how the humanities PhD has, can, and must be reimagined.

A central argument of this volume is that we must not expect a return to a previous steady state. Nor should we want such a return. There is no return to the narrow and flawed ways of preparing doctoral candidates in the humanities. Our reimagining must take us forward, not simply reify the status quo. Our response to the current crises we're facing must also include a reckoning with the fact that the humanities PhD has been underutilized for decades. We believe in a more expansive application of the humanities PhD. The competencies and skills acquired during doctoral training equip humanities PhDs for the questions, problems, and opportunities of the twenty-first century in unparalleled ways. And humanists are needed—now more than ever—in every possible field of endeavor.

We don't hold these beliefs in the abstract: each chapter in this volume focuses on practical ways the value and the applicability of the PhD can be realized, whether you are a PhD student, or whether you work with graduate students as a faculty member or administrator. *The Reimagined PhD* serves up stories of creative professional development programs, meaningful institutional and structural changes, innovative curricular reform, and inspiring digital humanities projects.

This volume builds on previous clarion calls for change in doctoral education.[1] In 2011, for example, James Grossman and Anthony Grafton's "No More Plan B: A Very Modest Proposal for Graduate Programs in History" proposed a cultural shift in graduate education, one that still needs to be fully realized. Noting that a narrow focus on training for tenure-track positions was a "disservice" to students, they pointed to the diverse careers outcomes for history PhDs, including "museum curators, archivists, historians in national parks, investment bankers, international business consultants, high school teachers, community college teachers, foundation officers, editors, journalists, [and] policy analysts at think tanks."[2] This range of outcomes pointed toward the fact that historians—like all PhDs in the humanities—acquire skills that equip them for a wide range of careers.

As the downward trend in the academic job market continues, more academics, graduate programs, and professional organizations have taken up the cause of reimagining doctoral education. Leonard Cassuto's *The Graduate School Mess: What Caused It and How We Can Fix It* laid out fundamental flaws in the system and placed them in historical context. Cassuto's opening sentence asks "Is graduate school 'broken'?" The answer is a definitive "yes" if graduate school is meant to prepare students only to become tenure-track professors in jobs that are scarcer each year. As Cassuto noted, there is a profound need for graduate programs to "revamp their curricula, structures, and standards in a way that prepares today's graduate students for a wider range of employment, not just academia."[3] In short, we begin to fix the mess when faculty, graduate students, and administrators of graduate programs adopt a revitalized raison d'être for twenty-first-century graduate education.

A reimagined PhD cannot be merely a response to the dearth of tenure-track positions. Within the new reality facing doctoral education, one of the more serious shifts that has to continue to occur is the way we judge success and failure. What if we looked at success for humanities PhDs differently? What if we learned to reimagine the ends and means of doctoral preparation so as to allow for more kaleidoscopic outcomes? In a landscape of reimagined PhD training we must attend more carefully to the cultures within higher education (often born and bred within academic departments) that reify the notion that there is one prescribed path for those in doctoral programs—preparing for a tenure-track job—and that all other outcomes are deviations from this norm.

We are convinced that hewing to this limited view of what constitutes successful outcomes for PhDs subordinates and at times even elides the success stories that we see on a daily basis. Humanities PhDs have—despite being largely ignored by the departments from which they emerged—gone on to remarkable successes beyond the academy. They've reimagined themselves and—despite limited institutional support—they've found ways to deploy their training in new and exciting ways. Many contributors to this volume recognize this trajectory as their own.

Career diversity has been happening at the margins: now it needs to be mainstreamed. Until recently, with the emergence and growth of the Graduate Career Consortium and the collating of resources on sites like Imagine PhD, graduate students in the humanities prepared for careers beyond the academy in a kind of shadowy, parallel universe to their doctoral preparation. There were conferences, coursework, and dissertation drafting, and then there were the professional development seminars, the career preparation exercises, and alumni panelists discussing careers beyond academia. These worlds didn't talk to each other, and each suffered because of this disconnect.

As we adopt new metrics for judging success, we must keep in mind that the changes that must come to doctoral education will work best if they make a collective, positive case for the value of the PhD, and do not merely collate a series of responses to the declines we've seen in tenure-track lines. It can't be business as usual, with a few tweaks.

Doctoral education has virtues and flaws that are rooted in institution-specific programs, histories, and experiences. And each doctoral program—and each student—represents a chance to remake it anew. The reimagined PhD thus also requires us to abandon our urge to view flaws in our own graduate programs as solely or primarily the effect of broader systemic issues across higher education—issues that are assumed to be beyond our control. It is time to stop thinking of doctoral programs as cogs in the machine of a discipline and instead view them as distinctive instances that serve their PhD students using the particular resources at their disposal. The work of reimagining the PhD must be systemic and local, worked out in professional associations and particular departments at once, and producing effects that help each PhD find meaningful ways to take their training into the world. Even as we attend to national trends, examine disciplinary data trends, and argue for comprehensive, intra-institutional changes, the reimagined PhD begins at home—in the departments around which so much of the life of a graduate student is centered.

The reimagined PhD recognizes doctoral education as a tool in the hand of the user, not the creation of a tool to be used in a system. PhDs are not created for a specific purpose, namely the tenure track. PhDs must be equipped for a variety of purposes, which they must have wide leeway to construct for themselves. For them, the PhD is not only training for a career. The experiences in graduate school constitute a small part, the beginning, of a long career. With this in mind we must reframe how we view the role of graduate education. Graduate study is professional experience, whether a student ultimately goes on to be a professor or inhabits the wider professional world.

Another part of this change is to see the divide between the academy and the world beyond the academy for what it is: a nonexistent binary. One seemingly innocuous way this manifests itself is in the way we describe the academy using prepositions that indicate some kind of spatial relation between the academy and other spaces. There are careers "in" academia and those "outside" of academia, while others are "on" or "off" the tenure track. Still others are "beyond"—a much better, but still spatially bound concept—the tenure track or academia itself.[4]

Collectively, the chapters that follow show that a range of collaborating stakeholders is what it takes to prepare the twenty-first-century PhD. *The Reimagined PhD* undercuts the insidious notion that career preparation is a zero-sum game in which time spent preparing for a range of careers detracts from professorial training. In doing so, this volume provides practical advice geared to help PhD students, faculty, and administrators incorporate professional skills into graduate training, build professional networks, and prepare PhDs for a range of careers.

Broadly speaking, this book is divided into two sections. The first five chapters make the case that embracing career diversity is essential: diverse career outcomes are a must if we are to have thriving graduate programs and graduate students.

In chapter 1, Robert Townsend draws on extensive statistical studies of the academic job market, bringing the post-2011 picture into focus. Specifically, he looks at the surplus of humanities PhDs on the market compared to the job openings posted annually. From this, it is clear that the job market has not shown signs of improvement. In fact, academic job prospects are possibly even dimmer since Grossman and Grafton's initial article. The numbers—each connecting back to a particular doctoral student with a particular lived experience—highlight the necessity of reimagining the PhD.

Robert Weisbuch draws on wide-ranging administrative experience to outline how systemic improvement can become more attractive for students, faculty, and administrators alike. Building upon the vision set forth by Grossman and Grafton, in chapter 2 Weisbuch suggests ways to create consensus among traditionally recalcitrant constituencies. This consensus is possible through a buffet of customized approaches to broadening the professional outcomes of graduate programs, and each option can be aligned to institutional needs and philosophies.

In chapter 3, Michael McGandy—senior editor at Cornell University Press and editorial director of Three Hills Press—examines how academic publishers maintain the old prestige regime and why it is time to reconsider these dynamics. This reification of an influence imbalance happens when a first-year assistant professor at Harvard with a degree from Stanford is always preferred over the University of Michigan PhD working in a think tank or the associate professor at Towson State with a degree from Penn State. McGandy shares practical professional issues that have arisen with the waning (but not death) of the old prestige regime. Most examples are drawn from his experience as an editor, and these anecdotes illuminate trends, showing how gatekeepers assess quality, authority, and relevance, and point a way forward for a reimagined vision of these processes.

Leonard Cassuto and James M. Van Wyck, in chapter 4, envision how relationships between advisers and advisees can be reimagined. Given the abiding importance of the advisor-advisee relationship, these new practices and attitudes represent a key beachhead for changing graduate programs. Graduate program faculty are often anxious about what advice to give a student who wants to prepare for a range of careers Cassuto and Van Wyck's advice is to create a graduate school experience that centers on graduate students every step of the way.

In the final chapter of the first part, Augusta Rohrbach discusses how to transition field-specific knowledge and activities into the larger research space. She argues that graduate students need to think of themselves as leaders. This important shift in mentality is difficult, she notes, because graduate students often feel disempowered. Drawing on her own career experiences within and beyond academia, Rohrbach shows the ways experiences open to all graduate students can translate in a variety of contexts.

The second section of this book continues to offer concrete suggestions: the last seven chapters highlight ways students, faculty, and administrators can actively cocreate the reimagined PhD and revamp doctoral preparation for the twenty-first century.

In chapter 6, Leanne M. Horinko and Jordan M. Reed point specifically to the experience of first-generation graduate students for inspiration. Drawing on their own experience as first-generation students, Horinko and Reed examine the nascent body of literature highlighting the isolating nature of this experience for graduate students. As it turns out, the profound challenges first-generation graduate students face are heightened versions of the challenges faced by the general graduate student population. Further, the authors highlight programs for first-generation students at Princeton University and the University of Washington as inspiration for graduate programs across the United States.

Joseph Vukov offers practical tips for jumpstarting (and then maintaining) a professional network in graduate school. In doing so, chapter 7 argues that building professional connections within and beyond the academy is not typically a matter of high-stakes networking. Rather, it is a matter of developing a set of practically oriented habits and social skills. In themselves, these habits and skills may seem inconsequential. But taken together and over time, they can help graduate students build a healthy professional network that will support them through graduate school and beyond.

In chapter 8, Melissa Dalgleish provides students, faculty, and administrators the information they need to find and assess the graduate student and postdoc professional development (GSPPD) programming offered at and outside their university. The chapter helps them make strategic decisions about their GSPPD learning and teaches them how to best advocate for more or different GSPPD when what is on offer is limited or lacking. These programs typically focus on transferable skills that are useful in faculty and careers beyond the academy and career development skills that can help students assess and explore their career preferences and future.

Karen Wilson and Stephen Aron outline the goals and results of a new kind of hybrid graduate seminar/workshop, "The Many Professions of History," through two iterations and document its reception by (and influence on) graduate students. The bulk of chapter 9 discusses how the course's focus and organization provide a viable approach for PhD programs in history and other fields to foster career exploration while enhancing students' understanding of the wide applicability of their skill sets. Offering an example of broadening the horizons and networks of graduate students, the chapter presents what happens when students are asked to engage with actual and potential roles of PhDs in twenty-first-century society while collaborating on an applied research project.

Vernita Burrell compels us to consider the ways that reimagining graduate education—and preparing humanities graduate students for a range of careers—requires a reimagination of the graduate pedagogical training. Incorporating her experiences as a community college professor, she argues in chapter 10 that programs that train PhD students in the humanities to teach should not expect them to end up at similar institutions but should instead create bespoke, student-centered pedagogical tracks that align with individual student goals and alumni outcomes—within and beyond academia. She reminds us that pedagogical training in graduate school need not be a homogenous set of activities that prepare humanities PhDs for university-level classroom but rather can be composed of modules focused on discrete skills needed by each PhD, regardless of career outcome. When we consider graduate pedagogical training in the humanities in this way, she argues, it will best serve our graduate students—and the broad array of audiences they'll engage post-PhD.

In chapter 11, William Fenton takes stock of the digital humanities (DH) job market and considers how graduate students might best prepare for a career in this evolving space. First, he describes the state of the DH market by canvassing higher education job boards, speaking with higher education experts, and interviewing DH leaders. After, he shows how DH creates candidates with skills transmissible to tenure-track and nonacademic positions within the academy. Fenton further shows how a DH portfolio can enable candidates to translate their academic work for potential careers at think tanks, consulting firms, galleries, libraries, archives, and museums.

Alexandra Lord explores how students can use internships, work for academic organizations, research, and classwork to build both a CV for an academic position and a resume for a careers beyond the academy. The final chapter also explores how students can navigate within academic culture to determine the type of career they, not their advisors or peers, want. This has ramifications for not just the students themselves but also the faculty and administrators who guide the mission and structure of graduate study at their respective universities.

The stakes are high for graduate students professionally and the institution of graduate study more generally. Ultimately, the benefits of a reimagined PhD transcend the academy itself. Cassuto observed in the closing pages of *The Graduate School Mess* that "we can advocate better for our vocation if humanists work throughout society, not just in universities." He saw a need for "a new higher education ethic."[5] That ethic informs the reimagined PhD that we know can and must emerge as career diversity and wide-ranging doctoral preparation become the norm for the twenty-first century. We hope students, faculty, and administrators alike find inspiration in the chapters that follow and then reimagine graduate education both locally and globally. The time is now, and the stakes are high.

Notes

1   See American Historical Association, "Career Diversity for Historians " (n.d.), https://www.historians.org/career-diversity; Connected Academics (n.d.), https://connect.mla.hcommons.org/.

2   Anthony T. Grafton and Jim Grossman, "No More Plan B: A Very Modest Proposal for Graduate Programs in History," *Perspectives on History*, October 2011, https://www.historians.org/publications-and-directories/perspectives-on-history/october-2011/no-more-plan-b.

3   Leonard Cassuto, *The Graduate School Mess: What Caused It and How We Can Fix It* (Harvard University Press, 2015).

4   James M. Van Wyck, "Academia Is Not a Container." *Inside Higher Ed,* November 2, 2020.

5   Cassuto, *Graduate School Mess*.

The Reimagined PhD

Part 1

A Call to Normalize Careers beyond the Academy

• •

1

An Honest Assessment

●●●●●●●●●●●●●●●●●●●●●

The State of Graduate Education

ROBERT TOWNSEND

In many ways, the new normal for graduate education in the humanities is the old normal. Throughout the twentieth century, humanities graduate programs focused their preparation of new PhDs on academic careers—and most often careers in research universities. Repeatedly, waves of academic hiring were followed by sharply receding waters that left numerous PhDs stranded. This appears in the annual reports of the disciplinary societies in the 1930s, the late 1960s and early 1970s, the 1990s, and again from 2009 to the time of this writing (mid-2020).

The ebbs and flows of the job market are nothing new, and yet they seem to come as a surprise to generation after generation of humanists. Three factors tend to exacerbate the problem and probably need to be placed at the start of any discussion. The academic job market has proven itself time and again to be far more elastic than the annual award of new PhDs in the humanities. For instance, in the modern languages and history, the available academic jobs fell by more than 30 percent in a few years after 1989 and again following the recession in 2008.[1] At the same time, the number of new PhDs managed to rise or hold steady for a decade or more after each collapse.

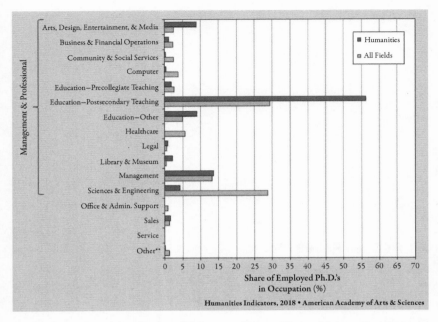

FIG. 1.1 Occupational distribution of PhDs, 2015. (Source: National Science Foundation, 2015 National Survey of College Graduates. Data analyzed and presented by the American Academy of Arts and Sciences' Humanities Indicators.)

The Present Challenge

Sudden swings in the academic job market hit the humanities especially hard because the field is unusually focused on academia as the primary job outcome. As shown in figure 1.1, as of 2015, humanities is the last field in which the vast majority of PhDs are employed in postsecondary teaching. Almost 60 percent of the employed PhDs from the humanities are employed in this area, as compared to less than a third of PhDs in the science fields. It has been two decades or more since the various STEM fields reached the crossover point when a majority of their PhDs were going into jobs outside the professoriate. This was due in large part to the more competitive salaries available in industry for their fields.[2]

Given their reliance on academic teaching jobs, the humanities face a twin set of challenges in the higher education sector. First, the field experienced a profound generational shift from the early 1990s to the mid-2000s, as a large cohort of tenured faculty hired in the late 1960s and early 1970s retired and were replaced by junior faculty who have only just entered mid-career. At the same time, since the recession the number of students majoring in the humanities (and by all accounts, enrolling in humanities courses) has fallen by more than 10 percent in almost every discipline. Viewed as a share of all undergraduate

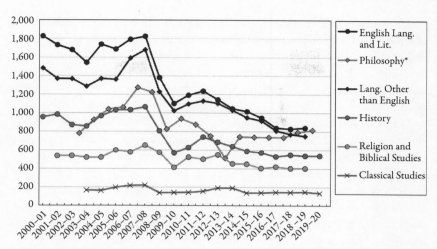

FIG. 1.2 Job advertisements at scholarly societies, 2000–2020. (Source: Information drawn from published data from the national scholarly society for each field. Data analyzed and presented by the American Academy of Arts and Sciences' Humanities Indicators.)

students, the losses for the humanities have been even greater. In 1967, the four largest humanities disciplines—English, history, languages and literatures, other than English, and philosophy—accounted for 17 percent of the bachelor's degrees awarded. As of 2018, they accounted for barely 4 percent of those degrees.

Taken together, these trends made it incredibly difficult to refill the limited number of positions that did come open, much less create pressure for additional tenure lines for humanities faculty. And the trend in job ads at the various scholarly societies bears this out (figure 1.2). After peaking in 2008, the number of job advertisements fell by 30 percent or more within three years in every discipline with available data, and their numbers remain at or below those levels up to the present.

In the past, the humanities have tended to experience extended periods of decline in periods of academic distress (such as the 1970s) and rise again in times of economic prosperity (such as the 1990s). But from an administrator's perspective, it is hard to judge when that might happen or to what degree. In the meantime, given the continued declines in the numbers of undergraduate students in humanities classes, administrators are choosing to hire adjuncts or visiting professors to replace open lines, or choosing to simply shift those positions over to departments where the student population is growing. And that was before colleges and universities crashed into a financial crisis caused by the COVID-19 pandemic, which will make it even more difficult to make the case for tenure lines in a field that was already losing students.

Many in the field attribute the collapse in available jobs to the replacement of tenure lines with adjunct appointments.[3] But the evidence shows that at the end of the previous job crisis in the 1990s, there were more humanities PhDs in tenure-track positions than before. And as of 2008, the major disciplinary societies were reporting nearly unprecedented numbers of tenure-track job openings for new PhDs.

When we just look at people employed in academia with a PhD, we find that about 70 percent of humanities PhD are full-time faculty, about 10 percent are part-time faculty, and the remaining 20 percent are in blended administrative or support roles in academia. This puts the humanities ahead of most other fields in academia, but it also masks some wide disciplinary differences in the field. In the modern language disciplines, the split is closer to 50–50 at four-year colleges according to a 2017 survey by the American Academy, while in history and philosophy, the ratio appears closer to the norm. Even though the number of job openings fell dramatically after 2008, the number of faculty in humanities departments and the share who were employed full-time were largely unchanged as of 2017.[4] Simply put, the problems for the humanities are far larger and more complex than the use of contingent faculty.

The Situation in Doctoral Programs

The recent trend in academic jobs is particularly difficult at the moment because the annual number of doctoral degrees awarded in the humanities has remained fairly stable since 2008, at precisely the same time the available jobs were taking such a dramatic tumble (figure 1.3).

To many observers, this seems irrational given the decline in academic jobs, but at least three factors converged to generate the current situation. Looking back, the number of students entering PhD programs as the recession hit actually increased for a few years, as a large number of people sought refuge in doctoral studies. And it also took a few years for departments to recognize that the crash was not going to be a short-term crisis specifically related to the recession. Indeed, many departments thought they were doing a favor to students by admitting them after the national unemployment rate soared. All these factors have been exacerbated by the amount of time it takes to earn a PhD in the humanities—an average of over seven years across the field. As a result, many of the students completing doctoral programs today started at a time of seeming prosperity in the job market—or at least a moment untainted by the current pessimism in the field.

A secondary effect of the extended time to degree is that, on average, humanities PhDs tend to be about three and a half years older than their counterparts in other fields (about thirty-four). This presents significant opportunity

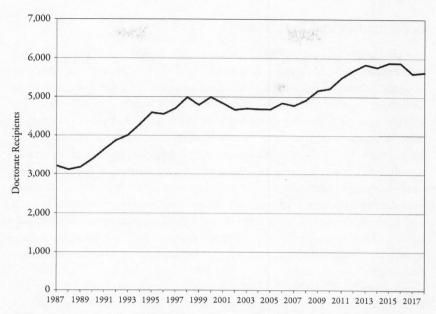

FIG. 1.3 Doctoral degrees awarded in humanities, 1987–2018. (Source: U.S. Department of Education, Integrated Postsecondary Data System. Data analyzed and presented by the American Academy of Arts and Sciences' Humanities Indicators.)

costs in terms of life experiences and potential earnings (as average salaries for faculty members tend to be lower than the salaries of those employed outside of academia). And there are other, more tangible, costs, as well. Looking back over about fifteen years, graduates from the humanities have consistently reported higher levels of debt from their graduate studies than their counterparts in the STEM fields, and the average debt levels have been rising fairly steadily since the recession. As a result, the costs of earning a PhD appear higher for those earning their degrees in the humanities.

The age and cost issues do have a flip side when compared to STEM PhDs. While only about 12 percent of humanities PhDs go on to postdoctoral studies, among graduates from the life and physical sciences that share is generally above 30 percent. So while humanities PhDs are entering the job market, many science PhDs are effectively continuing on in their studies, even though they have the degree. As a result, even though STEM PhDs tend to be considerably younger when they earn their degrees, they are only midway through their training journey. Another version of this in the humanities may be the growing use of adjuncts and signs that humanities PhDs are spending a growing number of years in contingent faculty employment before landing on the tenure track.

Opportunities and Outcomes

The challenges for humanities PhDs are widely known, but finding solutions seems much more challenging. In each of the job crises since the 1960s, the proposed responses have tended to fix on one set of actors as providing the key to a solution: if only departments would admit fewer students, or administrators would create more tenure-track jobs, or scholarly societies would dictate a preferred solution to both of them. In almost every case, these discussions are disconnected from a larger and more complex reality. The power to effect change is widely dispersed. Past efforts to reform doctoral training at the department level—either by shortening the time to degree or preparing doctoral students for a range of possible careers—have tended to flounder as soon as a key faculty leader leaves or the job market improves. Administrators make decisions based on their judgments about their own schools. And even though scholarly societies can articulate best practices, they lack the power to make demands of the others.

The response from the STEM fields is instructive, as they are belatedly acknowledging the change in employment outcomes for their students and have started to reassess the nature of their doctoral training. A recent report from the National Academies of Sciences, Engineering, and Medicine, for instance, noted that their fields have already substantially made a transition into serving jobs outside of academia and called on doctoral programs in the field to adjust their training models accordingly.[5] In the humanities, the American Historical Association and the Modern Language Association have undertaken similar initiatives, and the extended gap between academic jobs and new PhDs—as well as the continuing gap between academic jobs and PhDs—has prompted even elite departments to initiate career diversity programs.

Even in the present climate, I find that many faculty members remain resistant to career diversity programs, as they often argue that there are less expensive paths to careers beyond the academy. While that logic might make sense in a field where every new PhD was guaranteed the academic job for which they are trained, it ignores the historical patterns and the risks for any student undertaking doctoral studies. And even beyond that, it also accepts certain myths about the types of skills that are applicable only to academic employment or careers beyond the academy. According to an analysis of the National Survey of College Graduates, large shares of humanities PhDs in academia are engaged in administrative work, for instance, while among those employed outside of academia, substantial portions report doing traditional research and teaching activities. Assuming that picking up one set of skills or the other comes at the expense of the important work of graduate studies misses the point about the range of potential careers humanities PhDs will have after the degree—regardless of their place of employment.

For those who think these problems can be addressed only by lowering the number of new PhDs being conferred, there is some good news in a recent tracking study of students entering doctoral studies. According to the Council of Graduate Schools, the arts and humanities were nearly alone in seeing a decline in the number of new students—off nearly 3 percent from 2012 to 2017.[6] But the number of students in those programs remains at fairly high levels after more than two decades of rising admissions, so it will be some years before this change will have an impact on the number of new PhDs conferred.

Nevertheless, the recent trends suggest an important potential challenge for current efforts for reform. During the job crises of the 1970s and 1990s, the scholarly societies, doctoral programs, and some funders undertook initiatives similar to the current career diversity efforts. And in both cases, these initiatives largely evaporated when the annual number of new PhDs came back into alignment with the number of academic jobs. While it seems a distant prospect given the annual number of PhDs and the challenges for the humanities in academia, the declining numbers of new doctoral students point to a day when jobs and PhDs will come back into alignment as has been the case in the past. Given past experience, it remains to be seen whether the reform efforts of the present will survive that moment—even among those who know it will be fleeting.

Notes

1 See, e.g., David Laurence, "Demand for New Faculty Members, 1995–2016," *MLA Profession*, Winter 2019, https://profession.mla.org/demand-for-new-faculty-members-1995–2016/, and Robert B. Townsend and Julia Brookins, "The Troubled Academic Job Market for History," *Perspectives on History*, February 5, 2016, https://www.historians.org/publications-and-directories/perspectives-on-history/february-2016/the-troubled-academic-job-market-for-history.

2 Alan Leshner and Layne Scherer, eds., *Revitalizing Graduate STEM Education for the 21st Century* (National Academies Press, 2018).

3 Kevin Carey, "The Bleak Job Landscape of Adjunctopia for PhDs," *New York Times*, March 6, 2020, https://www.nytimes.com/2020/03/05/upshot/academic-job-crisis-phd.html.

4 Humanities Indicators, "The State of the Humanities in Four-Year Colleges and Universities" (American Academy of Arts and Sciences, 2020), https://www.amacad.org/sites/default/files/media/document/2020-05/hds3_the_state_of_the_humanities_in_colleges_and_universities.pdf.

5 Leshner and Scherer, *Revitalizing Graduate STEM Education for the 21st Century*.

6 Hironao Okahana and Enyu Zhou, *Graduate Enrollment and Degrees: 2007 to 2017* (Council of Graduate Schools, 2018).

2

The Liberal Arts at Work

• •

The Engaged PhD

ROBERT WEISBUCH

It's been forty-five years of standing around waiting for a change in doctoral education that would account for the dismal academic labor economy, but as Bob Dylan sang, "You can't rely no more to be standing around and waiting . . . / And there's a slow, slow train coming up around the bend." The MLA and the AHA—the professional organizations of English/foreign languages and history—represent the largest humanities disciplines. Both have established major initiatives that seek to redefine the goal of the PhD away from graduating the next generation of university faculty to graduating experts for all social sectors, the professoriate among them.[1]

Freeing the Doctorate

What are those other sectors? For starters: technology, media, public relations, academic administration, nonprofits, for-profits, and K–12 leadership. But the better answer might be "everything." And that's not just the hopeful, fuzzy feeling of an English professor lucky enough to have scaled the academic ladder. At a Woodrow Wilson National Fellowship Foundation forum, the then-head of Geico, Lou Simpson, noted that humanities PhDs are equipped for "just about anything." Simpson's reasoning was simple: "I can't teach a new employee how to think, write, do research, and teach others, but if someone comes with those skills, I can teach them a set of specific tasks in a few days."

Yet this sentiment—that PhDs can and should prepare for multiple possible careers—hasn't always found a ready reception in academe. A doctoral student in art history I recently met at a group discussion about PhD careers was skeptical. "This discussion makes me nervous," she explained, "I don't want to see the PhD turned into a professional degree."

"It already is that," I hastily blurted. But on reflection I agree with myself. The aim of replicating the faculty is a professional goal more than an intellectual one, and as an accepted goal it has evolved into a Ponzi scheme. I understand and share the pain of confronting the failure of an apprenticeship model that in many ways was lovely. But shouldn't one be made a great deal more nervous by the status quo?

A mere glance at the data can mislead. In my discipline of English, for instance, let's say one thousand new positions are listed for perhaps thirteen hundred graduating doctoral students. Not so bad. But half of those positions are temporary or non-tenure. Meanwhile, there are not only this year's graduates applying for the more promising positions but most of the graduates who did not achieve a permanent position in years past.

The economics have changed: far fewer replicants are required. One result? Our failure rate has soared. Of the students who begin a PhD in the humanities, one in ten will become a tenure-track assistant professor at a research university or selective college. Four or five of the ten will fail to complete the degree, with many exiting only after investing considerable time. The result? The university loses its investment in the student, and the student loses valuable earning years. Worst, our nation sacrifices the creative intelligence of thousands of potential leaders across the social spectrum.

Those who do graduate into this dire market will have spent typically eight years to be awarded a key that opens the door to a room that, for most, doesn't exist. And the training period stretches on and on. After all, why leave when a teaching assistant stipend is better than what comes next: adjuncting at minimum wage levels without benefits? Many see the benefit of slowly trodding through graduate school than taking a more direct route to Career Palookaville. *If replicating faculty is indeed the goal*, universities must then consider whether continuing programs with 80 to 90 percent career failure rate is a justifiable expenditure of university resources.

And while the academic market for bench scientists is healthier than in the humanities and social sciences, the doctoral experience is equally inept. In the STEM disciplines, half of all students do not want academic employment, though programs tend to assume they do. The typical time to degree of six years is lengthened by the near universal requirement of postdocs. The National

Academies of Science and Engineering's well-known screed, the COSEPUP report of 1995, concluded that science PhDs receive training that is "largely a byproduct of policies that support research." The writers of the report are forced to make the following assertion, which one might expect to be taken for granted: "The primary goal of graduate education is the education of students."[2] In the twenty years since the COSEPUP report, we've seen dozens of similar reports urging increases in training grants (that place the student interest at the center) at the expense of a reduction in research grants (awarded to faculty, whereby the graduate student becomes at best an apprentice, at worst cheap labor). Yet the trend has been in the opposite direction.

These are the defensive reasons why a growing minority has urged for years that doctoral degrees become less narrowly professional and at once more purely intellectual and more cosmopolitan. We need PhD programs that are more practically and variously engaged—not eschewing the theoretical but applying learning where apt. We need PhD training that does not fall into the binary trap of dissing either the benefits of a life of learning that are not all immediately translatable into the social realm or a greater interest in their social applicability.

But there is a far more important and positive reason for a broadened goal. The world needs PhDs and the PhD badly needs a more worldly perspective. Interpretation, research, discovery, and knowledge are crucial everywhere. The more hopeful and generous motive for rethinking the PhD is to expand the influence of academic learning throughout society. In reality, this is the doctoral aspect of a general move in the arts and sciences for a more socially engaged concept of colleges and universities, by which education is about more than either self-interest or self-luxuriating. Advocates for a more engaged PhD seek programs that capitalize on the versatility of expertise in the liberal arts disciplines, their enormous range of relevance and use—private and internal, public and political. Any social issue considered without the perspectives of history, the imaginative arts, religion, philosophy, anthropology, and the like—as well as biology, psychology, neuroscience, physics, and chemistry—is a thin-ice discussion prone to slipshod conclusions. In the STEM fields, engaging academic discovery in the ongoing life of a society is called tech transfer. It should apply equally to the humanities, arts, and social sciences. And while we might worry that thinking more about applicability sacrifices the traditional intellectual virtue of standing apart from the mainstream society in order to critique it, why should we settle for *critiquing* when we might play a far greater role in *constructing* the public world?

And on the more mundane level of personal fulfillment, various studies have shown that doctoral graduates who took nonacademic positions not only are happy in them but overwhelmingly affirm the graduate experience as relevant and worthwhile. If we can become more intentional and creative in exploring career outcomes and seek to evolve such efforts from our current practices, I believe that affirmation will grow further.

I also believe that faculty will be surprised twice, both times happily.

First, we will enjoy a great lift to the collective morale when our students graduate into a range of meaningful, consequential careers in and beyond academia. We have it within our compass to achieve years of full and meaningful employment for all of our graduates. Second, we will find that the innovations required to ensure full employment for our graduate students are not nearly as taxing as we may presume. They will alter the basic nature of the degree not radically but in an evolutionary manner. They do not require faculty members to retrain themselves radically. Granted, such reforms require administrative buy-in. For a prime example, in the case of career diversity, we academics do not usually know much about career opportunities beyond the professoriate. Thus a new effort must be undertaken to connect any graduate program to staff members in a career office who are specifically assigned to focus on doctoral students and their prospects—and then to connect both the program and those career staff to the alumni office for the simple reason that any graduate of a particular university (and not just doctoral graduates) has an emotional tie to current students from that same address.

But again, my point is that, apart perhaps from a change in attitude on the part of some members who fail to respect nonacademic employment, we professorial old dogs do not need to learn a bag of new tricks. To illustrate, I'll imagine the different solutions developed by four departments, all responding to the long-standing complaints about the PhD generally and the humanities PhD in particular. The doctorate

- takes too long;
- leads to diminishing career possibilities;
- gets ditched by nearly half the entrants and undercuts the passion of many others;
- leaves students wandering for years without sufficient mentoring;
- narrows interests and refuses the very versatility claimed by advocates of a liberal education;
- provides insufficient training in teaching, especially to a variety of audiences;
- lags behind business, the military, and almost every other social sector in recruiting African American, Hispanic, and Native American students and, in many disciplines, women students;
- and engages in a publishing arms race that results from the academic job shortage and lengthens the already nearly interminable time to degree.

Some of these issues are hardly recent but seem baked into a doctoral model that, as Leonard Cassuto has argued, attempted to combine the German emphasis on research with a soupçon of the British tradition of instruction.[3] As early as 1903, William James famously accused the PhD of creating "three magic letters we dangle before the eyes of their predestined victims, and they swarm to us like moths to an electric flame." And aside from the brief postwar period through the 1960s, James's humane condemnation holds. Indeed, his statement matches the Ponzi scheme of the present. It's a situation the Harvard-based scholar and successor of James, Louis Menand, recently decried: "Lives are warped because of the length and uncertainty of the doctoral education process." In the words of a 2001 report sponsored by the Pew Foundation, "The training doctoral students receive is not what they want, nor does it prepare them for the jobs they take." This constitutes what the Carnegie Fund for the Advancement of Teaching termed "a waste of human talent and energy in activities whose purpose is poorly understood." Derek Bok summed it up in 2013: "PhD programs are woefully out of alignment with the career opportunities available to graduates," and thus "graduate schools are the most poorly administered and badly designed of all the advanced degree programs in the university."[4]

Taking up Bok's challenge, we will look at how four hypothetical programs might decide to confront the future and then consider what it would require in the administration of the university to make any of them a reality. For that is our other question, well stated by David Damrosch several years ago when he chaired Columbia's English department: "If everybody knows what needs to be done, why isn't anyone doing it?"[5]

Four Paths to the Palace of Wisdom

Let's imagine that four humanities programs take a student survey to learn about the real lives of their students, as Damrosch convinced his colleagues in English at Columbia to undertake. Faculty at Columbia were surprised, for instance, to find that most of their students needed to spend many hours a week at a job to support themselves. Armed with findings like this one, faculty can start planning backward by considering the ultimate goals of their graduate training regimen.

Faster Yet Broader

The faculty of one of the four revised programs determine to focus most on a more economical use of student time even while broadening career opportunities. Their TTD (time to degree) program innovations take up Menand's challenge and develop a four-year degree with full financial support leading to a financed postdoc fifth year designed to allow graduates to explore career options via internships. If four years is the expectation for a BA, the TTD program reasons, four years is also a sensible period for developing in gifted students a usable expertise that will, after graduation, continue to develop. One need not consider the doctorate the final stage of intellectual growth.

For clarity, the four years begins with a written and verbally clarified timeline of expectations. In this program, a student will take several courses and complete a final, ambitious project, will teach over a two-year period in assignments that will develop pedagogical abilities, and will spend at least a semester or summer on a stipend to intern at a nonprofessorial off-campus site. For the dissertation, this program again modifies a suggestion from Menand, in this case replacing the book-length final project with a publishable major article. The final project can be either the traditional dissertation or two essays accepted for publication by refereed academic journals. But in either case, this project should be completed over one year and a half, with chapters of the traditional option of a dissertation limited to five and due on particular dates. During this time, mentors agree to meet with their students on a biweekly basis. Mentoring—and monitoring—begins with the first weeks of the first year and remains active throughout. In the postdoc year, another such internship occupies one semester, teaching at a community college or branch campus of a state university the second, thus broadening the ranges of both nonacademic career opportunities and academic ones.

To facilitate the economies in time and resources, the program agrees to admit only that number of students who can be adequately supported financially and that number equal to the number of graduates who secured dignified academic employment upon graduation two years earlier—whichever number is less. (I don't believe in doctoral birth control—surely a nation of 350 million can absorb and benefit from a mere 50,000 annual doctoral graduates. And I worry about the effect on curricular coherence of reducing student numbers. Still, we need to challenge ourselves to enlarge the cohort eventually by eliminating exploitative practices now.)

All-Purpose Pedagogy

In a second program, the faculty opts for a five-year program with a somewhat different goal of graduating educators who can succeed in the full range of institutions of higher learning. In this more traditional but broadened program, one course each in pedagogy, the landscape of higher education, and the history of the specific discipline are required, and two of twelve courses must be taken outside the department to provide academic breadth beyond a single discipline. Beyond that, we borrow from a reform of the 1980s and 1990s, Preparing Future Faculty (PFF), a technique that takes into account that the great majority of those graduates who do achieve academic employment will find themselves at institutions with missions very different from the research university where they are being educated. Thus, parts of two semesters are spent in a teaching assignment at a community college, small college, or public university branch campus, while a few students might consider the option of teaching or aiding in curricular design at a private or public high school. (One of the drawbacks of PFF had been that the graduate students merely "shadowed" faculty at these different institutions rather than actually teaching a course.) To minimize dropouts and meandering, the qualifying exam includes the dissertation prospectus and the curriculum is coordinated with decisions on the nature of the exam so that students prepare on their own only to a reasonable extent. The final project is either the traditional dissertation or a dissertation that emphasizes the consequences to teaching and learning of its discoveries.

The program requires of faculty only that they submit their own teaching to some scrutiny and explain more fully than in the current classroom norm the aims of any assignment. By such means, the program seeks to weaken the habit of secrecy that prevents any number of helpful exchanges on strategies for teaching and learning.

Career Diversity and Student Diversity

A third program goes all out for career diversity. It introduces students to not only the full range of academic options but nonacademic ones as well, and with equal standing. As well as establishing the links forged by the second program with a range of educational institutions, this program also emphasizes academic careers in administration that might allow doctoral graduates some teaching opportunities. Thus, it capitalizes on the fact that every university is a small city and funds internships for graduate students in various offices like Development, Public Relations, Publications, Admissions, and Student Affairs. (While some faculty might worry that they were turning their program into a Higher Ed Policy shop, the majority could remind doubters that this was only one set of options among many, still very much including the professoriate. They argue further that it would be beneficial to all if the leaders of such offices had developed their intellects fully, as the PhD would continue to do.)

But the main effort here is to get beyond the campus—not only this home campus but all of them—to propose impactful work in the social sectors. The overlap between career broadening and public engagement is natural, as doctoral students often bring with them a social idealism. And for these efforts, as noted above, the Career and Alumni offices come into play.

This program complements the goal of initiating students into the full range of academic opportunities by seeking to make the student cohort itself more diverse and representative of the new American population. It invents new forms of outreach in terms of both enrolling students and providing social engagements, a natural combination given the surveys that tell us students of color are especially concerned with applying their learning to social challenges. The program also develops a habit of considering how each new graduate policy and program innovation would best serve underrepresented groups of students. Mentoring would also be expanded beyond dissertation advising; mentors would need to instigate career discussions the moment a student enters the program, and the role of a mentor would extend beyond graduation. Career-long advising shouldn't be unheard of for our PhDs. And because it is unlikely that lifelong academics provide that a holistic perspective on nonacademic positions, an expanded graduate role for career offices is a prime necessity. So too is a revision of admissions standards necessary, so that students with nonacademic career goals are not discriminated against. Imagine how most programs today would react to an applicant who expressed an interest in technology applications of the discipline or in becoming a high school educator rather than in a college post. Finally, in addition to the dissertation, each student is required to explain in lingua franca the importance of her project, perhaps to a panel consisting of an undergraduate, a fellow graduate student in the program, and a graduate student in a largely unrelated discipline. That is because, in such a program as this, the notion of public intellectuals is a natural outgrowth.

All of the Above

A fourth program would combine the efforts of the three others. That's my ideal, and it may be where we end up finally. But we need to allow for short-term and longer-term goals, and any one of the several innovations mentioned here will require much trial-and-error adjustment. (A highly useful list of effective program practices is provided by the Mellon researchers in *Educating Scholars*.)[6] But that is why sophisticated assessment cannot occur only after the fact: the best assessment begins before the development of the redefined program to seek a consensus on goals and a means for learning backward from those goals. So too, the program sets aside retreats for mission time because what is most important is often not most pressing and so requires its own space. No one is prescient; the faculty of any program will need to make many adjustments along the route of an innovative practice, but at least we no longer will be blindly piloting the *Titanic*.

Clearing the Paths

A survey undertaken in 2000 by the National Association of Graduate Students led to this conclusion, anticipating Damrosch: "Instead of brainstorming about what should happen, those involved in enriching grad education should take well-considered suggestions that have already been made and turn those ideas into reality."[7] A report I coauthored with Leonard Cassuto for the Andrew Mellon Foundation reviewed a period of intensive reform activity undertaken by major foundations—Mellon, Woodrow Wilson, Carnegie Mellon University, the University of Washington team, the AGS effort in Preparing Future Faculty, and the Re-envisioning team at the University of Washington—between 1995 and 2005 that sought to treat the problems listed above and found that the results had been unanimously disappointing. Indeed, the researchers of Mellon's effort that expended $90 million in an effort to shorten time to degree and make the humanities doctorate more efficient faced near-total failure after a strenuous decade. They concluded with admirable frankness, "All told, redesigning doctoral education in the humanities has proved harder than imagined at the outset" and specified faculty skepticism as the main deterrent.[8]

In contrast, Carnegie Mellon's initiative was correct in assuming that nothing would get done if not approved by the faculty, and thus it emphasized the idea of self-study. Yet these self-studies resulted in not much change at all. This suggests a nasty joke often told by university leaders.

QUESTION: How many faculty members does it take to change a light bulb?
ANSWER: That light bulb doesn't need changing.

The PhD light bulb does need changing, and the refusal of many faculty to acknowledge that leaves doctoral education in the dark.

Yet shaming faculty is worse than useless. We love teaching gifted doctoral students. Yet those of us at research universities may not see that we are the winners of a competition in which there are far more losers. We have succeeded by ability as well as luck, but our experience is very far from the norm, and we need to internalize that fact rather than to retain a let-them-eat-cake superiority. I believe that many, perhaps most, faculty have not been given the full opportunity to learn about the realities of their students. And while academics may be as self-interested as the next person, we also have a larger dose than usual of idealism. That nobility must be fostered now. But it is also the case that a carrot and a stick can be of use. If faculty recalcitrance is a major roadblock, it may be because the other sharers of the widely held ideal of shared governance—upper administration—are strangely and radically absent. Who will provide the rewards or deprivations that should follow upon the success of a program for its students?

In a Carnegie volume of essays from leaders in the various disciplines of the arts and sciences on reforming the doctorate, Kenneth Prewitt notes that the ideas of his fellow essayists are bold but the means for realizing them are either timid or utterly absent. And he sees this as sadly symptomatic. "The genius of doctoral training in American higher education is that no one is in charge," he writes, but he adds that this is also a great difficulty: "That no one is in charge cannot be taken to mean that no one above the faculty level has responsibilities.... Goals and incentives are misaligned," and this "constitutes a leadership failure."[9]

At many universities, the position of dean of the graduate school doesn't exist or is subordinated to an inferior position in the Office of Research. And even when the office exists, it is typically a deanship with little authority or resources. Left to themselves in this era of dwindling academic employment, the most well-meaning faculty members cannot be expected to take on all the responsibilities required for the redefined PhD, especially in terms of career, as most of us have spent our entire lives in the academy. And more broadly, while faculty do need to become learners themselves about doctoral education, we would be foolish to require our professors to spend great chunks of time away from their pedagogy and scholarship to read up on everything regarding potential innovations.

The universities badly need empowered graduate deans with sufficient resources of money and personnel and authority to encourage student-first practices. We also need this empowered dean for intellectual reasons, for she is that key figure who can explain why the different disciplines exist on the same campus, can crosscut among them to make interdisciplinarity functional—for the great problems of any time do not come labeled in little packets marked "government" or "physics" or "literature."

Lacking a graduate dean, at the very least, a university must assign oversight of doctoral education to a single, authoritative individual with a strong staff and an ample budget. At the same time, where such a structure does not exist, there may still be an opportunity for individual programs to improve if the central administration makes such improvement a cause. James Grossman, the executive director of the American Historical Association, has noted that doctoral education consists of three cohorts—students, faculty, administrators—and that each blames the other two for blocking sensible change. Yet typically, in a situation where a graduate chair feels bullied by a provost who counts only Ivy-like student outcomes as worthy, no one from the department has even opened the conversation to redefine program success more broadly, something most provosts in my experience would welcome. Lacking that understanding and encouragement from upper administration, I am sorry to acknowledge, it would be folly for any program to undertake basic renovation.

A second structural necessity concerns something like making friends—establishing mutual-advantage relationships with other programs, including in the so-called professional schools, and with university offices such as publications, admissions, and development where students might replace retiring staffers or allow for new efforts. And again, in any program intended to foster a more creative sense of career opportunities, a strengthened relation to the Career Office and the Alumni Relations Office is crucial.

A final administrative requirement is for assessment as defined above, which includes but is not limited to far better tracking of graduates (and of students who leave) than most departments now practice. When I briefly served as graduate dean at the University of Michigan, we had reams of information—exit interviews, visits with current students in every program once every three years—but it was hit or miss whether the information we developed was shared with the program's faculty. The first task of a real assessment program is the establishment of goals, and that also requires an expertise that often does not exist within the faculty. Everything will depend on agreed-upon goals (no more than three, with room for subgoals), and that is why the careful choice of a faculty-friendly consultant is key.[10]

Getting There

These consultants are key because reform is hard. Changing one aspect of a program may well lead to considering how it could affect other facets; it may call for greater faculty effort and thus raise the legitimate question of what current faculty activity might be sacrificed to make way for, say, improved mentoring. Consider how much effort would be required should a program determine that graduate students should teach different courses through their years that develop their pedagogy, so that they begin in a closely supervised situation and graduate to more and more independence. Since in many programs the graduate student teaches whatever introductory course the faculty member prefers not to teach, this will require revisions of assignments—and a more generous mindset. Or again, persuading the career office that it must not limit its efforts to undergraduates may require discussion, collaboration, greater mutual understanding, and respect. And whatever the innovation, coordinating the new program and the existing one, so as not to penalize enrolled students, will be essential and laborious.

Most of all, change requires patience and courage. No program will get everything right on the first try, which is the reason for continuing evaluation, so that midcourse corrections can be made. And there will be times when an innovation simply doesn't succeed. One of the reasons for faculty conservatism is the conviction that, at a university, once you start something it is nearly impossible to stop it. To defeat that fear, every new practice should come with clear goals, a specified date for review, and a stated means for discontinuing the practice or changing it.

That's to say we academics are great at locating weaknesses in any idea—I am aware myself that, as I read a proposal, even when I am enthusiastic I find myself looking for problems, like a car with a bias toward one or another curb. We are less great at entrepreneurship, what Daniel Weiss, the head of the Metropolitan Museum of Art, terms "managing risk" rather than avoiding it. That is why we can benefit from an administrative push, but what is best is if we can give ourselves that friendly shove.

How then to engage the faculty while not permitting discussion to delay and even illegitimately replace innovation, rather than to lead to student-first improvements? The Carnegie initiative offered faculty three questions: what are the goals of the program, how does each practice achieve one or another of those goals, and how do you know that this is the case? Coupled with a survey of recent graduates and program leavers and some carefully selected brief readings, these questions provide an apt beginning. But there needs to be a time limit—a summer and a semester at most—to these contemplations and a stated intention of change, so that debate issues in meaningful reform. And again, determining a few major goals and working backwards from them all the way to first steps is essential.

A New World Doctorate

We must reimagine the doctorate so that it opens the doors and windows of the library and lab and classroom to mingle our charged and challenging moment with well-earned traditions, the semipermanent standards of validity, and methods for discovery that have been developed and sustained over decades, in most fields over centuries. The move to a less sheltered doctorate recalls a deep national origin for higher education. That origin informs Emerson's definition in 1837 of the "American scholar" as a public intellectual, "one who raises himself from private considerations and lives on public and illustrious thoughts."

It explains the insistence seven decades later of Woodrow Wilson, president of Wesleyan and Princeton and then the United States, that "we are not put into this world to sit still and know; we are put here to act." Unsurprisingly, the notion of the worldly intellectual runs throughout the writings of John Dewey, as when he urges, "give the pupils something to do, not something to learn; and the doing is of such a nature as to demand thinking. . . . learning naturally results" just as Melville's Ishmael earlier had proclaimed "a whale-ship . . . my Yale College and Harvard." And speaking from the civic side of this partnership, John F. Kennedy declared in 1963, "I look forward to an America which will steadily raise the standards of artistic accomplishment and which will steadily enlarge opportunity for all of our citizens. And I look forward to an America which commands respect throughout the world not only for its strength but for its civilization as well."[11]

Now that is a job description fit for humanists, one that can be enacted in myriad ways in unnumbered contexts. "If your Nerve deny you," Emily Dickinson advises, "go above your Nerve." Slow train coming up around the bend. Deep breath, athletic leap, and we are onto Dylan's train and, thank God, finally moving again, on a route with many fine destinations.

Notes

1 The American Historical Association's Career Diversity initiative and the Modern Language Association's Connected Academics initiative, both funded by the Andrew Mellon Foundation. The former president of the foundation, Earl Lewis, has been highly influential in encouraging a rethinking of doctoral education in the humanities, and James Grossman, the director of the AHA, has been an especially active and effective leader. See, for example, his essay coauthored with Anthony T. Grafton. Anthony T. Grafton and Jim Grossman, "No More Plan B," *Chronicle of Higher Education*, October 9, 2011, https://www.chronicle.com/article/No-More-Plan-B/129293.

2 Committee on Science, Engineering, and Public Policy, *Reshaping the Graduate Education of Scientists and Engineers* (National Academies Press, 1995), 5.

3 See Leonard Cassuto, *The Graduate School Mess: What Caused It and How We Can Fix It* (Harvard University Press, 2015).

4 William James, "The PhD Octopus," *Harvard Monthly*, March 1903; Louis Menand, *The Marketplace of Ideas: Reform and Resistance in the American University* (Norton, 2010), 151–152; Chris M. Golde and Timothy M. Dore, "At Cross Purposes: What the Experiences of Doctoral Students Reveal about Doctoral Education" (Pew Charitable Trusts, 2001), 5, www.phd-survey.org; George E. Walker et al., *The Formation of Scholars: Rethinking Doctoral Education for the Twenty-First Century* (Jossey-Bass, 2008), 5; Derek Bok, *Higher Education in America* (Princeton University Press, 2013), 232, 240.

5 David Damrosch, "Vectors of Change," in *Envisioning the Future of Doctoral Education: Preparing Stewards of the Discipline*, ed. Chris M. Golde and George E. Walker (Jossey-Bass, 2006), 34.

6 Ronald G. Ehrenberg, Harriet Zuckerman, Jeffrey A. Groen, and Sharon M. Brucker, *Educating Scholars: Doctoral Education in the Humanities* (Princeton University Press, 2009), 59–61.

7 Quoted in Donald H. Wulff and Ann E. Austin, *Paths to the Professoriate: Strategies for Enriching the Preparation of Future Faculty* (Jossey-Bass, 2004), 88.

8 Ronald G. Ehrenberg et al., *Educating Scholars: Doctoral Education in the Humanities* (Princeton University Press, 2009), 248.

9 Kenneth Prewitt, "Who Should Do What," in Golde and Walker, *Envisioning the Future of Doctoral Education*, 23–24.

10 Perhaps the most germane book for academics on strategic planning, which emphasizes planning backward from consensual ultimate goals, is David Grant, *The Social Profit Handbook: The Essential Guide to Setting Goals, Assessing Outcomes, and Achieving Success for Mission-Driven Organizations* (Chelsea Green, 2015).

11 Ralph Waldo Emerson, "The American Scholar (1837)," in *Selected Writings*,
    ed. Stephen E. Whicher (Houghton Mifflin, 1957), 73; Wilson Woodrow and
    Arthur S. Link, "Princeton for the National Service (1902)," in *The Papers of
    Woodrow Wilson*, vol. 16 (Princeton University Press, 1972), 228; John Dewey,
    Democracy and Education: Introduction to the Philosophy of Education (Macmillan,
    1916), 181; John F. Kennedy, "Remarks at Amherst College" (1963), http://arts.gov
    /about/kennedy.

3

Diverse Careers, the Waning of the Prestige Regime, and the Rise of the Influence Economy in Academic Publishing

•••••••••••••••••••••

MICHAEL J. McGANDY

As the academic marketplace constricts, and more humanities and social science PhDs are making careers outside of traditional tenure-track positions, a new flexibility is required of gatekeepers like book acquisitions editors. Publishing opportunities are rising for scholars working outside the academy or with so-called alternative careers inside the academy. For authors and editors alike, these are exciting and uncertain times.

The old prestige regime—wherein the first-year assistant professor at Harvard with a doctorate from Stanford is automatically preferred as an author over the University of Toledo PhD working in a think tank—no longer works well for editors. That system—which favors elite credentials and pedigrees of training—leaves out too many talented researchers and authors with high-quality book projects. Moreover, editors are forming new estimations of the value of influence in the public sphere. PhDs on career tracks beyond the academy, because they are in jobs that connect them to the media, public programming, and policy and outreach professionals who can promote and disseminate their work, are oftentimes more likely to command sizeable readerships. These are qualities in authors—summarized by the shorthand term "platform"—that an editor cannot ignore.

The prestige regime has not disappeared, of course, and gatekeepers hold onto old habits of classification even as they establish new systems for decision making. Prestige still works and editors continue to employ its fuzzy metrics when making decisions regarding the potential of book projects and their likely sales. Moreover, influence has a larger effect in the case of some books and a more modest one with others; author platform is not going to make every book budget work, and alternative career scholars with robust professional networks continue to write standard monographs with limited readerships. Editors, who continually assess a welter of book proposals for quality, authority, and relevance, search for better techniques to reduce the noise, focus attention, limit labor, and (fingers crossed) increase book sales.[1] Adding measures of public impact contributes to that work of sorting.

Systems of prestige and economies of influence, while they serve a common function of directing decision making, are distinct from and sometimes in tension with one another. This is a basic uncertainty for editors and authors at this moment. Whereas systems of prestige are largely internal to the academy, economies of influence look to audiences beyond academia. For editors and authors new rules are being written (and then revised and revised again) for determining which authors are well situated to command broader audiences and drive book sales.

University presses are aptly named: they are hosted and often funded by a university and serve the needs of that school as well as other colleges and universities.[2] The key function of university presses is peer review. They vet book-length work prior to publication so as to ensure that only good to excellent scholarship is published, and that that work represents an advance in the relevant field. (Commercial academic presses play a similar role, with key differences pertaining to funding and mission regarding mandatory peer review.)[3] University presses thus uphold the quality of academic discourse. They also confer to scholars in the humanities and social sciences a form of recognition—a published book—that signals to their home institution colleagues and peers around the world that their scholarship is worthy of attention and that they are also worthy of being hired, tenured, and promoted. Academic publishers keep the meritocratic system of colleges and universities functioning. Merit and prestige are so closely connected that any challenge to the centrality of prestige in the world of scholarly publishing will have systematic effects on what sorts of academic work is rewarded and what sorts of scholars are valued.

The developments in the sorting rules used by editors have a real (but indeterminate) effect on the shared work of authors and editors. How to weigh prestige and how to assess influence? What balance are editors striking or what imbalance are they accepting? Authors, even as they pursue their research agendas and draft their book manuscripts, are especially keen to have an estimation on how desirable their work will be in the literary marketplace and what they can do to make their work more sought after. Even as authors are making these plans, often with imperfect information, acquisitions editors are sussing out which sort of author profile will best support a specific sort of book.[4] The strategic work of authors and editors is constant and mutually influencing. Despite this close association, author perceptions of the motivations and goals of editors are often unclear. Many authors are frankly confused—and with reason—about how new demands for relevance fit into the traditional, meritocratic prestige system. They want to succeed at the game—getting a book contract and being published—but the rules of the game are not clear.

The importance of author platform is now commonplace for authors and editors.[5] (Both book proposals and editorial board presentations include explicit consideration of platform.)[6] The problem is that it is not easy to determine which type of platform is best for a given book, and, in the absence of such knowledge, an author will have to make choices regarding how best to spend their time, energy, and, yes, money to establish standing in one or more relevant communities. Ancillary works like conference papers and blog posts are ways to get one's scholarship noticed and establish networks of supporters who, one anticipates, will buy the book when it is published, assign it in class, urge it on friends, write complimentary comments on Amazon, and provide glowing reviews in magazines and journals. So an author will want to know whether attending a core subdisciplinary group meeting makes their work more valuable than, say, writing a blog post or pitching op-eds to newspapers. Which set of readers is to be preferred? An acquisitions editor, if she is being frank, will tell an author to do both—i.e., develop standing within the prestige economy while also establishing themself as a public scholar—so as to cover both potential audiences. But not every or even most authors will be able to do that, and some choices will need to be made.

In this essay, I articulate trends in academic publishing that have resulted in this uncertain moment.[7] More authors with diverse career paths have opportunities to publish important books with academic presses.[8] At the same time, more and more is being asked of all authors in order to demonstrate their reach in the literary marketplace and then to publicize the books to these readerships. My aim here is to offer, based on my twenty years of professional experience at commercial and academic presses, a practical analysis of the decline of the prestige regime and the rise of the influence economy that stops short of guidance of a how-to sort.[9] There are clear trends, and if one follows the lines then some action-guiding conclusions can be reached in the context of individual careers. More generally, in this essay I want to clearly describe the uncertainty and messiness that characterize the work of acquisitions editors and the larger enterprise of academic presses.

This essay was begun prior to the Covid-19 pandemic. The pandemic has put pressure on academic institutions, hobbled traditional publishing practices, and created financial confusion at academic presses. Current events, then, amplify the uncertainty analyzed here. That uncertainty, driven by the crisis in public health, in my preliminary assessment will only amplify the trends charted here.

Acquisitions editors, publicists, and press directors in academic book publishing talk a lot about markets and sales. Managing costs and maximizing income from sales are basic principles that run through conversations that editors have with everyone ranging from authors to university administrators. That dollars-and-cents economy, which we erroneously like to think is distinct from the meritocracy, has long been associated with a system of prestige wherein presses look to acquire the best work from the best authors so as to produce the best books that go on to win the best book prizes.

A reputation for publishing excellent books makes a press highly desirable to authors because the prestige of the press carries over to authors and their books. And the prestige of these prize-winning authors supports the publishing operation. A press must enhance its own brand, a senior editor at a large private university press shared with me. As such, being affiliated with scholars who are on the tenure track and likely to be academic leaders of the future is a sound strategy to maintain or improve its standing in the academic and literary marketplace.[10] In this system, prestige is the basic unit of value, and when functioning properly, that value cycles among presses, the home institutions of presses, authors, and the home institutions of authors. It is not a zero-sum game, but it is one premised on exclusivity with better scholars necessarily publishing with the better presses and the rest of the academic field publishing with the rest of the presses.

The accrual of prestige on the part of an academic press has arguably been more important than profit-and-loss statements for individual books. So long as publishing professionals played our part in the prestige system, then book sales took care of themselves and the financial support of our home institutions would be reliable. As testimony to that, it is no coincidence that the informal gradient of prestige among university presses maps well onto the formal system of classification, by levels of annual income, generated by the Association of University Press. The so-called Group 4 presses, all with annual income in excess of $6 million, are almost uniformly considered the elite presses when assessed by prestige.[11] Financial success has traditionally gone with academic standing.

For decades after World War II the prestige economy of academic publishing worked just fine. When university presses and their commercial counterparts like Palgrave Macmillan and Rowman & Littlefield could count on the reasonable financial health of and steady administrative governance at American colleges and universities, the meritocratic principles of academic presses functioned in concert with meritocratic academic institutions. (Like most other parts of meritocratic systems, the set of relations became, over time, insular; the Bancroft Prize—winning senior scholar at an Ivy League institution would introduce her PhD student to a choice book editor at a top press and the clubby cycle would continue.) Dollars spent on humanities and social science faculty hires worked in tandem with library acquisitions plans that supported those subject areas such that the published books from those faculty members filled the library shelves of colleges and universities across the United States and around the world. The practices of hiring, offering tenure, and granting promotion were in synch with the financial health of presses. The perennial free-rider problem—where the vast majority of colleges and universities benefit from the work of university presses while not paying directly for that common good by supporting their own presses—was mitigated by library spending on university press books by schools without presses.[12]

It is an old story, not in need of much rehearsing, of how this system came undone beginning in the late 1980s.[13] Whether one attributes it to Reagan-era policies, an infatuation with new digital technologies, or the rise of the not-yet-labeled STEM disciplines (and their journals), faculty lines in the humanities and social sciences went unfunded, fewer courses in the humanities and social sciences were taught, fewer books were assigned, and library acquisitions budgets for the books written by those same aspiring faculty members were rolled back. The budgets of academic presses accordingly took a hit, and the hits kept coming. We editors largely remained committed to supporting the prestige regime, chasing after the best students of the best scholars and aiming to publish books that would win the best prizes on offer in the academy. But we also saw our sales drop and witnessed, even as we continued to develop our lists, retrenchment and austerity at our presses. Prestige was not dead in the humanities and social sciences. Prestige was not even discredited. It just no longer was sufficient to pay the bills.

The failure of the prestige regime in academic departments, libraries, and presses had three related effects.

- First, doctoral students who could not get tenure-track jobs or even steady employment in universities sought out careers beyond the tenure track.[14] Years of academic training were channeled into nonteaching jobs and applied to support nonacademic institutions often with broad public missions. There was, in effect, a brain drain in the humanities and social sciences.

- Second, academic presses had to establish new economic models and reconfigure expectations regarding the books that editors acquire. With library budgets for books in free fall beginning in the 2010s, book sales outside the academy were deemed necessary to make any title's profit-and-loss statement work. It was around this time that editors began talking with scholarly authors—including authors of first books based on dissertations—about so-called crossover books with an emphasis on the interests of vaguely identified educated lay readers.
- Third, the coinage of terms like "outward facing," "translational research," and "publicly engaged scholarship" came at just this time as departments in the humanities and social sciences, with the support of administrators, sought ways to establish and then magnify the impact of faculty scholarship beyond the academy.

These three effects describe an incipient and informal system in which faculty, administrators, and editors were all looking outside the academy to justify their academic training, defend their institutions, and balance their budgets.

The demand for relevance has resulted in the rise of influence as a sometime companion to and sometime competitor with academic prestige. The intersection of academic prestige with public influence is nothing new. (Consider the careers of scholars like historian Drew Gilpin Faust, economist Joseph Stiglitz, and sociologist Elijah Anderson; years of acclaimed academic scholarship made each of them a sought-after commentator, consultant, and leader in the public sphere.) What is novel about the relationship of prestige and influence in the 2010s and 2020s is how influence operates on its own terms, has its own spheres, and accrues its own rewards. Influence is now as often achieved by stepping outside the prestige system of the academy as it is by building up a reputation inside the academy. Moreover, many of the key venues and institutions of the influence economy are not controlled by academic institutions.

In the influence economy, success is measured by the capacity one has to set the agenda for discussion of public matters. As an editor who is active on Twitter, no doubt my assessment of the importance of that medium is exaggerated. Allowing for that, it strikes me as necessary to be on Twitter in order to steer early critical conversations, introduce one's opinion as relevant, and then establish a key node (e.g., have you thought about that in *this* way?) in the ongoing conversation on Twitter and other media. Those verbs—*steering, introducing,* and *establishing*—all have their actuality in public discourse and not in scholarship. Scholarship will be referred to and it will be deployed in argument, but in the influence economy no one is waiting on the next research agenda. People on Twitter, people who are adding to and reading the comments on op-eds, people downloading podcasts—they are all looking to get direction that will shape their thinking. They will later seek out the matter itself—the datasets or the historical argument—but first they want a frame for their thought and action. Those who are successful in the influence economy provide just that. And that work is largely being done in media other than peer-reviewed books and journal articles.

An ideal author in the influence economy will do more than a few of the following:

- speak publicly in contexts beyond the academy;
- contribute to Twitter, Instagram, and/or TikTok;
- contribute regularly to current events blogs and write op-eds for legacy media;
- be listed by a home institution or other organization as an expert for media contacts in new media like podcasts and legacy media;
- serve as a partner or trustee with one or more relevant nonprofit organizations;
- stand as a public advocate for a cause allied to a research and writing agenda.

This list could be extended, and as any public scholar will tell you, keeping up with Twitter and being a strategic op-ed writer require significant amounts of time and constant attention.[15] Indeed what even this short list shows is how much work is required to be a vital part of the influence economy and how different that work is from the traditional labor of teaching, researching, and writing associated with developing one's stature in an academic subdiscipline.[16] This also underscores how academic uses of social media—for promoting talks, asking for help with syllabi, and the like—is a different employment of these technologies than those that are part of the influence economy. The spheres of influence and prestige are not contrary to one another. They are, however, distinct, and success in each area requires scholars to develop different skills, address different audiences, and seek different outcomes for the reception of their scholarship.

Even as we seek out excellent scholarship certified by the meritocracy of the prestige regime, editors are looking to networks of influence to boost the reception of that work. (And we are also looking for books that cannot be seen as scholarly contributions but are exclusively oriented to achieve public impact.) Academic authors, goaded by administrators with new metrics for relevance and tasked with encouraging translational research, are often leading the way.[17] As an executive editor at a large public university press related, "Regardless of career trajectory of the author, a platform and the capacity to boost visibility for their work is really a huge positive." This editor noted that no matter the intrinsic quality of the work—whether it is groundbreaking and beautifully wrought—if the author doesn't "have some level of following on social media and beyond, then our own promotional efforts become more of an uphill struggle."[18] Another executive editor, at a large private university press, underlined this point, sharing that "when an author can use an extensive network to help get the word out not merely among her colleagues but to the wider world, we can see that reflected in sales and publicity attention." This editor added that the extra help with marketing "makes no difference in terms of vetting the project, but it is a bonus when considering projects to sign up."[19] But while it does not figure into peer review (where the meritocratic model still reigns), platform (and the associated prospective sales) may be a key consideration as to whether a book manuscript even goes out to peer review and thus has a chance for contract. As gatekeepers, acquiring editors are assessing influence at that very first threshold.

Once through that initial door, authors are asked to keep paying out services to maintain their fund of relevance. Indeed, one of the trends in academic publishing has been to rely on authors to engage closely with and sometimes lead marketing efforts. Some of this has been guided by common sense—i.e., the author actually knows (and has the email addresses of) his core audience, and personal promotions are more effective than those launched by a marketing assistant whose email message might get caught in a spam filter. But the push to have the author lead is also testimony to years of retrenchment when most academic presses have tried to do more with less and more again with even less. At this moment of tight budgets and uncertain revenues, if an author does not do some key things to market his book they just might not get done. In that context, platform is synonymous with effective marketing itself, and that puts all the work of establishing relevance on the author.

The baseline labor of acquiring editors is finding, developing, and publishing work that develops scholarly disciplines. But that work, in itself, is not sufficient to make budget. Too many first books based on revised dissertations do not break even, and too many scholarly works by midlevel or even senior scholars just scrape by financially.[20] The university administrators who sign our paychecks are more eager to know what public partnerships we have formed than how many tenure books we have sponsored. Like our authors, editors are feeling the pressure to be relevant.

Editors are joining the economy of influence by seeking out authors with profiles that register in the public sphere and then encouraging them to develop their work so as to have an impact beyond the academy. As an acquisitions editor at a midsize public university press commented, this trend is "encouraging us to broaden our definition of who belongs in academia and who can publish books with university presses." This editor reported seeing "growing numbers of university administrators, lawyers, archivists, librarians, museum specialists, and other non-tenure-track staff members" proposing books. This new openness and an expanding pool of authors are certainly positive signs and offer the prospect, as this editor stated, of "more conversations, more research, more knowledge, and more engagement."[21]

Judging from the assessments of my acquisitions colleagues at other university presses, the influence economy is working well or at least as well as the old prestige regime. That may be so. I am hardly in a position to argue against my more sanguine colleagues because, in the professional community of the Association of University Presses, we lack hard numbers on or official assessments of what is driving acquisitions trends and fostering publishing success. Lacking those, acquisitions editors like me fall back on anecdote and personal experience. My take on the trends giving rise to the influence economy and the decline of the prestige regime is that they are in tension, and the tensions are posing new challenges for authors and editors even as new opportunities are created.

First, it must be noted that a scholar pursuing relevance ignores the prestige regime at their peril. This is particularly true of younger scholars who have yet to develop a robust network outside the academy. Administrators, senior department faculty, and editors all tend conservatively to approach relevance as the plus to a solid academic CV. Developing a profile in the world of prestige is a foundation on which one can build a larger reputation in the influence economy. For an editor like myself, the solid CV and a reliable set of relations in the academy are assurance that the book will review well in the scholarly journals and that people will buy and assign the book as a professional courtesy that is part of cultivating and maintaining good relations within a community of scholars. The scholars who fails to pay heed to these folkways of the academy may see their book neglected by journals (no one jumps to review the book) and passed over by readers. Knowing this, editors rightfully worry that the books of authors working outside the prestige regime will not sell as well as the books of those who have played the prestige game well.

I certainly can associate solid sales in the academy to having access to and cultivating the right prestige networks. And I can correlate a failure to do that with poor sales in the academy. An executive editor at a large university press has had similar experiences, noting that PhDs beyond academia who "are not present in those communities or have dwindling networks of partners or visibility (whether on campus or at conferences)" make publishing the book more challenging. (Another editor reminded me, however, that in some fields like diplomatic history and military history scholars associated with think tanks or the federal government are common and they stay well connected to relevant academic communities; so differences in fields and subfields matter here.)[22] This person recalled that, when working at another large university press, senior managers "wondered how the lack of a clear academic affiliation would impact the book's market and potential in the long run." Their questions, often framed along the lines of "What does this Plan B track do for us?" may have been crass. But, as this editor noted, the data showed that the books of authors without academic affiliations consistently sold less well.[23]

Of course, an author who is very successful in the influence economy can compensate for a lack of standing in the academy. But that means that she has to have already achieved that success and, as the earlier description of the desirable author who is relevant outside of the mainline scholarly community shows, it is no easy thing to attain that standing. So any presumed equity between tenure-track scholars working the prestige system and alternative career scholars laboring in the influence economy ignores the basic difference of their starting points. With the right PhD, a scholar takes his first job already well positioned in the prestige system. With the right PhD, a scholar taking an alternative route is beginning from scratch and has to amass a whole new set of connections in order to be able to activate the power of relevance.

Moreover, once achieved, influence has to be maintained. The work of tapping into trends of relevance and ensuring one's own relevance as a scholar is ceaseless. Track the Twitter feeds of the most influential of scholars in the humanities and social sciences or consider their public speaking (in person and for podcasts and radio interviews) schedules, and a reasonable response is to wonder how they get any research done. They do, of course, and they also continue to write books. Their success, and the tireless activity that makes it possible, shows that scholars working in the influence economy cannot rest on padded CVs and cannot let too many news cycles pass them by.

The labor of being relevant is daunting, and when it is achieved the very fact of success might be held against an author. Some editors frankly wonder if a scholar can do both well—be a scholar and a pundit. As one senior editor at a midsize private university press commented, "I do not doubt that there are enhancements of reputation and impact to be made through these channels, but they do not figure in the decision-making on books that I sponsor." This person went on to state that "when I see scholars whose social-media presence is to my mind excessive, I worry. I think the term 'public intellectual' is overused, and even suspect."[24] Meritocracy has its problems, but editors know how it works and we can count on the scholarly goods it produces. Pushing for influence, by contrast, can seem risky.

The senior scholar ensconced in an endowed chair, while a bit of a stereotype, remains a valuable asset in the prestige regime. Administrators in higher education push for outward-facing scholarship and translational research, but they still substantially reward basic scholarship and continue to recognize standing in disciplines as fundamental to the university. So the scholar with the prize-winning first book will, by the time she is an associate professor and developing her second or third book project, likely have a pot of funds for research and even some that she can throw at graphics for her book and perhaps enough for a cash subvention to make the book budget look better for her chosen press. (In this regard, it is worth underlining the importance of subventions to making individual book budgets work and keeping whole presses running at something like breakeven.) She may not be active on Twitter and may not be adept at connecting her research to headlines, but this associate professor knows how to work the academic and scholarly publishing systems. The prestige regime, as negotiated by such an associate professor, still offers a breakeven proposition for an academic press. And for university presses breakeven is financial success. The books from junior scholars in the academy or pursuing careers outside the tenure track, though, seldom get to breakeven.

As much as university presses (among the larger cohort of academic presses) have stepped forward into the influence economy, we still see our standing connected to the estimation in which we are held by our home institutions and by the academy more generally.[25] More and more we look to align our lists with the subject area expertise for which our home institutions are best known. Increasingly we are publishing work in open-access channels (e.g., the Toward an Open Monograph Ecosystem and Sustainable History Monograph Pilot programs) and for distribution through aggregator services (i.e., Project MUSE, JSTOR, De Gruyter). Both of these trends in distribution are more associated with the prestige regime than the influence economy. They are not about the presumed payoff of publishing relevant books—with above-average books sales and the recognition of driving public conversation. Rather the rise of open access and aggregators is about scholarly communication. At university presses, no matter the rise of the influence economy, economic basics like financial support from home institutions and the income from the use (but, note, no longer the *sale*) of our books are tied to the prestige regime.

Finally, and further underscoring the tension between promoting public relevance and building scholarship, the influence economy is not aligned with the credentialing function that academic presses serve for hiring, tenure, and promotion. For most every tenure post in the humanities and for many in the social sciences a successfully published book is necessary for promotion to associate professor and highly desired for tenure. At academic presses, roughly half of the books we publish are first books that are needed to establish a person in the prestige regime. While it is true that university administrators seldom praise academic presses for keeping this system running—and, to be frank, they have intentionally defunded this system by slashing library acquisitions budgets for books in the humanities and social sciences—they fully expect the accreditation system to keep running to serve their faculty. But each slot on our limited lists of books that goes to a scholar pursuing a career outside the academy means there is one less slot for an assistant professor who needs a published book for tenure. The situation is not quite zero-sum, but academic presses with limited resources cannot just keep adding books to our lists.

The relationship between these two missions is unstable. The influence of economy shows great promise but also requires a tremendous amount of work on the part of the author and requires academic presses to push the limits of traditional practices and standards. The prestige regime is tried and true, but it does not pay the bills and appears to disregard new administrative demands to show relevance and support translational research. Despite these tensions, authors and editors must decide which way specific book projects will be framed and which audiences to which to aspire.

I think it is shortsighted to assess the role of influence as a bit of polish applied at the end of the process and mostly a concern for marketing. Estimations regarding influence are affecting which books acquisitions editors accept into the peer-review process and which ones we are actively commissioning. As before, sales potential and the role of platform figure into the earliest assessments of book projects.

We also need to consider the impact of the number of each type of author on our lists. An acquiring editor who goes all-in on relevance will have some explaining to do as to why she is turning away so many revised dissertations and passing up on feeding the scholarly system with content. The editor who hews to the tried-and-true prestige system will be asked why he cannot find some books that sell better and why he is not promoting translational research.

Most editors, of course, strike a balance between the two missions, and their middle position can be confounding for authors who feel they must make a choice between the prestige system and the economy of influence. When an editor encourages an author to see the two systems as complementary, what he is asking the author to do is effectively double her work—that is, do everything to have a solid position in the prestige system and then build a public platform of value in the influence economy. That is easily requested but hard to achieve. As an acquisitions editor at a midsize public university press reflected on working with PhDs beyond the tenure track, "I've found that sometimes I need to build extra time into the schedule to give these authors an opportunity to write and revise, because they're often working full-time jobs at the same time as researching and writing." This editor went on to underline the basic fact that "without institutional support, researching and writing can be difficult."[26]

Evaluating the status of the influence economy in 2021, I would say that *relevance* is the watchword of publishing, and *uncertain* is its role in academic publishing. For publishing professionals and, in specific, acquisitions editors it comes down to financial numbers and institutional and personal ethics.

The numbers are pretty clear and provide direction to acquisitions editors acting as gatekeepers. Seeking to publish books that are more relevant and have readerships outside the academy is necessary to bolster income at a time when we are seeing continued declines in once-staple markets like library purchases and course adoptions. Income from aggregators like JSTOR is substantial, but academic presses need to maintain a diverse portfolio of books for different readerships that are sold, as we like to say, in different channels. Books that are driven by relevance or fit neatly into current events offer sales potential that most academic books that forthrightly contribute to the literature cannot. They also appeal to different readerships. Some of these relevant books will flop, of course, and sometimes presses will pay, in the form of cash advances, too much for them; their potential is significant enough to warrant staying the course and pursuing relevant work that addresses readers beyond the academy and is sometimes authored by experts outside the academy.

Those numbers, measured in actual and potential sales, mean that editors will be open to and sometimes actively court authors working outside the academy and active in the economy of influence. PhDs working beyond the academy are a key part of a cohort of likely authors—including journalists, activists, and legal and medical experts—who are plugged into this new system, can write with authority, and can then effectively get the word out about their books.

There are, however, another set of numbers beyond sales figures that guide what acquisitions editors should be thinking. Alternative career authors are also readers and book buyers. Keeping PhDs beyond the tenure track engaged with the production of knowledge and tied into the academic publishing world is a way to ensure that this cohort remains a set of active book buyers. As much as an editor wants to tap a successful scholar in the economy of influence for his next book, that editor should want to make sure that that scholar thinks that academic presses are still relevant to his reading for work and pleasure. The demonstrated drain of knowledge and experience that career diversity have signified for the academy also represents a drain of readers for academic publishers.

So there are clear economic incentives for academic presses to participate in the influence economy and cultivate those scholars who contribute to its existence while working outside the academy. There are also ethical issues to consider, and these too favor support of PhDs beyond the academy. For even when we are not chasing the promise of improved sales, acquisitions editors have a responsibility to publish the best scholarship and best books they can find that support their presses' missions and build their specific lists. "I've always looked at the inherent qualities of manuscripts, no matter the author credentials," said a senior editor with a long career at midsize commercial academic presses. "I try to stay alert to the fact that there are many excellent scholars among nontenured faculty."[27] The prestige regime is a meritocracy that, like all such systems, can degenerate into a club that unfairly favors one set of accomplished scholars over another. As editors and gatekeepers, we have a charge to develop the best books no matter an author's background or regardless of nontraditional experience represented on her CV. In that broader context, in which ethnic, racial, gender, sexual, and socioeconomic forms of diversity are highlighted and cultivated, we need to add the factor of career diversity. The idea of open knowledge is heuristic, no doubt, but it is a useful ideal for editors and their presses.

The ethical issue of inclusion also applies in the economy of influence, which can become almost as insular as the world that runs on prestige. As one executive editor at a large private university press reminded me, "We frequently publish books where the author has a very limited platform, whether inside or outside the academy, and we see one of our services as a publisher to help the author build that platform through publishing their work."[28] Our work at academic presses should be to introduce people to relevant conversations and not just ride the name recognition of already known figures toward more influence and greater book sales. We should not aspire to create an alternative salon of relevance to match the club of prestige.

Editors then have good reasons to see prestige and influence within a rubric of both/and. If we have both qualities in a single author, there is good reason to think the book will do well inside and outside the academy. And prestige is not a drag on influence; the scholar with impeccable bona fides in the academy can be relevant so long as she puts in the work.

The emphasis on *work* is key here. For authors, I think the relationship of prestige and influence is more complicated than for editors, and scarcity of time, energy, and money will force hard choices. Editors will encourage a both-end approach in which PhDs beyond the tenure track develop their academic and public profiles at the same time. That encouragement then meets with the facts of finitude in which authors need to decide between spending on conference travel and paying for personal websites or between writing articles for academic journals and writing and pitching op-eds. PhDs beyond the tenure track will also have to grapple with the fact that the rush after relevance on the part of editors has been guided by a desire for work that reaches beyond the academy and has the potential to be popular. What of the work of PhDs beyond the tenure track who are writing for scholars and forthrightly contributing to the literature? Their day jobs at think tanks or in museums might give them entrée with the general public and a good feel for conveying relevance, but their explicitly scholarly work is not easily supported by a good profile in the economy of influence. What chance do they have to interest an editor in their book projects?

Authors need to stick to their principles and remain true to the reasons they embarked on their book projects. The literary marketplace is uncertain at best, and editors are pursuing acquisitions strategies that mix the values of the prestige system with those of the influence economy. The academic literary marketplace is, frankly, a bit of a mess. So, for the PhD beyond the tenure track, there is little sense in putting a finger in the air; the winds shift too often and vary in velocity from press to press and even editor to editor at a single press.

A PhD beyond the tenure track who is committed to being a force in the influence economy will want to be an active participant in public discussion and write books that are meant to have impact outside the academy. Acquisitions editors will be waiting to hear from her about her work. A so-called "alt-ac" scholar with an influential day job who wants to pursue academic scholarship will need to be more strategic and ready to face the skepticism of editors who will wonder how his work will fare when his connections in the academy are limited and waning. Grappling with those challenges, emphasizing influence in some cases and prestige in others, will require a good understanding of the complex academic publishing world.

Once a work passes early tests from an editor, is reviewed, and then is developed under contract, an acquiring editor will collaborate with that author to make the book excellent according to the appropriate standards. As an executive editor at a large private university press stated, "In terms of project development, I would say that the author's goals for the book matter, be it a scholar who identifies as on an alternative career track or who is intentionally writing for a particular audience regardless of rank/position." This person added, "It helps to know what the author's hopes and dreams for a book are and to be able to gauge whether those are goals the press can realistically help an author reach."[29] With a modicum of self-knowledge, some savvy, and a good support network a strategy can be developed, and a research and writing career can be maintained that runs parallel to a scholar's public career.[30] Editors are there to support those aspirations.

The uncertainty of the present moment is not an accident, and it certainly is not the product of the fickle tastes of acquisitions editors. It is built into the dollars-and-cents economy of academic publishing and other complex trends in the developing missions of the academy.[31] Clear direction awaits thoughtful decisions on the part of university administrators as to what they want from their faculty and what place university presses (and to some degree commercial academic presses) fit into the academic mission. That way we editors would understand better how to balance the worlds and sometime competing interests of the system of prestige and the influence economy. Until then, editors and authors will muddle along and enjoy some of the excitement that comes with the revision of institutions, standards, and expectations. As we muddle along, it is incumbent on all of us to be honest about what we expect our books to achieve and what we require our authors to do.

Notes

I thank Eric Crahan, Nicole Hemmer, Alison E. Isenberg, Derek Krissoff, Dylan Ruediger, and Karen Wulf for reading earlier drafts of this essay and for their insightful comments. This essay was conceived and drafted in full prior to the COVID-19 pandemic. The economic effects of the pandemic surely will make the narrow career goal of securing a professorial position still more unlikely for the majority of doctoral graduates, but it also may provide the impetus for accelerating the move to a student-centered, career-diverse, and socially engaged PhD.

1   See the essays in Peter Ginna's edited volume, *What Editors Do: The Art, Craft, and Business of Book Editing* (University of Chicago Press, 2017), for descriptions of all facets of an acquisitions editor's work.

2   For basic information on university presses, see the website of the Association of University Presses, https://aupresses.org/.

3   An example of a commercial academic press is Rowman & Littlefield. For this essay, the place that larger commercial presses with strong lists in the humanities and social sciences have—e.g., Knopf, Basic, Norton—is not considered.

4   In this essay, the place of teaching and administrative work on the part of scholars in the academy is not highlighted. For a textured composite portrait of faculty experience and responsibilities beyond research and writing, see the edited volume from Robert Zemsky, Gregory R Wegner, and Ann J. Duffield, *Making Sense of the College Curriculum: Faculty Stories of Change, Conflict, and Accommodation* (Rutgers University Press, 2018).

5   A search for "author platform" will turn up tens of hits, most of them useful. Jane Friedman's summary account, bundled in with advice on how to develop an author platform, is succinct and helpful, July 25, 2016, https://www.janefriedman.com/author-platform-definition/. See also her book, *The Business of Being a Writer* (University of Chicago Press, 2018).

6   Correspondence, Editor H, April 12, 2019. In order for each editor quoted in this essay to speak freely, their comments are listed here tied to a letter rather than their actual name.

7   My take on the state of academic publishing and the place of alternative career scholars is informed by many conversations, some of which are used in this essay. My survey of the opinions of colleagues was highly informal and incomplete. I collected ten responses from acquisition editors with varying experience in terms of time of service (first acquisitions editor job to executive editors) and types of press. All are editors in the humanities and social sciences; seven of them work at university presses and three at commercial academic presses. Their opinions here are meant to be illustrative of different opinions on key issues pertaining to alternative career authors. They are not mean to be definitive or statistically significant.

8   More professional academic organizations are developing outlooks on career diversity and making it part of the data they collect on organization members and a facet of the services they offer to members. In my experience, the American Historical Association has a model program, https://www.historians.org/jobs-and-professional-development/career-diversity-for-historians, regarding career diversity.

9   There is no lack of excellent books that direct authors on how to develop writing projects, revise dissertations, and pitch and successfully publish books. William Germano's *Getting It Published: A Guide for Scholars and Anyone Else Serious about Serious Books*, 3rd ed. (University of Chicago Press, 2016) remains the class of its field. I also recommend Susan Rabiner and Alfred Fortunato's *Thinking Like Your Editor: How to Write Great Serious Nonfiction—and Get It Published* (W. W. Norton, 2003), Germano's *From Dissertation to Book*, 2nd ed. (University of Chicago Press, 2013), and Beth Luey's *Revising Your Dissertation: Advice from Leading Editors* (University of California Press, 2007).

10   Correspondence, Editor B, January 27, 2019.

11   List of university presses, identified by their income bracket, provided by Lynn A. Benedetto, Director Finance and Production, Cornell University Press. For a

deeper analysis of the types and position of different university presses, see
Robert C. Schonfeld's "A Taxonomy of University Presses Today," The Scholarly
Kitchen, October 13, 2016, https://scholarlykitchen.sspnet.org/2016/10/13/a
-taxonomy-of-university-presses-today/.

12 The Association of University Presses counts 140 institutions, the vast majority
U.S. based, as members. In 2019, *U.S. News & World Report* found there to be
more than 4,000 degree-granting institutions in American higher education. See
"A Guide to the Changing Number of U.S. Universities," *U.S. News & World
Report*, February 15, 2019, https://www.usnews.com/education/best-colleges
/articles/2019-02-15/how-many-universities-are-in-the-us-and-why-that-number-is
-changing; accessed July 24, 2020. For an overview on free riding in scholarly
book publishing, see Paul N. Courant and Terri Geitgey, "Preliminary Examination of 'Free Riding' in US Monograph Publication," *Journal of Electronic
Publishing* 19, no. 1 (Summer 2016), https://quod.lib.umich.edu/j/jep/3336451
.0019.101?view=text;rgn=main.

13 A search for "crisis" and "academic publishing" will turn up lots of hits with
overviews of this period of transition. For good perspectives on the changes in
scholarly publishing that are often labeled crisis, The Scholarly Kitchen, https://
scholarlykitchen.sspnet.org/, is an excellent community of publishing, library,
and scholarly professionals. Analyses and opinion pieces there lean toward
scientific communication, but there is ample dialogue addressing the social
sciences and the humanities.

14 It is a fraught choice deciding on the term best suited to describe scholars with
doctorates who do not earn their living in a college setting teaching and researching in the field in which they earned their degree. (See the American Historical
Association's statement on career diversity: https://www.historians.org/jobs-and
-professional-development/career-diversity-for-historians/about-career-diversity.)
In this essay I use, despite its limitations, "alternative careers" and eschew the
language of "Plan B."

15 See Arlene Stein and Jessie Daniels's *Going Public: A Guide to Social Scientists*
(Chicago, 2017) for a full account of the labor and strategizing require.

16 See Friedman's *The Business of Being a Writer*.

17 The twenty-year-old *Journal of Higher Education Outreach and Engagement* (an
open access resource published through a partnership of the University of
Georgia's Office of the Vice President for Public Service and Outreach, the
Institute of Higher Education, and University Extension) is a great place to start
in order to chart the growth of engagement as part of the mission of higher
education.

18 Correspondence, Editor C, January 23, 2019.

19 Correspondence, Editor D, January 17, 2019.

20 In 2016, Donald J. Waters wrote, summarizing a Mellon Foundation-funded
study into costs associated with producing academic monographs: "In a recently
published Mellon-funded study, the university presses at Indiana and Michigan
put the average costs respectively at $26,700 and $27,600. The Ithaka cost study
attempts to get at full costs of the first digital file; that is, excluding the costs of
printing and distribution of print copies, but including marketing and overhead.
The study reports average costs ranging from $30,000 per book for the group of
the smallest university presses to more than $49,000 per book for the group of the
largest presses. These are costs for monograph publication only; the costs of

innovative long-form genres that are non-linear, data-intensive, or multimedia rich are still not yet well understood. These cost estimates are sobering: 3,000 books a year, at an average per book cost of $30,000, yields a total cost of approximately $90 million in the US alone" (*Against the Grain*, June 2016, pp. 17–20), https://www.charleston-hub.com/wp-content/uploads/2016/07/ATG_fea_waters_v28-3.pdf. Given those costs, inclusive of overhead but not considering printing and distribution (not inconsiderable expenses), a standard university press book that sell 300 copies in the first year and earns $12,000 is not coming close to breaking even.

21 Correspondence, Editor E, January 17, 2019.

22 Correspondence, Editor G, January 23, 2019.

23 Correspondence, Editor B, January 27, 2019.

24 Correspondence, Editor A, January 18, 2019.

25 Regarding institutional alignment, see these essays as jumping off points: Anthony Cond's "University Press Redux," The Scholarly Kitchen, February 21, 2018, https://scholarlykitchen.sspnet.org/2018/02/21/guest-post-institutional-alignment-university-press-redux/; Heather Staine's "Mission Alignment: University Presses versus Institutional Visions," Learned Publishing, November 28, 2020, https://onlinelibrary.wiley.com/doi/abs/10.1002/leap.1346.

26 Correspondence, Editor E, January 17, 2019.

27 Correspondence, Editor J, April 12, 2019.

28 Correspondence, Editor B, January 27, 2019.

29 Correspondence, Editor F, January 10, 2019.

30 The topic of academic publishing for alternative career scholars was addressed at a panel, "Writing a Book from Beyond the Professoriate," at the 2020 annual meeting of the American Historical Association, https://aha.confex.com/aha/2020/webprogram/Session20004.html.

31 John V. Lombardi's *How Universities Work* (Johns Hopkins University Press, 2013) is a useful overview for university structures and processes, which is a foundation for thinking about developing missions.

4

The PhD Adviser-Advisee Relationship Reimagined for the Twenty-First Century

•••••••••••••••••••••••

LEONARD CASSUTO AND

JAMES M. VAN WYCK

What's the most important factor in successfully navigating graduate school? An invested adviser.[1] What does a good adviser do? Cede control.

Given that one of the other names sometimes given to a dissertation adviser is "director," that suggestion may seem to go against the grain. We don't mean that advisers should turn away from their advisees and become uninvolved. Instead, they should collaborate with their students on the students' goals.

If that sounds obvious, it hasn't proved so in practice. Graduate school has traditionally centered on the faculty, with students' concerns spinning off from faculty interests. This fact shows most clearly in the bench sciences, where student projects are typically carved out of faculty lab agendas. But it's also true in the humanistic fields: think of how often professors base their graduate seminars on whatever they're working on at the time, not the foundational knowledge of the discipline that students should acquire. We've had a lot of contact with graduate students across campuses and disciplines, and we hear numerous stories of how graduate students struggle under their advisers' controlling views of what they ought to be doing.

On the adviser's side, there's a long-enshrined expectation that student advisees should be "mini-mes" who take their places in a lineage that extends from the past into the future. That sense of generational determinism creates habits and assumptions that can be hard to break. As a result, advisers don't always realize when they're pressuring their students, and their students often feel too anxious to tell them when they do so.

Maybe the most important moment in James's time as a PhD advisee was when his adviser—Lenny—pointed away from himself to another source of knowledge and advice. The moment came early on in James's ABD (all but dissertation) stage: he had just selected Lenny as an adviser and was looking for guidance on how to apply for an administrative fellowship in the graduate school. If he got the award, it would replace his year's teaching and open up a new career horizon.

The position was newly invented, and its title was a mouthful: "fellow in higher education leadership," located in the Graduate School of Arts and Sciences. James wanted to work there, but he knew little about it and had no contacts in the GSAS. Lenny didn't hesitate to both validate the opportunity and also acknowledge that he wasn't the go-to person to consult about it. While he had held different administrative positions within the English department, he had only limited interaction with the graduate school administration.

It can be hard for a tenured professor to say "I don't know," but that's what Lenny did when James asked him about this job. Instead, he suggested someone who might know more. If Lenny had known this person himself, he would have brokered the contact. Because he didn't, he offered some guidance to James about how to do so.

Lenny made sure that James drove the connection: he invited James to forge the relationship himself. This moment exemplifies at least two needful characteristics of the adviser-advisee relation: James was being empowered, and he wasn't being dictated to. As important, the moment broke with the adviser-student dyad model that prevails in doctoral education. James learned through his own experience that it takes a village to raise a graduate student, particularly when the post-PhD path is no longer a track (as in tenure track) and more of a Rorschach blot.

James won the administrative fellowship and finished his dissertation. Keeping his academic options open, he also published an article in a prestigious peer-reviewed journal along the way. But his experience as graduate fellow—and the subsequent administrative opportunities that followed from it—convinced him that his immediate future lay beyond the tenure track. The hands-on administrative experience he got during graduate school led to his current job as an assistant dean.

James's experience broke new ground for Lenny too. None of his previous PhD students had sought a career in academic administration, so he made sure to learn as much as he could from James. He questioned James carefully about his work and incorporated James's experiences into his advising practices afterward. He has also referred students to James for advice that James could offer firsthand, and he learned even more about the importance of networking to secure jobs beyond the tenure track.

That story of James's journey is the fulcrum for this essay. It conveys two important ideas: First, the adviser-advisee relation is a partnership, not an employer/employee relationship. That partnership centers on the student's education, not the teacher's research. Which brings us to the second idea: the student's needs should guide that partnership. Lenny speaks to a lot of graduate student audiences around the country, and one thing he tells them all is: You are the CEO of your own graduate education.

Graduate students should be able to decide on the goals of their graduate education—and that's what James did when he decided to apply for an administrative internship. The adviser's job is to support those goals. Lenny didn't know a lot about James's chosen path, but he was able to make suggestions, learn with him, and become a knowledgeable partner as James crafted a career path around his degree.

Both adviser and advisee grew through this process of discovery. James gained experience in self-direction, and Lenny got past some ideas of what an adviser "should" do and made himself more comfortable saying, "You're right that you should know this, but I don't know the answer. Here's where you might look for it—and when you find it, share it with me too."

James could design and pursue his own outcome because the questions Lenny asked about careers were open-ended, not leading. They drew on his experience as a teacher, including his desire to challenge James to identify his own goals—because challenging questions act as learning tools in ways that leading questions don't. By asking questions that invited James to consider a variety of careers, desires, and paths, Lenny validated a true inventory of James's skills and ambitions.

These questions about preferences and strengths made it clear to James that the advice he was getting was bespoke. As it became clear that James liked to build (and not merely critique) programs, choices about the kinds of activities he could take part in grew clearer to him. He steered toward the kinds of roles that gave him a chance to advise and direct other graduate students, going "meta" at every opportunity.

There is no received wisdom for the twenty-first-century PhD adviser, nor for the twenty-first-century PhD advisee. There is only an ever-changing next.

For both adviser and advisee, the only way forward into the reimagined world of twenty-first-century PhD advising is to assume the position of the learner. The learner's stance requires a kind of intellectual and practical humility that can be difficult for professors—and graduate students too. Advisers learn while they teach. We shouldn't forget that advising is a form of teaching.

Like any form of teaching done right, both parties are teaching and learning at the same time.

In practice, that teaching-learning equilibrium can be harder to achieve than it sounds. The difficulty arises from the tension between "learner" and "expert." Academics (faculty and students both) are socialized into an intellectual world that demands, rewards, and credentials expertise. Professors are taught to view themselves as specialized experts, and they teach their students to do the same. It can be hard to teach (and learn) in a world of "I'm not sure"—or worse, "I don't know"—but it can be done. And we have to do it together.[2]

"Together" means more than two people. Committees need to do more than just ratify the work of student and adviser, and they need to be more open and flexible. If a graduate student wants a career in government, for example, her committee can and should include an expert already working in that field. The way forward lies beyond the apprenticeship model of one-to-one knowledge and skills transferal.[3] Instead of a graduate student "belonging" to his or her adviser, we should think in terms of a community of experts upon whom the student may draw. The twenty-first-century graduate adviser will continue to play a pivotal role in a graduate student's education, but it should be more as an organizing point person, rather than a directing force. Advisers will open up vistas (or call attention to those already open) and help students sort through a range of options. And they won't hesitate to say "I don't know." Now more than ever, doctoral advising calls for humility, and for advisors who are confident enough to cede control.

The Challenges of a New Advising Model

The Avital Ronell case of 2018 brought more publicity to graduate advising than it had ever had before—for all the wrong reasons. Ronell's prurient flirtations with her graduate student advisee Nimrod Reitman proved tabloid catnip and resulted in her suspension from teaching for a year for sexual harassment.[4]

The Ronell case looks at first like a bizarre outlier, but it's really just a grotesque version of something ordinary that we've seen for years.[5] Most graduate advisers don't send their students mash notes, but advisers have been known to use their influence to push their students toward choices that the students don't necessarily wish for themselves. We won't dish here, but if you're skeptical, get a few graduate students together, assure them that they're off the record, and listen to the stories.

When advisers push, and students get pushed, the action points to a structural leadership problem and an individual leadership problem at the same time. It's a structural leadership problem because the adviser has enough power, both bureaucratic and personal, to make such behavior both possible and tempting.

Sometimes advisers don't even know they're engaging in it. It's an individual leadership problem because the student often doesn't push back.

All of which suggests that we ought to think about advising more capaciously. Advisers and graduate students need to work together—and they ought to lead together. When things are going well, the student holds the reins, and the adviser—or advisers—are there to help the student negotiate terrain that may be familiar to one, and less so to the other.

This new kind of advising goes against the historical grain. When a student chooses an adviser, it can seem as though the student is withdrawing from a program's common culture to enter the adviser's private world. We act that way because of long-standing tradition. The hierarchical adviser-student dyad has been enshrined—or we might say entrenched—in American academia for over a century. It goes back even further in Europe, where the idea of the professor as a charismatic "master" (not a mere teacher) surrounded by his acolytes informed the structure of doctoral instruction when research universities came to the United States beginning in the late nineteenth century.[6] In this model, the student entered the adviser's circle and was in effect taken out of academic circulation.

It's telling that the German word for dissertation adviser is *Doktorvater*, or literally, "doctor-father." That sense of family relation—and of lineage—long ago carried over into American practice.[7] Academic genealogy is a popular hobby, especially among tenure-stream academics. Discussions and examples proliferate.[8] These genealogies (my students, myself, my adviser, my adviser's adviser, and so on) may seem harmless, but they can be subtly coercive. Note, for example, how they quietly erase the professional lives of PhDs whose career choices take them beyond academia.

This elision of nonprofessorial careers shows how advisers have construed the cultural work of the PhD too narrowly for too long—and how they've taught their students to do the same. When advisers operate under this limitation, even by doing something as simple as publishing an academic family tree, it constrains the advice that they give. If we think only in terms of what is lost when students don't obtain the tenure-track jobs that everyone knows they are qualified for, we can miss the other careers and landing spots for them and, worse, teach them that those places are somehow unsuitable.

In the same spirit, we might also reconsider the term "mentor," which we have deliberately refrained from using in this essay. Professors and students alike use "mentor" interchangeably with "adviser," but the word carries thousands of years of freight. In the *Odyssey*, the venerable Mentor earns the trust of Odysseus, who assigns Mentor to educate his son, Telemachus. In this position, Mentor does not partner with Telemachus so much as dispense wisdom to his student from on high—and the hierarchical distance between them is further emphasized when Athena, the goddess of wisdom herself, disguises herself as Mentor to dispense some of the most important advice that the young man receives during the story.[9]

Most contemporary users of the term "mentor" probably won't think of those particulars, but the word conveys many of them by implication. A mentor-mentee relation runs strictly vertically—and for that reason, it might be time to jettison "mentor" as a name for a graduate school adviser. We make no pronouncements, except one: to use names with care, and an eye to their implications. Academia is already conservative, but graduate school is a conservative version of academia, so things change particularly slowly there. Old words carry old assumptions, and these can get in the way of doing things in new and different ways.

Chief among those new ways is a new conception: the need to air out the adviser-student dyad. For generations now, advisers have apprenticed their doctoral students, parceling out instruction and recommendations in exchange for loyalty (and in the case of the bench sciences, hours of labor in the lab). We've needed to ventilate that relation for a while, to prevent potential manipulation.[10] But we really need to open it outward now, because graduate school is different now. During the postwar generation of abundance, doctoral education was an apprenticeship. For those who finished, the apprenticeship led to a professor's job.[11] That one postwar generation created what has been taken to be the standard path for academics—a kind of assumed norm for PhD outcomes. And because that path was strewn with such happy outcomes, academics quickly grew very attached to it. So when the burgeoning higher education sector filled and stabilized, and then was politicized by the traumas of the 1960s, and the academic job market contracted, professors' first response was to wait for it to recover. Their second and third responses were the same as the first. Not until the crash of 2008 caused an already-desiccated market to wither still further did academics begin to realize that a time for a reckoning—and a reimagining—had arrived.

The result: graduate school isn't simply an apprenticeship for would-be professors anymore. Today we need to prepare graduate students for a diversity of possible outcomes. That means that each graduate student's advising team needs a diversity of skills.

Accordingly, graduate school needs to be public facing. Graduate students need to be more public facing. They need to look toward a world that needs their contributions, whether from inside or outside the academy. Graduate advising needs to reflect these necessities. Advisers help their students when they model what an academic in public should look like. But more important, they should be able to point their advisees toward a range of possibilities for being scholars in public themselves.[12]

So here's some advice to students who are scoping out an adviser. First, think about what you're doing in graduate school. You need to reflect on your own mission and goals before you can think about what your graduate adviser (and your graduate school) can do for you. Second, beware the prospective adviser who doesn't mention other faculty, graduate students, postdocs, or on-campus resources. If you already have an advisor who doesn't connect you, then supplement your adviser's advice by consulting with a range of other people yourself. In fact, you should make this a policy regardless of whether your adviser is a good connector or not.

And here's a takeaway for advisors: this isn't about you. It's about your student. It's not about your legacy or the perpetuation of your discipline. It's about teaching your student in the here and now.

It's a Matter of Leadership

We're saying that both advisers and students need to be good leaders—but what does leadership even mean? In this final section, we argue that twenty-first-century graduate school calls for the emergence of the PhD student as leader. The long-enshrined tradition of infantilizing the PhD student needs to end.

The meaning of leadership depends on the situation. Rather than a clear approach, studies of leadership often assemble a pastiche of anecdotes. The literature about leadership traffics more often in equivocation than definition. That's okay, because most of us are aware that definitions fail to capture what it means to benefit from good leadership. Further, who among us can discern the moment when we tipped from followership to leadership? (Tellingly, the English language has very few words that describe leadership, or the advising relationship for that matter.) And isn't every leader leading only in particular contexts and for a limited amount of time? Even if we are acknowledged as leaders, we are only temporary stewards of the role.

Systematically studying leadership has so far proved chimerical. Reflecting on a Harvard Business School Colloquium on the subject, J. Richard Hackman described leadership as "little more than a semantic inkblot, an ambiguous word onto which people project their personal fantasies, hopes, and anxieties about what it takes to make a difference." Hackman backs away from this quickly, however: "because there really *is* something there. The challenge is to find it, tame it, and set it off on a course that generates knowledge."[13] The same can be said about doctoral advising.

So leadership is an ineffable quality that can be identified, but it's hard to isolate. In a section titled simply "It," Hackman concludes with a conundrum: it's hard to understand *it* "in part because people who have it are unable to explain what it is but also because they may be disinclined to tell us even if they could." Hackman recalls how he "once asked someone who quite clearly had it if I could follow him around for a month or so over the summer to try to understand his superb capabilities. 'No,' he said. 'That wouldn't be a good use of your time. And, besides, to do that would be wrong.' He meant it. He knew he had something special, but he seemed fearful that if someone were to closely inspect and analyze whatever it was, he just might lose it."[14]

Good doctoral advisers may be just as reluctant to pick apart their advising practice to see what makes it work. And doctoral advisees are ill placed to do so: they have only one committee, so they have little to contrast their experience with, other than the stories they hear from their peers around the proverbial water cooler.[15]

Yet those stories matter. We're encouraging each graduate student to "fill your space," and we're calling on advisers to make room for graduate student partnerships. Whether they do or not, students need to fill that leadership space at the head of their own education. If they do not, then it will get filled all right—but not by them, because leadership abhors a vacuum. The result: narratives that discourage initiative and creativity. When those stories get told around the water cooler, they poison the air that graduate students breathe.

The inability to define leadership (and the relative lack of on-the-ground analyses of graduate adviser best practices) means that the stories we tell ourselves about leadership matter more than ever. That's particularly the case when we're looking to replace one mode of leadership with another, as we are with doctoral advising. But it also means that we need to avail ourselves of all the communications tools at our disposal—and perhaps invent a few new ones—in order to provide doctoral students the best chance to navigate graduate school and beyond in ways that benefit them. Throughout this chapter—and in many of the chapters it rubs shoulders within this volume—we've suggested the following:

a   We can derive some general principles for doctoral advising—what it is, isn't, and should be in the ideal.
b   These principles should focus more on the agency of the advisee, who is the CEO of their own graduate education.
c   Further, good graduate advisers can be known by the stories that are told about them, but they can also be located by taking advantage of the transparency afforded by the world of digital sharing that we live in now.
d   Leadership in the context of doctoral advising will always be difficult to pinpoint, but if graduate programs institute systematic, periodic self-reflections, doctoral advisers and committees will be prompted to consider the ways they lead, colead, and help their advisees direct the shape of their own graduate education.

Reviewing this list, it seems to us that rethinking leadership in the context of the adviser-advisee relationship can't come quickly enough. We would suggest that all efforts to change the adviser-advisee relationship should give the advisee agency—that is, the power to choose, to pivot, to innovate, and to imagine multiple futures. Practices that don't embrace student agency belong to a tradition that sees the PhD still as the passing down of lore (a vertical movement), rather than a living, malleable set of practices that shape the lives of particular people.

Advisers need to rethink leadership—their own, to be sure, but also that of their advisees. Old-school advisers want their PhD students to lead the kind of scholarly life that they entered in their own idealized and independent pasts. To such advisers, PhD students have freedom to choose their own course, as long as their choice leads toward academia. Instead, advisers need to help their advisees lead whenever possible—even if they lead toward unfamiliar places.

Leadership in its most capacious sense doesn't involve someone in front and someone following behind. In the hopeful future we envision, leadership becomes a kind of service, not a continuous act of directing and instructing.[16] Advisers create spaces in which students can grow into their own leadership, or augment leaderly aspects of themselves that they had before coming into graduate education.

The best kinds of leaders don't try to clone themselves. The goal is to create other leaders, not pale imitations of themselves. Accordingly, academic advisers need to reinvent their approach for each advisee: if academic advising isn't personalized, individualized, specialized, delimited, and contoured to the needs of each advisee, then it won't work in a professional world that no longer sends its PhDs toward a single chute.

Both advisers and advisees should lead in the same way that PhD students move through their training. For the graduate student, the process of getting through a PhD should grow not only disciplinary knowledge but also self-knowledge. Students necessarily negotiate requirements in the world. When they do so, they take control of their own experience. In this updated relation, productive disagreement with your adviser can lead to learning on both sides. By contrast, a sycophantic relation in which no conflict ever appears suggests a failure of leadership on both sides.

What does this shared and mutual leadership through advising look like in practice? Let's look at an example. At Princeton, the GradFUTURES University Administrative Fellowship Program places over forty fellows throughout the institution to work with and be advised by senior administrators (many of whom have PhDs). The program is split between shadowing and mentoring (two to three hours a week) and work on a project (two to four hours, for a total average of six hours a week). One of the outcomes of the project is that the fellows gain another person to vouch for their abilities in spaces beyond academia. In one instance, a fellow—we'll call her Lori—wanted to pursue a career in science policy. After completing a fellowship in an office charged with outreach to foundations, Lori was able to use a letter of recommendation from her supervisor in this office to secure her first post in Washington.

Advisers ought to welcome such stories because they show that advisers need not do it all. And these scenarios empower advisees, who need not get all their advice from one source. Advisers worthy of the name recognize that advising PhDs today requires teamwork. Even the best-intentioned, most well-caffeinated, Twitter-following, *Inside Higher Ed*–addicted adviser may never be able to stay abreast of employment trends or best practices for crafting cover letters for jobs at ed-tech startups. But that's the point. Advisers need not—and should not—do this work alone. Good advisers follow the spirit of this passage from the Hippocratic oath: "I will not be ashamed to say 'I know not,' nor will I fail to call on my colleagues when the skills of another are needed for a patient's recovery."[17]

This bespoke work sounds time-consuming. How might an adviser do it? Again: it should not be done alone. Graduate schools are investing in resources that curate and extend the supports available on campus, including hiring graduate career specialists in career services offices. We need to make sure that we make these resources visible to graduate students from the time that they enter their programs, not just at the job market moment.[18] And there's also tremendous value in the peer network, and in particular the recent alumni-to-student relationship.

Leadership in the context of doctoral advising is certainly not about giving orders. Advisers give advice, not commands—and if they're doing their job properly, the student will take the adviser's advice seriously.

Everyone arrives at the start of PhD training with different experiences, needs, and goals. Advising cannot, therefore, be reduced to a standard set of practices. (Though some are obvious: accessibility, transparency, and timely feedback, for example.)[19] And advisers have places to go for some of the answers. Compared to a few years ago, the resources for being a twenty-first-century academic are now myriad. Take, for example, the National Center for Faculty Development and Diversity, ImaginePhD, and the pay-to-play resources offered by the Professor Is In or Beyond the Professoriate.[20]

Advisers may send their advisees to these sites—and vice versa—for general advice. But advice needs to be tailored and fit to the particular student, who attends a particular institution at a particular time. Any style of graduate advising that doesn't consider a student's previous experience—whether as a first-generation undergraduate, for example, or one with a prior career—rests upon a mistaken central assumption that "graduate school" and "graduate student" are largely homogeneous categories. They never were, and to continue to treat them as such substitutes stereotypes for real people.

Prioritizing students means focusing on them. Advisers have to take cues from their students. In Robert Greenleaf's classic essay "The Servant as Leader," he calls for "a sustained intentness of listening." Because the adviser should be working for the student, good advising is reactive as well as active—and listening is key. So is asking the right questions.

Advisers try to lead students to insights (that will never change), but those insights aren't all about the content of the discipline. In particular, graduate advisers and committees need to make sure that their advisees do the work of finding out (and then periodically reassessing) what it is they want out of their PhD. This work cannot be left undone, nor should advisers assume they know what advisees want. In too many PhD programs, the default message is that the advisee will have to make the case for doing something other than what has been typically done in the past. Part of being a good leader as a doctoral adviser, then, is to make sure that everyone involved is doing the work of self-assessment and self-understanding, recognizing strengths and weaknesses, and thinking about the big picture along with the scholarly details.

It is the adviser's job to help students to be the best version of themselves that they want to be. This dynamic is particularly at odds with the commonly heard phrase "my adviser won't let me do it." The relation described by that phrase is not one of advising at all (are you an adviser if you're controlling the actions of your advisee?) and belies a structural and relational imbalance that is out of proportion. Should doctoral advisers be allowed to determine whether or not graduate students take up a part-time job or serve on a university-wide committee? Consider that an adviser may feel empowered to tell a PhD student in anthropology who came to graduate school after completing a JD and working around the globe that she cannot take up a fellowship, while the same adviser would not say the same to an undergraduate whom this PhD candidate herself is teaching as a TA. (The reason for this disjunction does not always lie in the funding of graduate education: departments, programs, and graduate schools are generally more inclined to permit extracurricular activities that graduate advisers are unwilling to approve.) "My adviser won't let me" is a phrase that ought never to be heard again.

This postulate leads to a concluding example, of a fellow contributor to this volume: Will Fenton. Will's first job post-PhD—director of scholarly innovation at the Library Company of Philadelphia—didn't exist before he originated it. He found the job by networking, by thinking and acting differently from other PhD students, and by seeing unmet needs in the research and scholarly communities in which he circulated. Will, a recently minted PhD, has produced scholarship that already rivals that of more established scholars. Will got to his position with the help of lots of advisers. Even at this early stage, his career shows that the strength of the adviser-advisee relationship in the twenty-first century will be determined by the degree to which we learn—structurally and at the individual level—to break up and expand the adviser-advisee dyad.

Notes

1   Jennifer Bloom et al., "Graduate Students' Perceptions of Outstanding Graduate Advisor Characteristics," *NACADA Journal* 27, no. 2 (2007): 28–35.

2   See Leonard Cassuto, "Can You Train Your PhDs for Diverse Careers When You Don't Have One?," *Chronicle of Higher Education*, August 22, 2018, https://www.chronicle.com/article/Can-You-Train-Your-PhDs-for/244323.

3   At the University of Louisville, dissertation committee structures in some departments explicitly allow for nonaffiliated committee members (including those without a PhD, such as nurses or other practitioners).

4   See, for example, Andrew O'Hehir, "When a Woman Is Accused of Sexual Misconduct: The Strange Case of Avital Ronell," *Salon*, August 18, 2018, https://www.salon.com/2018/08/18/when-a-woman-is-accused-of-sexual-misconduct-the-strange-case-of-avital-ronell/.

5   See Leonard Cassuto, "The Overlooked Lesson of the Ronell-Reitman Case," *Chronicle of Higher Education*, September 16, 2018, https://www.chronicle.com/article/The-Overlooked-Lesson-of-the/244508.

6   We use the male pronoun advisedly. For a European account of the emergence of the "master," see William Clark, *Academic Charisma and the Origins of the Research University*, reprint ed. (University of Chicago Press, 2007). For a historical view of how the idea of the master was refracted in the United States, see Laurence R. Veysey, *The Emergence of the American University* (University of Chicago Press, 1965).

7   For a valuable reading of the "Doktorvater" term, see Jim Grossman, "Hierarchy and Needs: How to Dislodge Outdated Notions of Advising," *Perspectives on History*, September 1, 2018, https://www.historians.org/publications-and-directories/perspectives-on-history/september-2018/hierarchy-and-needs-how-to-dislodge-outdated-notions-of-advising.

8   See, for example, https://www.lorentz.leidenuniv.nl/history/explosion/APS_back_page.html.

9   See Edward Mendelson, "Old Saul and Young Saul," *New York Review of Books*, September 26, 2013, https://www.nybooks.com/articles/2013/09/26/old-saul-and-young-saul-bellow/ The disguised Athena advises Telemachus on how to deal with his mother's suitors.

10   We're borrowing the ventilation metaphor from Thomas Bender. See "Expanding the Domain of History," in *Envisioning the Future of Doctoral Education: Preparing Stewards of the Discipline*, ed.Chris M. Golde and George E. Walker (Jossey-Bass, 2006), 295–310, 305.

11   It's worth pointing out that even during that brief time when anyone who finished a PhD could get a professorship, finishing was no trivial matter: graduate school attrition rates were very high, even higher than the still-amazing 50 percent rate that prevails now. In his memoir, *One Hundred Semesters: My Adventures as Student, Professor, and University President, and What I Learned along the Way* (Princeton University Press, 2006), William Chace recalls that about 80 percent of his entering English department cohort at Berkeley in the early sixties failed to complete the degree.

12   For a detailed discussion of public scholarship with examples drawn from across the disciplines, see Leonard Cassuto and Robert Weisbuch, *The New PhD: How to*

Build a Better Graduate Education (Johns Hopkins University Press, 2021), esp. chapter 10.

13 J. Richard Hackman, "What Is This Thing Called Leadership?," in *Handbook of Leadership Theory and Practice*, ed. Nitin Nohria and Rakesh Kurana (Harvard Business Review Press, 2010), 107–118, 107.

14 Hackman, "What Is This Thing Called Leadership?," 117–118.

15 There's only one book that we know of on doctoral advising, Bruce M. Shore's *The Graduate Advisor Handbook: A Student-Centered Approach* (University of Chicago Press, 2014). As his subtitle suggests, Shore has some valuable things to say about student-centered advising, but his advice applies most readily to social science fields such as his own.

16 For the best meditation on the view of leadership as service, see Robert Greenleaf's seminal 1970 essay, "The Servant as Leader," http://www.ediguys.net/Robert_K _Greenleaf_The_Servant_as_Leader.pdf. (Servant leadership is a term that has been co-opted and used in ways that Greenleaf warns against, but this essay serves as a good starting point for rethinking the advisor-advisee dynamic.)

17 See James M. Van Wyck, "How Graduate Advisers Can Bolster Their Career Guidance," *Inside Higher Ed*, June 11, 2018.

18 For a good example of what that practice might look like, see Jim Grossman, "Imagining Ph.D. Orientation in 2022," *Chronicle of Higher Education*, August 28, 2017, https://www.chronicle.com/article/Imagining-PhD-Orientation -in/240995.

19 The 2020 "Report from the MLA Task Force on Ethical Conduct in Graduate Education" provides a useful summary of certain best practices. https://www.mla .org/About-Us/Governance/Executive-Council/Executive-Council-Actions/2020 /Report-of-the-MLA-Task-Force-on-Ethical-Conduct-in-Graduate-Education.

20 See https://www.facultydiversity.org/; https://www.imaginephd.com/; http:// theprofessorisin.com/; https://beyondprof.com/.

5

Out of the Field and into the Woods

• •

The PhD as Professional Compass

AUGUSTA ROHRBACH

It's not just the job market for people with PhDs that is under threat, facing the demand to provide that they "add value" and bring a "return on invest-ment."[1] The major challenge beating down higher education and its research enterprise—from granting advanced degrees to doing basic science, scholarship, and translational research—is two-pronged. On the one hand, there is the man-date to uphold a standard of inquiry that has long been defined along disci-plinary lines. On the other, there is a pressing need to address complex, multilayered problems in a nuanced and sophisticated way—be that by prepar-ing students for the workforce or providing thoughtful contributions to meet the human needs in the world around us. For many, higher education's mission for decades—maybe even from its inception—treated these two goals as com-plementary.[2] What is different about the present moment (now confounded exponentially by the pressures brought on by the COVID-19 pandemic) is the confluence of forces galvanized by rapidly evolving digital technologies that are pushing the boundaries of and reinventing the methodologies for how we teach, learn, and conduct research—no matter what field or discipline. In the face of dynamic change, we notice with alarm the winnowing of interest in conventional subjects, the uncertainty of the funding landscape, and the sheer magnitude of the challenges around us. As dire as the situation seems to many, including those in the STEM fields, people with training in the humanities and social sciences have a particular skill set to bring to bear on what appears to be a surfeit of ambiguity. What is needed, however, is a more active agenda coming out of higher education that empowers PhDs to be agents of change at this important time.

Rather than theorize on my own, I took the question to the experts—querying those holding or pursuing a degree in the humanities and social sciences. To learn more about what others holding a PhD thought, I posted a survey to a variety of listservs and other social media outlets.[3] I framed my request for information like this:

> Calling all of you who have thought about the humanities and/or advanced degrees: Share your thoughts with me for a piece I am calling "Out of the Field and into the Woods" exploring the importance of the humanities PhD outside traditional scholarly classroom activities. . . . Please go to: PhD into the Woods Survey to access a survey, and/or send your ideas to me offline by March 9. Very happy to acknowledge you if you do the survey—there's a space for self-identification. Or, take the survey anonymously. . . . Specific anecdotes and references will be especially valuable to help readers grapple with and move beyond otherwise abstract arguments that characterize training in humanities as "critical thinking." Feel free to share the link with your networks. Many thanks for considering.[4]

The survey reached a PhD-rich audience—almost 95 percent of those who responded either have or are working toward a PhD.[5] Importantly for the present discussion, 71 percent have worked outside of academia.[6] I turned to this group of respondents to help me better contextualize my own experience bridging the gap between what people generally understand as the value of the PhD and the actual functions for which this training can and should be utilized.

More than 85 percent of those responding to the survey believe the PhD will be (or is) an asset to seeking employment outside of academia. These results tell me that it is time, as Nicholas B. Dirks, a former chancellor of the University of California, Berkeley, says, "to do more than tell our story better. We may have to change the story we tell."[7] Following Dirks, I am looking for more than professional recuperation for PhDs and higher education. Rather, my goal is to plumb the survey data for an actionable agenda—and one that is meaningful to publics beyond academe—as to how advanced academic training can functionally serve the public good.

In reviewing the 184 responses I received, one central message was clear. For all the ways in which respondents had suggestions, criticisms, and disappointments, there is a fundamental idealism embedded deep within the commitment to attain the degree itself that we just don't fully reckon as valuable. Of those surveyed, 48 percent believe the PhD was an asset to obtaining their jobs. What this tells me is that not enough has been said about the elemental belief in the power of thought and study shared by those who invest the time, money, and heart into an advanced degree. This key value and the transformative power it holds, evidenced in the sheer magnitude of the investment in training, registers a remarkable commitment to quality—a commitment that will benefit large-scale, ambitious projects that require intellectual stamina. Just because those in conventional academic positions are defined by institutional demands to produce tangible results according to disciplinary norms and traditions does not mean that PhDs are limited by those norms or traditions. The message is clear: keep feeding the idealistic spirit that attracts people to academia because it can and will animate its future.[8]

A core principle for those who make getting a PhD a goal is that we are (or should be!) invested in the notion that culture is participatory; we believe that individuals can be active agents rather than passive recipients of received wisdom. Treating texts and contexts as implicitly biased is an accepted fact, underpinning the prime directive to interrogate them. Such a deep understanding of complexly interwoven context and purpose is essential to creating well-informed and carefully reasoned decisions. Such analytic training positions people "to sift through thousands of pages in order to locate answers to questions" as well as anticipate objections and gaps in reasoning. Respondents agree that PhD training enhances capacity to do large-scale information processing, producing evidence-based, data-driven decision makers. We undersell the indispensable role research plays not just in decision making but in the broader process of what business speak calls "buy-in." Rather than just solve problems, as one respondent indicated, PhD training emphasizes the importance of offering a "methodology," in order to show the logic of change, helping others see shifts as neither "arbitrary or personal." Administrators and program directors can use the ethos of participatory culture to create opportunities for scholars across disciplines to merge approaches. At Tufts, we've been thinking about launching a program that creates a role for those currently pursuing a PhD to develop research opportunities in cross-disciplinary collaboration. The PhD Externship program, developed in partnership with PhD-granting departments, provides time and space for students to learn how to contribute to field-defining research outside of their chosen disciplines; it also incentivizes inclusion by offering a small stipend to support the initiative in the form of a supplement to existing fellowship funding.[9] By design, this program presents what one respondent thinks is the biggest advantage higher education has to offer: "an opportunity to build a wide range of skills and experiences while having some safety net of structure and financial support."[10] This program would create cross-disciplinary opportunities and instruction for PhDs in training from other disciplines while also serving as a potential method to grow innovation outside the norms of the primary research group with which the student is working. The PhD Externship program aims to enhance opportunities for PhDs in training beyond traditional roles typically associated with their chosen disciplines. A goal of the program, as a long-term investment in broadening the way disciplines interact, is to teach people to speak a variety of languages and grow innovation through diverse perspectives.

For as much as we all talk about the importance of disruption and the need to think outside of the box, the truth is that truly interdisciplinary research is a skill that needs to be taught and takes time, patience, practice, and that magic elixir of life: money. Today, many educators are focused on developing programs for cross-disciplinary innovation at the middle school level, incorporating STEM approaches through "maker curriculums," for instance.[11] But at the upper levels of our talent pool—the soon-to-be, recent, or established PhDs— there are few or no opportunities to learn the practices that so many agree fuel discovery. The capacity to move across disciplines has remained too embedded in the training itself and by the need to produce predictable results. We need to be more explicit about how and why our training prepares us for a multitude of roles and take an active interest in working outside our comfort zones. Indeed, 90 percent of those who responded to the question in the survey affirming the value of their training articulated concrete ways in which preparation for the PhD helped them meet (and often enhance) the goals of their position. One respondent explained that the training improved the "ability to do high level management work," while another found lessons on diversity and inclusion provided by graduate education essential preparation for the workplace: "The advanced training I received prepared me to teach in a non-traditional setting. Working with individuals who thought their opinions, beliefs, and culture were the standard platform for advancement, I then surpassed the learning curves presented as a disqualifier initially. Cultural competencies, prejudiced social consciousness were revealed and addressed as team building and teamwork strategies in order to achieve the goals of the team."[12] In particular, one respondent argued that "the intellectual, procedural, and motivational rigor that goes into a dissertation have been essential for all the kinds of work done outside of research. Working with other people in particular and being able to see large projects and ideas in terms of stages and components is a particular skill learned through dissertation writing."

One major qualification that PhDs have and should be foregrounded is our ability to collect and use evidence-based approaches to advance long-range theories and/or action plans. PhDs have an enhanced ability to communicate research goals to various stakeholders, a skill that is essential in a knowledge economy. Yet outside of academic departments, a PhD in English is, at best, often valued as a writing credential. Despite the continual emphasis on "critical thinking" that many use to position the English major, when it comes to the PhD, this message has little or no purchase in the working world.[13] Those responding to my survey had much more to say about the value of their training. One respondent noted that the PhD was preparation for "having an idea that is too big to really grapple with except over the course of multiple stages of inquiry."[14] They concluded that the degree was a contributing factor in helping people wrestle with some of life's most dire circumstances, such as cancer treatment and end-of-life care. While no other respondents cited such weighty outlets for their training, roughly 90 percent of those responding to the question used words like "essential," "vital," in addition to "required" when describing how doctoral training helped them get the position in which they are currently.

What the respondents seem to agree on is that there is a set of transferable skills that allowed them to cogently analyze complex ideas and communicate them in a trustworthy manner. Thus, though institutions are notoriously slow to change, those who emerge from them with a PhD have skills that are essential in the effort to move ideas from the lab and the library to the world around us. These very skills are among the characteristics needed to render abstract research and scholarship toward a social purpose. As participants in a knowledge economy, PhDs innovate by virtue of their ability to translate systems of thought into discrete actions, would that we simply be more tactical and explicit in our approaches. What can we do to help others see the important value we bring? Be ready with a clear example to help people understand your contribution in concrete terms. One of my respondents shared this story: "I worked with a Computer Science colleague to help him with a pitch to University leadership for a financial investment in a project he imagined. I presented with him, and it was clear that my presentation skills won the day for him. He's brilliant, but he considers me to be a brilliant communicator—a skill he can't approximate (just as I can't approximate his programming skills)."[15] This story makes clear that the ability to express complex ideas to an audience outside of your peers is indispensable. The proposal would have failed had it not been pitched properly.

PhDs have an important role to play as navigators of complex systems. They are trained in the kind of nuanced thinking required to fit solutions to the real-life context in which problems are situated. Many funders incentivize research to be more adaptive—supporting proposals that are large in scope, address problems that have complex causes, require new technologies, treatments, or policies, and have real-world relevance.[16] These requirements are meant to create a fertile nexus between three strands: *research*, *policy*, and *practice*. Humanists are accustomed to braiding these three components together, fostering innovation within the norms of existing communities because they are trained to do this work without losing sight of the ultimate goal. As one respondent noted, "Working with other people in particular and being able to see large projects and ideas in terms of stages and components is a particular skill learned through dissertation writing."[17] Many PhDs pivot between two axes—as scholars seeking to understand, explore, and expand knowledge and as educators looking to share knowledge. Combined, these two modalities provide the dexterity required to traverse the intricate set of relationships that characterize current needs for education, research, and scholarship inside *and* outside the academy. We can further facilitate this kind of training by providing opportunities during graduate school through a variety of programming.

As editor-in-chief of *ESQ: A Journal of Nineteenth-Century American Literature and Culture*, I looked for ways to instill the value of participatory culture broadly, emphasizing its purpose across multiple constituencies. To that end, I developed an outreach program for graduate students that helped them be active producers of knowledge others could use by reporting on scholarly proceedings at major academic conferences. Using a networked model of distributed communication, graduate students met and worked together to produce a report from the field that captured the current conversation and framed possibilities for future collaborations. Dubbed "The Year in Conferences," this program remains in practice today because it creates opportunities across several sectors while emphasizing the purpose of research rather than by simply archiving it.

As a literary scholar, I wanted to understand fundamental currents that shaped U.S. literary realism. I used the lens of business history to reread literary history when writing *Truth Stranger Than Fiction: Race, Realism and the U.S. Literary Marketplace*. What I found by studying literature from a market perspective was that slave narratives were a taproot for realism—one of the most popular genres in nineteenth-century U.S. literature, a genre long seen as the province of white men. I saw it differently, tracing in African American literary form and realism a shared aesthetic, an emphasis on the nitty-gritty details, and the importance of money and finances, as the tools by which plot is advanced. Prior to the work I did for my first book, there was no identifiable link between the African American literary form and realism, a popular fictional form dominated by white middle-class (mostly male) writers.

The rhetorical modes that my earlier training in close reading equipped me with weren't sufficient for the task of convincing other literary scholars to accept my theory as anything more than a coincidental stylistic similarity.[18] Putting aside the monumental differences between stories about slavery and white middle-class life, I focused instead on the common denominator: these two genres shared a medium—print—and a market. It was in the print marketplace that I found demonstrable evidence of how anxiety about the remarkable success of slave narratives might have provided a model for white writers eager to succeed as literary authors. Slave narratives flourished by telling stories in graphic detail for a moral purpose, tapping into the evangelical capitalism of the period and thus circulated broadly through a variety of print mediums. I believed that realism essentially adapted this strategy in the effort to galvanize the interest of middle-class white people to see their plight as meaningful.

I could have tried to bolster my literary analysis with other field-specific approaches, but instead I chose to frame my analysis in a manner more accessible to those beyond my field of study. I followed the money, taking a systems-level approach to how knowledge is created and disseminated through a study of the literary marketplace. Framing my analysis this way, paradoxically, made it resound all the more with my fellow literary scholars.

None of this is to say that the road is easy or straightforward. But my point here is that the discipline's utility is real—what is holding it back is our own fear of change. Bridget McKenzie in "Towards the Sociocratic Museum" argues that the answer to museums' existential crisis in the digital era is "not in the familiar question 'how can museums survive?' but in 'how can museums do work that matters?'" The same question is at the heart of discussions about reforming the PhD conducted by major organizational leaders like the Modern Language Association and the American Historical Association. So too have funders supportive of the humanities begun to play their role in fomenting change—with public scholar programs sponsored by the National Endowment for the Humanities, incentives to retrain and undertake cross-disciplinary training like the Burkhardt fellowship, sponsored by the American Council of Learned Societies, and Mellon's New Directions fellowships aimed at helping midcareer scholars advance their studies while also transforming educational prospects.

Though these opportunities are far fewer in number than there is need for, what they portend is a willingness to support change holistically, rather than simply let the professoriate die on the vine. The Mellon Foundation has also developed a dedicated funding stream toward enriching humanistic study. Through programs like the Sawyer Seminar, clusters of institutions are provided "support for comparative research on the historical and cultural sources of contemporary developments."[19] Importantly, Sawyer Seminar support is meant not to build on established institutional structures—like centers—but rather to create a fluid space for dialogues that would otherwise be difficult to pursue in an institutional setting—a kind of pop-up market of ideas. Fueled by a start-up mentality, preference is given to proposals that include a diverse set of participants—from all levels of the academy both inside and outside of the institution. This emphasis on inclusion is one way the foundation intends to create greater communication across a number of constituencies. These baked-in requirements, like those in place from the United States Agency for

International Development (USAID) for established, in-country partners, create necessary conditions for lasting change. The challenge programs like this offer is to move from more sedentary forms of reflection to critical thinking in real time, prompting academics to be agents of change among themselves and across disciplines.[20]

Let us heed the message being sent by Mellon and USAID alike. PhDs are well suited for this kind of work. After all, folks in the humanities and the social sciences were theorizing alternate models of identity long before the federal government took up legislation around such controversial topics as discrimination in the military or gender-neutral bathrooms. Yet few of its thought leaders have engaged in the public dialogue around these issues. One rarely hears of a professor of gender studies giving expert testimony to Congress, and yet these are precisely the spaces where change happens—even if slow and incremental.[21] Humanists excel at the iterative and use threaded discussions and other pedagogies to generate and implement change, yet the role of policy influencer is usually reserved for people who are in the hard sciences. It would seem to me that insights drawn from literary studies would greatly advance the work of many other disciplines if the field worked harder at sharing its lessons.[22]

This is not to say that literary studies is without its flaws or limits. Like so many other disciplines, it can also be functionally blind to its hamartia. Our efforts to claim value can alienate the public, especially when we emphasize our value as exclusive. As former chancellor Dirks observes, "When we say we have a 17-percent acceptance rate, the public hears that we have an 83-percent rejection rate."[23] And rather than sneer smugly at the parochial view of the *New York Times* whenever the Modern Language Association comes to town for its annual convention, we might try a little harder at helping those not committed to the monastic life of the academy to see the value in the "Jane Austen and the Masturbating Girl" session famously derided by the *New York Times*.[24] It's the ultimate challenge to bring your knowledge and expertise to outside audiences—to test its value and your own for a larger purpose.

To help me keep a healthy perspective, I prefer to tarry on Twitter feeds like this tweet from @ShitAcademicsSay for the bracing effect of self-awareness it provides: "just wondering if you had time to grab a coffee to discuss how busy we all are."[25] We fail when we forget how much liberty we have to dwell in our own thoughts about our own problems—no matter how real or imagined. However, once the laughter subsides, I am reminded of how easy it is to recede back into the cynicism that threatens much of the joy this work can create. According to the survey results, we flunk most detrimentally when it comes to creating a positive affect around the work we do. An overwhelming number of respondents agreed that the PhD has not contributed to a sense of job satisfaction. Indeed many believe that the residue of feeling around the degree is primarily negative—no matter where one works. Thus we all must answer one major and important existential question: Why is it so difficult to claim the idealism that fuels the hard work we do?

Training for the PhD teaches the ability to disentangle discrete narrative strands—tracking historical events, aesthetic conventions, social and political norms, and economic conditions, as well as a myriad of other factors that go into shaping events. But we can't let ourselves forget what a privilege it is to have access to time and the opportunity to be reflective. As shown in this tweet by @ShitAcademicsSay, "I don't always get emotional. But when I do I call it affect."[26] We, as specialists, must help others recognize that this skill is extremely valuable in today's global context, where to be effective, one must be able to negotiate complex and multilayered systems on the ground and in real time. Being able to think across and between multiple narratives while maintaining the discrete distinctions of each is precisely what the PhD trains its recipients to do. Why do so few—including ourselves—proclaim the value of this training?

It is not only the federal agencies and for-profit and nonprofit funding organizations that are increasingly changing the type of proposals they support, but rather the needs, hopes, problems, and desires that arise out of our twenty-first-century global context. Agencies as different as USAID and the MacArthur Foundation agree that discoveries made in the silos of academia are far from ready to enter the world.[27] As one respondent to my survey explained, training in the humanities has "made it easier to access work which stretches across categories such as diversity, access, and institutional change," providing the language needed to successfully communicate and prompt transformation in "a variety of different work environments."[28] Another person emphasized the way in which the training has contributed to an ability to "do high-level management work," made successful by the ability to justify policy and decisions in real time.[29]

As many have already argued, clarifying the value of the PhD becomes even more urgent when considering graduate education, especially during a period when colleges are closing and PhDs are less in demand than ever before. What did those who responded to the survey say when asked if they would recommend getting a PhD in the current job market? A mere 1.2 percent responded with an unequivocal "yes." However, all others, including most of those who would not recommend getting a PhD, urged those interested in pursuing a degree to be prepared to accept employment outside an R1 institution.[30] Those who responded to this question emphasize the importance of purpose, ensuring that the work we're undertaking can improve the future of thinking *by doing*.

As a writer, advancing the value of the PhD has meant undertaking projects that bring unlikely subjects into fruitful juxtaposition—like drawing a through line from nineteenth-century publication practices to the political and ideological goals afforded by social media as I did in *Thinking Outside the Book*.[31] Though I was interested in the historical mechanisms that promoted certain writing strategies in the nineteenth century, I was just as interested in what those strategies could tell us about our current cultural moment and the digital tools that inform it. Bringing the past into contact with the present is one way that humanists can help others have a longer, more hopeful view. For those designing programs, directing dissertations, or working with graduate students in general, encouraging students to make connections between discipline-specific content and the world around us is essential. Requiring, for instance, at least one assignment be directed to the public will train students to contribute to what the National Science Foundation (NSF) calls "broader impacts," requiring grantees to articulate a plan to share the knowledge generated with a larger public than the community of researchers with whom scientists typically communicate.[32] Better yet, why not require a chapter in each dissertation dedicated to such "broader impacts" just as NSF requires its grantees to do?

As an administrator, my background as a scholar and educator has helped me understand, in concrete ways, what the stakes are when we consider change on a structural level and how important it is to preserve the discrete values epitomized by the various fields of study—as well as their unique contributions. In each of these cases, academic training gave me the vision and the discipline to launch these efforts, engage others in their development, and sustain them over the course of years.

Like with other professions, the world around us shapes both the content and forms research and scholarship take. As a result, literary studies produce important and useful insights—though, like any other form of expertise, such insights often require a degree of translation for them to be comprehensible to those not trained in the discipline. Far from being "economically irrelevant, unaffordable luxuries," research-intensive humanities degrees enrich nondisciplinary professional outcomes in part because this training demands taking the long view.[33] At a recent industry relations panel that assembled representatives from pharma, tech, and venture capital, for instance, speakers agreed that a major incentive in partnering with academic researchers is the fact that academics are *not* driven by the business calendar but rather seek results unencumbered by those limitations. Academic training emphasizes the pursuit of knowledge for the sake of inquiry, operating in the kind of "what if" mode that often fuels innovation. Instead of relying strictly on fee-for-service, business-oriented research and development units, industry looks to the university for the ways in which disciplinary norms ensure high-level thinking and results that have been developed in terms of the broadest possibilities. Our belief in the possibility of truth provides an important, even if not always convenient, contribution. Part of what the PhD certifies is what Leonard Cassuto calls "an ethic." As he defines it, an ethic " provides a way to rethink day-to-day actions and a basis for large-scale engagement."[34]

What the panelists emphasized as a drawback, however, was that academic partners undermine their value when communication is too slow and/or too vague. Although results may not be available as planned in the third quarter, for instance, industry partners still need to allocate resources for the next quarter. Failing to submit a report on the current state of the project—especially when plans are not aligned with the agreed-upon schedule—is tantamount to students expecting to receive a passing grade on an assignment never turned in. This same lesson follows when transitioning from an academic job to an administrative one. Just as syllabi are due and classes take place at a given time, research-related work products also need to meet firm deadlines. Being reluctant to communicate honestly about the state of research—what's taking place and what's not—is the deal breaker. Just as we accept—and expect—students to run into sudden and unexpected pitfalls as they try to complete assignments, researchers doing high-level thinking cannot anticipate all that may arise through inquiry. But what we can do—and need to do more of—is be more transparent about the steps in the thinking we're doing, and why continuing to think deeply will result in the kind of thoughtful and intelligent change that most people want to see define the work they do. In my administrative role, I try to bring this process-oriented approach to projects and take great joy in finding ways to open up conversations to ideas and practices from all corners. For instance, when we were in the information- gathering stage of the Research and Scholarship Strategic Plan at Tufts, we found that there was much more to learn from faculty than the time we had put aside would permit.[35] Instead of sticking with our plan, we extended our study period, adding additional focus groups. At the same time, the commitment to specific goals and a timeline helped advance this work at a pace that satisfied the need for productivity while also creating an opportunity for innovation and much-needed growth. Sometimes, the commitment to objectivity can surface as a too rigid demand for autonomy. What we forget at these times is that we are in a partnership working toward a common goal and it just doesn't pay to finish a job that doesn't suit the purpose. In our case, our purpose was to enhance opportunities for research and scholarship at Tufts, not just create a tidy narrative about what we thought that might look like.

Truthfully, the elite educational background I have been afforded infuses what many would call a privileged view of work—that it should be more than just financially remunerative but also personally rewarding. I have also had the luxury of a fully funded education financed by teaching and research assistantships. Since getting my PhD, I have taught in elite settings and been employed by research-intensive colleges and universities like Tufts—where I am currently employed. I got my PhD during the height of the "canon wars," as literary studies were striving toward inclusion. My interests were conditioned by those social and political concerns—about what wasn't getting talked about in academic settings and why. My first project, in which I reread literary history through the lens of business history, allowed me to reframe the rise of canonical literature as a market phenomenon, driven by the need to make authorship pay more than prestige. In some ways the argument I am making here mirrors the one nineteenth-century authors had to make—we need to earn money, not just respect—to survive in this capitalist society. Indeed, what drew me to higher education and the pursuit of the PhD was precisely the desire to do work that was both intellectual and useful. The PhD required that I devote myself to the twin purposes of teaching and learning. And though I spent over a decade in pursuit of a tenure-track position, I did not restrict myself—or my value— to the limits of academic activity. As I continue to work outside of my field, I find I have countless opportunities to continue to chase those goals—and find new ways to fulfill them. I agree with the survey respondent who linked success and job satisfaction to how advanced training not only made an attractive non-faculty role possible but also provided the resources and perspective needed to grow the role itself.[36]

We can heed Daniel Lee Kleinman's clarion call that "all public higher-education leaders should be making a specific argument for the employment relevance of liberal arts and humanities education and taking this case directly to the economically concerned and utility-oriented citizens of these states."[37] But not enough of us with a humanities background have made it clear why we are well positioned to foster the kind of intelligent growth in research and scholarship most needed to meet the demands presented by the twenty-first-century global context. From focusing on infrastructure and programming to foster innovation to breaking new ground through targeted investments and creating opportunities to braid together resources made possible by their strong liberal arts tradition, universities are poised to do more than reclaim the respect of an earlier era. That reputation had its roots in a siloed ivory tower, removed from the day-to-day world around it. Today's universities have more to offer as long as they keep an eye on the business proposition: extended and deep thinking over time is a value-add. Survey respondents emphasize "training and practical experience in a wide variety of research methods, analysis, and learning how to learn new things independently" as a key contribution. Another respondent noted the impact of advanced training on the ability to take on the role of collaborator, improving work products over time by deepening team conversations with the express purpose of advancing them.[38]

Humanities PhDs need to take a more vocal stance on why their skill set should be seen as "the most effective way to increase the creativity and innovation in their business and technology" as scholars Rafael Alvarado and Paul Humphries claim.[39] Career options outside of the professoriate require radical acts of creativity—and this is, in part, what drew me away from my tenured position. Alvarado and Humphries caution that if we can't "responsibly generalize in our readings and our representations, the possibility of collective public life is imperiled."[40] Now more than ever, PhDs are needed in the workforce to bring to bear the large-scale complex analyses that are at the heart of the training the degree represents. Indeed, as Alvarado and Humphries argue, "the increasing pace and consciousness of globalization have made thinking on a wider scale of space, at least, a scholarly imperative. Consciousness of planetary forces and problems, such as environmental destruction, species extinction, and global warming, have also forced a reckoning with the long-term processes behind these developments—and the vast extent of their impact."[41] The abilities to conduct intensive literary analysis and communicate the insights generated, especially when made legible to people outside academia, have all the elements of leadership. People with PhDs are people who have studied complex systems and learned to conduct multilayered analyses, often driven by key principles such as equity, democracy, and access. PhDs are problem solvers because they are problem finders. We are trained to be critical, an important asset that can be diminished by an inability or aversion to collaboration. Working outside the academy incentivizes collaboration as it is simply required to succeed. As many PhDs take to the internet, mobilize using hashtag activism, and crowdsource syllabi to satisfy the need to create change and expand our audience, they may just as significantly use those impulses to put words into action by shaping policy, informing organizations, and advancing other humanistic goals all across society.[42]

In other words, taking a research-intensive degree into a context not defined by the disciplinary norms that were used to produce it requires those norms to be examined and repurposed with a view toward utility and efforts to advance goals that can be enormously satisfying.[43] Being careful, and critical, about what one's "value add" is to a shared goal may seem like a departure from the rigors and solitary practices of the scholar, but I suggest answers to such questions provide a healthy and ultimately rewarding antidote to what can be a corrosive anxiety about the true legitimacy and social purpose of expertise. As one respondent to my survey commented, "Working outside my discipline has helped me think more critically about the meaning of the discipline itself and the many ways that my scholarly work informs the agendas I most care about."

Notes

A hearty thanks to Henry Louis Gates Jr. for posting my survey and to all those who filled out the survey, including those who self-identified: Nicole Blair, Paula Chambers, Javier de la Rosa, Edoardo Frezet, Amod Lele, Quentin McAndrew, Keith

Newlin, Elizabeth Padilla, Jodine Perkins, J. Jeanine Ruhsam, Sandy Vaughn Suazo, Gustavo Vargas, Katherine Walden.

1 See Robert Weisbuch and Leonard Cassuto, "Reforming Doctoral Education, 1990 to 2015 Recent Initiatives and Future Prospects" (Andrew W. Mellon Foundation, June 2, 2016), https://mellon.org/media/filer_public/35/32/3532f16c -20c4-4213-805d-356f85251a98/report-on-doctoral-education-reform_june-2016 .pdf. As they say, "More recently, academic positions in the sciences have been in decline as federal and state support of higher education continues to decrease. Time to degree has remained terribly long, with over eight years from the start of a program to graduation now the norm in the humanities. And the cyclical grant-making mechanism of the sciences built a structure that relies on student populations to staff laboratories to do the work that would allow the grants to be renewed. Such research exigencies, then and now, have severely compromised the academic development of doctoral students."

2 Studies from Burton Bledstein, *The Culture of Professionalism: The Middle Class and the Development of Higher Education in America* (Norton, 1965), up through more recent studies of the university as a neoliberal institution such as Christopher Newfield's *Ivy and Industry* all recognize the effort of higher education to "serve" the public.

3 The survey was posted on the C19 list, the Boston Digital Humanities list, my Facebook and LinkedIn pages, the Hutchins Center Facebook page, and multiple Twitter accounts. I received 189 responses. The survey ran March 2–10, 2019.

4 Augusta Rohrbach, "LinkedIn Post Announcing Survey," March 5, 2019.

5 Among the fields represented were varieties of education, language, literature, history, philosophy, religion, and one outlier with a PhD in cognitive psychology.

6 I defined "outside academia" as "in a non-teaching position" so my results do not exclude those in academic administration.

7 Quoted in Karin Fischer, "It's a New Assault on the University," *Chronicle of Higher Education*, February 18, 2019, https://www.chronicle.com/interactives /Trend19-Intrusion-Main.

8 For more the need to promote community among academics, sharing ideas and work, see Jane Tompkins and Gerald Graff, "Can We Talk?," in *Professions: Conversations on the Future of Literary and Cultural Studies*, ed. Donald E. Hall (University of Illinois Press, 2001); Maggie Berg and Barbara K. Seeber, *The Slow Professor: Challenging the Culture of Speed in the Academy*, reprint ed. (University of Toronto Press, 2017). Maggie Berg and Barbara Seeber blame the corporatization of the university; I see the problem as stretching well beyond the effort to use business principles to support educational and research institutions.

9 Unlike other programs, Tufts plans to grow collaboration through the interaction of grad students together with faculty. Other programs include students, but usually undergrads, or they strictly focus on grad students *or* faculty. For a program that focuses on grad students that was recently funded by NSF, see, for instance, a recent grant that Texas Tech got from NSF, Developing Reflective Engineers, and Mcubed at the University of Michigan, which focuses on faculty. Another way of thinking about it is as a mini-IGERT program without the risk and stresses on students and faculty to support students across degree requirements from different schools and departments. Ryan C. Campbell et al., "Fostering Reflective Engineers: Outcomes of an Arts- and Humanities-Infused

Graduate Course," in *2018 World Engineering Education Forum—Global Engineering Deans Council (WEEF-GEDC)* (IEEE, 2018), 1–6, https://doi.org/10.1109/WEEF-GEDC.2018.8629714; Mcubed, "Mcubed 3.0 Essentials," https://mcubed.umich.edu/mcubed-essentials; "Welcome to IGERT.Org," http://www.igert.org/.

10 Response to Q11, submitted to Augusta Rohrbach (n.d.).

11 K–12 Blueprint, "Maker & STEM," May 13, 2014, https://www.k12blueprint.com/toolkits/maker-stem.

12 Responses 10 and 32 to question 10 submitted to Augusta Rohrbach (n.d.).

13 Sam Fallon's article in the *Chronicle of Higher Education* provides a recent example of how academics contribute to the popular notion that professors bluster over moot points rather than contribute to a larger discussion. Fallon, "The Rise of the Pedantic Professor," *Chronicle of Higher Education*, March 1, 2019, https://www.chronicle.com/article/The-Rise-of-the-Pedantic/245808?cid=cr&utm_source=cr&utm_medium=en&elqTrackId=60196e66569c4f408ce4f8b152facc8&elq=427facbf3df345769ded4ab02c33776c&elqaid=22469&elqat=1&elqCampaignId=11084.

14 Survey response to question 10 submitted to Augusta Rohrbach (n.d.).

15 Survey response to question 10 submitted to Augusta Rohrbach (n.d.).

16 Educational Advisory Board, "For the Greater Good: Boosting the Value of Industry Partnerships " (2017), https://attachment.eab.com/wp-content/uploads/2019/07/For_Greater_Good_URF_Finals.pdf#page=21.

17 Survey response to question 10 submitted to Augusta Rohrbach (n.d.).

18 Today's scholars can use digital tools to refine analyses of style and word frequencies such as those described by Ted Underwood in "The Stone and the Shell." However, even when leveraging the most sophisticated tools to establish patterns across the large digital corpora available today, I wonder how much weight that kind of evidence would hold for those outside of the humanities. Underwood, "The Stone and the Shell" (n.d.), https://tedunderwood.com/.

19 See https://mellon.org/programs/higher-learning/sawyer-seminars/ for a full description of the Sawyer Seminar program.

20 Institutionalized forms seem to promise innovation but often outlive their purpose. As Mark Garrett Cooper and John Marx explain about the failure of centers to galvanize change, centers exerted "a compelling pull on the intellectual life of the period, humanities centers supported grand agenda-setting projects for the humanities, but they addressed niche audiences habituated to the academic star system." In this case, taking a business model approach that includes a sun-setting clause, I would agree, is a useful hedge against institutional forms outliving their function. Marx and Cooper, *Media U: How the Need to Win Audiences Has Shaped Higher Education* (Columbia University Press, 2018), 213.

21 There are exceptions, of course. Research on electromagnetic interference by Dr. Elaine Scarry, Walter M. Cabot Professor of Aesthetics and the General Theory of Value, Harvard University, made its way into the National Transportation Safety Board's report. See Emily Eakin, "Professor Scarry Has a Theory," *New York Times Magazine*, November 19, 2000, https://archive.nytimes.com/www.nytimes.com/library/magazine/home/20001119mag-scarry.html ; Nathan Schneider, "A Literary Scholar's Voice in the Wilderness," *Chronicle of Higher Education*, February 17, 2014, https://www.chronicle.com/article/A-Literary-Scholars-Voice-in-/144733.

22 See Thomas Koenigs's argument for "the workplace value of the kind of supposi-
tional reasoning and conjectural thinking inherent in the reading of fiction" in
"Fictionality Risen: Early America, the Common Core Curriculum, and How We
Argue about Fiction Today," ed. Osucha Batker and Augusta Rohrbach, *American
Literature* 89, no. 2 (June 1, 2017): 225–253, https://doi.org/10.1215/00029831
-3861493.

23 Fischer, "It's a New Assault on the University."

24 Nick Gillespie, "Who's Afraid of the MLA?," *Reason*, December 27, 2005,
https://reason.com/2005/12/27/whos-afraid-of-the-mla/.

25 Shit Academics Say (@AcademicsSay), "Just Wondering If You Had Time to Grab
a Coffee to Discuss How Busy We All Are," Twitter, February 21, 2019, https://
twitter.com/AcademicsSay/status/1098647081965768707.

26 Shit Academics Say (@AcademicsSay), "I Don't Always Get Emotional. But
When I Do I Call It Affect," Twitter, March 25, 2015, https://twitter.com
/academicssay/status/580693264904359936?lang=en.

27 For more information on USAID and the MacArthur Foundation, see US Aid,
"What We Do," February 16, 2018, https://www.usaid.gov/what-we-do; Crain's
Chicago Business, "A New Nonprofit Helps Match Donors with Causes,"
February 28, 2019, https://www.chicagobusiness.com/nonprofits-philanthropy
/new-nonprofit-helps-match-donors-causes.

28 Survey response to question 10 submitted to Augusta Rohrbach (n.d.).

29 Survey response to question 10 submitted to Augusta Rohrbach (n.d.).

30 Breakdown of responses to Q12—"Would you recommend getting a PhD in the
humanities in the current job market? If so, why? If not, why not?" Total $n = 50$;
Y = 6; Yb = 17; N = 17; Nb = 6; n/a = 4.

31 Augusta Rohrbach, *Thinking Outside the Book* (University of Massachusetts Press,
2014).

32 NSF defines its Broader Impacts criterion by offering a series of questions: "How
well does the activity advance discovery and understanding while promoting
teaching, training, and learning? How well does the proposed activity broaden the
participation of underrepresented groups (e.g., gender, ethnicity, disability,
geographic, etc.)? To what extent will it enhance the infrastructure for research
and education, such as facilities, instrumentation, networks, and partnerships?
Will the results be disseminated broadly to enhance scientific and technological
understanding? What may be the benefits of the proposed activity to society?"
Peter March, "Broader Impacts Review Criterion—Dear Colleague Letter "
(National Science Foundation, n.d.). https://www.nsf.gov/pubs/2007/nsf07046
/nsf07046.jsp.

33 Roger L. Geiger et al., *A New Deal for the Humanities: Liberal Arts and the Future
of Public Higher Education*, ed. Gordon Hutner and Feisal G. Mohamed (Rutgers
University Press, 2015), 86–100.

34 Leonard Cassuto, *The Graduate School Mess: What Caused It and How We Can
Fix It* (Harvard University Press, 2015), 210.

35 For information on Tufts' Research and Scholarship Strategic Plan, see https://
viceprovost.tufts.edu/research-scholarship-strategic-plan.

36 Response to question 11 submitted to Augusta Rohrbach (n.d.).

37 Daniel Lee Klienman, "Sticking Up for Liberal Arts and Humanities Education:
Governance, Leadership, and Fiscal Crisis," *New Deal for the Humanities*, 86–87.

38 Response to question 10 submitted to Augusta Rohrbach (n.d.).

39 Rafael Alvarado and Paul Humphries, "Big Data, Thick Mediation, and Represen-
    tational Opacity," *New Literary History* 48 (2017): 786.
40 Alvarado and Humphries, "Big Data," 784.
41 Alvarado and Humphries, "Big Data," 784.
42 See Augusta Rohrbach, "Realism 2.0," in *The Oxford Handbook to American
    Literary Realism*, ed. Keith Newlin (Oxford University Press, 2019), for further
    thoughts on the impact of web 2.0 capabilities on the active roles educators and
    scholars can now take.
43 In *The Graduate School Mess*, Cassuto reminds readers that utility was in the
    DNA of U.S. higher education. With its origins in the Morrill Act of 1862, the
    land-grant university was conceived in order to "advance all kinds of professions in
    utilitarian as well as theoretical ways." Cassuto, *Graduate School Mess*, 12.

Part 2

Beyond Plan B

• •

Preparing for What's Next

6

First-Generation Students and the Mission of Graduate Study

• •

LEANNE M. HORINKO

AND JORDAN M. REED

There is a vast literature on the needs of first-generation undergraduate students. It is known that they need strong mentors, defined access to resources, and a student body and faculty that represent diverse perspectives. The literature on these first-generation students shows how overwhelming and alienating the college experience can be. They struggle with testing, getting acclimated to the old traditions of a college or university setting, balancing their academic work with familial responsibilities, and translating their academic work to their family members who have not gone to college. But what happens when these same students decide to enroll in a graduate program? For a group of students who entered college without the academic cultural capital other students already possess, graduate school can be an even more daunting prospect. Despite this reality, when compared to the first-generation college experience, the first-generation graduate student experience is relatively unexamined, save for a few scattered articles.[1]

The graduate student experience is considerably different from the undergraduate student experience for all students. On some level it is inherently overwhelming and, at times, alienating for all students. Graduate school brings with it complex relationships with faculty mentors, enhanced expectations in seminar-style classes, ambiguous exams, thesis defenses, language exams, field-work, internships, or any number of program-specific or discipline-specific requirements. At the doctoral level, students are trying to balance collegial rela-tionships with other PhD students and postdocs, while also knowing they will soon be competing for academic positions with these colleagues. Likewise, the staple of doctoral work, research projects, can be daunting. The act of pro-ducing original research, especially in the humanities and social sciences, is about going off on your own to complete and compile your contribution to your field—an isolating experience for any student population. That isolation can be exacerbated for first-generation graduate students who do not have a family support system that understands what they do. First-generation graduate stu-dents are clearly capable of serious contributions to their respective fields. Their otherness as first-generation students should not stand in the way of allowing them to fully commit to their research and training. Reforms are needed in graduate school to remedy the challenges and disadvantages that first-generation students face.

Alicia Peaker and Katie Shives noted the obstacles they met as first-generation graduate students coming off successful careers as undergraduates. Simply figuring out how they best worked within this new environment of iso-lated research was a challenge. At the center of graduate study is the lone researcher, venturing out into the archives or setting off to collect data to later be compiled into journal articles and a dissertation. However, feelings of isola-tion are not restricted to research endeavors. They are a staple of graduate school coursework and social life. Further, graduate school is often a highly competi-tive environment with students competing for scholarship opportunities, fund-ing packages, prizes, and places in publications and conferences and sometimes competing for the attention of faculty and mentors. The result of this isolating experience and competitive environment is often imposter syndrome. Peaker and Shives described their situation perfectly:

> When I started my graduate program I realized that I did not know how to really read primary literature. For the life of me I could not figure out how my peers were able to cover all the journal articles for class, and I was so embar-rassed that I couldn't keep up. For a while I thought it was due to me being from a smaller state school while many of my peers were from private institu-tions and had impressive credentials, so surely they were smarter than me and that was why I couldn't keep up. Nope! Turns out most of the other students skimmed the figures and discussion sections just enough to discuss them in class. It had nothing to do with my intelligence—I just didn't know about a common shortcut because I hadn't had experience with high-volume coursework.[2]

This scenario is embedded in the psyche of just about every graduate student. Whether sitting in a seminar discussion or around a pub table, listening to their peers rattle off names and concepts that are not familiar can make students feel like they are behind their peers. Every graduate student feels some anxiety of being found out, revealed to their colleagues as the inferior student who slipped past the gatekeepers into this prestigious ivory tower system. For first-generation graduate students, this also brings up feelings of internal conflict and a heightened sense that they do not belong. Despite offers of admission to graduate programs with full funding and after receiving stellar grades as an undergraduate, they do not feel they belong in this prestigious place.

Imposter syndrome is far from the only challenge first-generation students experience at a heightened level. Being first-generation students ourselves and the authors of this chapter, we have firsthand experience navigating the challenges Peaker and Shives described. We felt out of place during much of our graduate school experience. In retrospect, there is a lot of information we wish we had known when we set out for graduate school. We wish we had better understood how a particular program's structure can impact graduate study or how varied the experience can be from institution to institution. We wish we had known the unwritten rules and what is often referred to as the "hidden curriculum." In essence, we wish we had known what questions to ask and when to ask them. Instead, we learned through experience and met each challenge as it presented itself. During our journey, questions constantly arose. Some were business-oriented questions of funding and completing goals—Who should I speak to at the university to apply for extra travel funding? How much work should I dedicate to publishing ASAP? By the way, how do I publish? Others were more personal and complex questions about managing graduate school— How do I balance the need to dedicate myself to research and bring in enough income to survive, especially given the expectations of research fellows and teaching assistants for little compensation?

In light of our experiences, it is time for a harder look at first-generation graduate student academic and professional life. From this, it is possible to discover how systemic problems in the graduate school ecosystem can be solved, not only for first-generation students but for all graduate students. This can take the form of revised policies or educational programs, but each should be created with a unifying purpose. We should take the necessary steps to aid first-generation students in their transition to graduate study effectively. The fruits of these efforts will likely benefit all graduate students. First-generation students, many of them underrepresented and so-called nontraditional students, are exactly what the academy needs to innovate and develop. If we want to serve students better and diversify the professoriate, we need to look at those students we are welcoming into graduate schools and see their wants and needs. What follows in this chapter is a breakdown of some key issues and experiences where there is potential to improve the graduate student experience in ways that speak directly to the challenges faced by first-generation students. We focus on some particular challenges faced and examine ways that institutions can implement policies and programs deliberately crafted to address first-generation students' needs and, by extension, the needs of graduate students more generally.

Perhaps the most enduring challenge first-generation graduate students face is the gap between their family's background and their own educational attainment. The undergraduate experience has been brought into the public eye enough so family members without a bachelor's can understand what their first-generation student is doing when they are studying for and completing their bachelor's degree. There are now seminars and programs designed to introduce students to the fundamental aspects of pursuing a college education and learning about funding their education. Perhaps more importantly, the general public understands the value of a college degree on the job market. The bachelor's diploma is the presumed golden ticket to the middle class. It was our family members who did not have a college education who encouraged both of us to go to college so that we could find well-paying jobs.

What these family members do not understand, however, is how complicated the job outcomes and earning potential for a graduate student in the humanities or social sciences can become. The math is rather simple for a college degree. Though the precise dollar amount depends on the study, a college degree is worth well more than a high school degree. The Association of Public and Land-Grant Universities estimates that a bachelor's degree holder earns $2,268,000 over a lifetime compared to the $1,547,000 earned by someone with only a high school degree. For an advanced degree, either a master's or a doctorate, an individual is expected to earn $2,671,000.[3] This advanced degree category is particularly tricky. It does not differentiate between MA, MS, MAT, MBA, EdD, MD, or PhD, each of which have vastly different earning potentials. Humanities and social science PhDs, in particular, will face challenging job markets and likely lower salaries upon graduation. None of these figures take into account the seven to ten years it takes to earn a PhD in many disciplines compared to three years for an MBA or JD or four years for an MD. These considerations are particularly challenging for any first-generation graduate student who is more likely to be wholly reliant on undergraduate advisers for experienced guidance in pursuing graduate education.

This is even more challenging when considering the decidedly intellectual outcomes of a PhD program in the humanities compared to a more professionally oriented graduate program. Explaining to your parents, grandparents, aunts, and uncles how studying an obscure research topic will help you on the job market can be difficult. Many tend to view the PhD as training for a specific job—teaching or the abstract notion of being a tenured professor. While this expectation is wholly reasonable, and the ideal for many PhD students, it is simply not the reality of the present academic job market and the growing focus on career diversity. Indeed, it can be challenging to explain to parents how the better part of a decade's worth of education could lead to limited job prospects and earning potential. To them, a doctorate means a six-figure salary and guaranteed job prospects. To a humanities PhD student—first-generation or not—the reality is much different.

Further, there is a fundamental disconnect between how first-generation families perceive graduate-level study. As graduate students, we understand the intellectual considerations that go into every methodological decision we make and every sentence we write. We think of our work as a serious endeavor. Hearing your reading and research referred to as "homework" (which we have both experienced) can feel diminishing. As graduate students, we prefer to think of our writing as articles, critical essays, and, if we're lucky, book manuscripts. It can be disheartening to hear well-intentioned family members ask how your "paper" is going. Graduate students who have family members already well versed in the academic world have a different perception of these essential elements of graduate study. To them, the act of creating scholarship is different, an essential element of the academic profession, that is not obvious to many first-generation families. Jess Waggoner wrote eloquently about this particular challenge with her own family when she was a graduate student. She faced questions such as "When are you finishing up? You've been in school for a long time. I thought you were a teacher, not a student. What are you studying again?"[4]

In personal conversations, it can be challenging to confide in loved ones who do not understand the academic culture, academic work, and job market during and after graduate school. Their advice, while appreciated, can be counterproductive and add to the frustration. Questions like "how much longer until you're done?," while innocent enough, may hammer on a student's insecurities about their progress. Blithe optimism about the job market, while intended as reassuring, may remind students of the long road of applications and possible rejection ahead of them. These remarks can feel alienating and add to the isolation felt by far too many graduate students struggling in silence. Waggoner astutely recommended a particular approach to these conversations, recommending first-generation graduate students "stay positive . . . and emphasize what you've learned or your most recent accomplishments."[5] Talk about conference travel or great feedback from a colleague. Chances are relatives of first-generation students will recognize these accomplishments for what they are—an integral and exciting part of graduate study.

However, these circumstances do not even begin to address the financial concerns first-generation students possess. All of this can be especially challenging with paltry funding packages supplied by most universities. Any student may find it difficult to live on a graduate student stipend. However, a first-generation graduate student may have the extra financial pressure of needing to contribute to the family household. It is a situation commonly discussed for first-generation undergraduate students but often overlooked for graduate students.[6] This issue is further complicated by the fact that graduate students are in a stage of life where financial concerns may prohibit them from big life events, namely home ownership, marriage, and parenthood.

To make ends meet, graduate students may feel pressure to live up to a certain expectation of style, which has its own financial repercussions. Waggoner summed up this expectation nicely : "The expectation [is] that we dress, speak, and professionalize as if we were making $40K+, while living on a stipend often less than $15K."[7] This comment does not even take into account the challenges of socializing with better-off peers who go out to the local pub for a drink. It also does not take into account cooking at home on a budget when healthier foods tend to cost more and eating poorly can translate into decrease wellness. This, by extension, has effects on performance in seminars and independent research. For first-generation students, already more anxious about these things than the average graduate student, this can cause a vicious cycle that affects overall performance, heightens imposter syndrome, and makes graduate school feel less than welcoming.

Over the past few years, a number of articles have appeared to provide advice and guidance for first-generation students working their way through graduate school. Broadly speaking, this advice falls into a few key categories. First, it encourages first-generation students to expand their professional networks. This can take the form of seeking career advice from colleagues or developing close connections to mentors and advisers. These articles also encourage the development of confidence and habits that counteract imposter syndrome. Finding like-minded colleagues and mentors is key, as is finding experience beyond coursework and research tasks. Last, first-generation students are encouraged to make use of essential campus services—career services, administrative offices, student organizations, and committees.[8] These recommendations are, indeed, wise. Many of the chapters in this book dig deeply into the particular ways graduate students, faculty, and administrators can develop these exact resources and skills. However, administrators and faculty need to be mindful that students who already feel like outsiders may not seek out these resources on their own. Going to the career center or setting up a meeting with a reference librarian may feel like asking for help and play into the same insecurities that are feeding their imposter syndrome. Graduate programs need to be proactive about bringing these resources to students in a way that feels integrated into the entire graduate student experience. Further, simply cultivating these skills does not make it any easier for first-generation students, who are predisposed to feel like outsiders in graduate school, to feel more comfortable with these skills. It also does not make up for the tremendous gap in generational knowledge that simply being a first-generation student entails. In the following pages, we discuss how universities can cultivate programs and policies specifically tailored to the needs of this student population.

Demystifying Graduate Programs and Admissions

Graduate school admissions processes are notoriously opaque and idiosyncratic.[9] What's more, the admissions process is not structured in a way to make it easy for students to gain more information. Students are often left questioning how GRE scores and GPAs factor into a committee's review. It's not clear whether a semester their grades suffered in college because they had to take on a second job to help with family finances will preclude them from admission. They do not know if a strong writing sample will be enough to convince a committee they deserve a spot in the incoming class, despite a mediocre GRE score. Letters of recommendation can be particularly confusing. Common questions include: What should they do if they've been out of a college setting for a few years? Will their professors even remember them enough to write letters of recommendation? Is it better to get a more recent letter of recommendation from an employer? Is it okay to ask about funding during the admission process, or is graduate admissions like a job interview? Is it improper to discuss finances until you know you have a spot? Can discussing financial packages prior to admission negatively impact your chances at an admission offer?

Of course the answers to these questions range from institution to institution, but they are usually more positive than many first-generation students would expect. The reality is many graduate programs welcome, even hope for, students with professional experience before embarking on a PhD. We were two students in this situation. Not every enrolled student comes straight from a BA or MA program. Students should be encouraged to reach out to their academic mentors, no matter how many years since their formal education. Chances are, if a student cares enough about a given subject to pursue a PhD, they already made a lasting impression on a potential recommender that will last a while. Absolutely, it is acceptable to ask about financial aid packages at the appropriate stage in the admissions process, after a student has expressed genuine, thought-out interest in a program for academic reasons. Administrators and faculty know that for many students this is an essential component to figure out if graduate study is even possible. The key is asking professionally and with tact. All of these questions and answers are natural additions for any graduate department's frequently asked questions web page.

Within the admissions system, the typical first-generation graduate student is reliant on a vague department website and an amalgamation of advice from past mentors and scattered graduate school guides to gain a full picture of a program and life as a graduate student. The savviest students will read articles and attempt to piece together information. The opacity of the admissions process puts first-generation students at a disadvantage, especially on issues of financial support and student life. Departments tend to obscure their financial aid and assistantship packages. Many students do not know the full picture of their finances until they have already committed to joining a program. The same is true of social life on campus. Many universities pay to have all accepted students visit campus as part of their efforts to get students to commit to their program. But in reality, by that time it is already too late for many students to gain a full understanding of graduate study. That effort needs to begin much sooner in the admissions cycle. Fortunately, some universities have already made strides in this direction, and their model can serve as inspiration for others.

Princeton University's Graduate School's Access, Diversity, and Inclusion Team hosts a Prospective PhD Preview (P3) program, which encourages first-generation students, low-income students, and students from historically under-represented groups to come to campus prior to admission and learn about life and academics at Princeton from faculty and current students.[10] This effort works hand in hand with other existing efforts to bring a more diverse student body to Princeton's campus.[11] In reality, many of the initiatives that colleges and universities are currently implementing to recruit a diverse body of undergraduate students can be extended to graduate students. As we mentioned at the beginning of this chapter, the population of first-generation undergraduate students is not wholly dissimilar from first-generation graduate students. Both groups need more experience and insight into navigating higher education institutions. Simply put, one of those groups—the undergraduates—has received more attention to date.

Of course, not every institution has access to the plentiful resources of Princeton. The feasibility of such a program can be more questionable at less prestigious, private institutions or a state institution under budget constraints. However, we encourage faculty and administrators to look for low-budget ways to create similar programs, even if it means not being able to pay for prospective students' travel and accommodations. The key goal here is education, no matter the delivery method—on campus or virtually.

Other programs, like HSI Pathways to the Professoriate, work across institutions to educate students about graduate school and "to cultivate a faculty that mirrors the nation's growing ethnic and racial diversity."[12] This particular program emphasizes graduate study for Hispanic students, a key group of first-generation graduate students. It focuses on students from Hispanic-serving institutions such as Florida International University, the University of Texas at El Paso, and California State University, Northridge. The Andrew W. Mellon Foundation supplied $5.1 million in support, which includes visits from mentors who get to know the fellows in the program as they prepare for graduate school. There is a six-week "boot camp" that includes extensive training where "students learn theories and methods, how to write a statement of purpose, how to take on original research projects and how to present at conferences." In addition, "they learn about addressing their mental health, how to navigate the politics of a campus, how to negotiate a PhD offer and how to select potential faculty advisors in graduate school, among other skills." As undergraduates, they receive a stipend and can get funding for laptops, books, conference travel, and even housing during their time as graduate students.[13] All of these areas address key challenges for first-generation students outlined throughout this chapter. Perhaps it is time for more programs like HSI Pathways to be funded nationwide. The impact for first-generation students could be profound.

Moreover, these programs address long-standing challenges faculty and administrators have been trying to solve. Academics have been working toward diversifying the professoriate for a number of years. One of the methods to address these diversity initiatives involves feeding the pipeline for future faculty by enrolling a more diverse graduate student population. Not only do we need first-generation graduate students and graduate students from underrepresented backgrounds to enroll in graduate programs and then become faculty to build a faculty body to better serve and mirror the college students of the future. It's also essential for quality scholarship and pedagogy to diversify our faculty pool. A diverse population of graduate students and faculty leads to a richer intellectual life for everyone. Students who are coming to graduate school for the first time offer a fresh perspective on scholarship and educational practice. They know how to cross new social and cultural boundaries and spread information.

Aside from the broader, far-reaching impact these programs can have on higher education, it is important to take a moment to reflect on the micro level—the individual students affected. First-generation students may feel like they do not belong in graduate school. However, they should find comfort in the knowledge that graduate schools are seeking them out. Although graduate programs and the application process can seem hugely intimidating, it is crucial for first-generation, underrepresented, and nontraditional students to know that graduate programs are actively looking for them! These programs can go a long way toward making progress in closing these gaps in cultural capital and assuaging the early onset of imposter syndrome. The more deliberately we incorporate the needs of first-generation students into the graduate school recruitment process, the better.

Improved Orientations and Community

Introducing students to a graduate school culture needs to begin at the prospective student stage and continue through enrollment (and possibly commencement). It is essential for graduate schools and departments to make information readily available and host workshops to introduce them to and teach them how to complete tasks fundamental to graduate education such as presenting at conferences, publishing, creating a CV, writing grants, building a syllabus, and so on. These information sessions can and should be targeted to every phase of graduate study itself to transitioning from graduate study and entering the job market. Ideally, these sessions include not just faculty but current student perspectives, as well as alumni and professionals from around the institution and outside the academy.

The best structure of these orientations and information sessions depends on the institution's size and resources. For example, Princeton graduate history students attend a two-day orientation organized by the Graduate School, plus a series of events organized by the department. The Graduate History Association, a student-led body, puts together several information sessions on navigating resources and graduate school with a student-to-student perspective. The department staff coordinates brief information sessions on navigating the university's funding platforms and the departmental dossier service. Additionally, Princeton graduate students are fortunate enough to have a team of professionals in the Graduate School's Professional Development office (also known as Grad-FUTURES) and the university's Career Center. These offices organize events, workshops, and boot camps dedicated to helping students learn how to navigate the job market, gain experience in a variety of professional areas in paid fellowship positions, hone their professional communication, and build their professional skills as educators. Workshops and information sessions at an institution the size of Princeton are virtually endless. If a student has difficulty finding information already being pushed to them, they can reach out to faculty or staff in their program, department, graduate school office, and centers to get information. Indeed, many of these initiatives are advocated in other chapters throughout this book for the benefit of all graduate students.

The University of Washington uses another approach, one that is likely much more feasible for all institutions regardless of their financial situation and size. The UW Graduate School maintains a website specifically for first-generation student audiences. The website states four objectives. It strives to "create visibility," "reduce stigma," "foster a sense of belonging," and "develop sustainable and supportive programming." The site offers direct links to connect to resources and the emails and phone numbers for the offices that can help provide assistance as well as a calendar of relevant events. Perhaps most importantly, it includes profiles of graduate students who identify as first-generation.[14]

There is no more powerful way to make first-generation students feel like they belong as graduate students than to make them realize they are not alone. The University of Washington at Tacoma's "We Are First Generation" web page accomplishes this quite well. The site's tagline labels first-generation students as "aspirational," "multilingual," "empowered," and "resilient." It acknowledges first-generation students ties to family and their community as well as their need to navigate the world of graduate study. At the moment, graduate student profiles are mixed into the site, which remains predominantly focused on undergraduate students. However, the graduate student profiles that populate the page are inspiring and would make anyone feel welcome. Angela Jones, an MEd candidate at the university, provides some advice for students: "It is not the challenge or obstacle that makes the difference in your life, it is how you handle those challenges that makes the greatest impact and leaves a lasting impression on the individual you are striving to become."[15]

Perhaps most importantly for first-generation students, a professor is identified as first-generation on the site. Jeffrey Cohen, assistant professor of social work, writes,

> Being a first-generation college student has long been a source of pride for me. While finishing high school and continuing to college was something my parents had always hoped for my siblings and I, I did not grow up with a sense that a college degree was in my future. I struggled in high school and was not academically prepared to attend a four-year college upon graduating. Instead, I attended a community college for a year in order to earn college credit and improve my grades. . . . For me, it was a real challenge to acclimate to college life. I had no idea what to expect and neither of my parents were able to prepare me based on their own experiences. I struggled to get a sense of what was expected of me both in and out of the classroom. I didn't know how to interact with faculty or staff. In order to help support myself and not be a financial burden to my family, I had to work in addition to taking classes.[16]

Cohen speaks to every core issue first-generation students face. He acknowledges that he felt out of place during his undergraduate years. He reflects on his academic struggles. Expectations were ambiguous and anxiety-inducing. Speaking with faculty and staff felt foreign, and there was a significant amount of pressure not to be a burden to loved ones who already struggled to stay afloat financially. From this excerpt, it is clear that his reflections are primarily focused on the undergraduate experience, but it is difficult to overstate how essential this type of honesty is for graduate students as well. Faculty are an integral part of the graduate student experience. If they make a deliberate effort to speak to the first-generation graduate student experience alongside administrative programs, much progress can be made.

The University of Washington's efforts to reach first-generation graduate students likely came from the top. David Eaton, the former dean of the Graduate School, self-identifies as a first-generation student from Montana. His narrative sheds light on another key area of need for these students—mentorship.

Eaton recalls a time early on in his graduate school experience when he was a student in the biochemistry program at the University of Kansas, but deeply unhappy. His career took a turn after he scheduled a meeting with the department chair to discuss his options. Specifically, Eaton was eyeing the pharmacology program, his eventual field of study. The meeting went well. In Eaton's memory, the chair "must have taken a liking to [him]" and offered Eaton a spot in the pharmacology program.[17] Eaton's story is the type that needs to be shared more freely in graduate school. Indeed, he received good mentorship during his time as a first-generation graduate student. Fortunately, he used this as an opportunity to share his story with a new generation of first-generation graduate students. In some ways, his experience is likely unique, but it can serve as a worthy model for faculty and administrators to emulate at their institutions. Good mentorship can be difficult to find in graduate school, especially for first-generation students who are likely to feel like they do not belong or lack the same cultural capital as their colleagues and faculty advisers. This is precisely why there is a need to think beyond the traditional models of mentorship in graduate school communities in favor of a more expansive view. Indeed, some of our greatest mentors in our own graduate school experience have been outside of our institution's faculty or dissertation committees.

The University of Washington also provides its own philosophical statement of what good mentorship is for students. For the purposes of this chapter, the statement also provides a useful mission statement for making graduate school less daunting for first-generation students. They promote mentorship that "engages students in conversation" and "demystifies graduate school." In comments and feedback, they advocate for "constructive" remarks and "encouragement." Last, and most important, the graduate school encourages students to find a mentor who "fosters networks and multiple mentors."[18] Together, these statements provide a framework for how graduate school can be made more comfortable and suitable for first-generation students, but the same can be said for all graduate students. Each chapter in this book provides useful strategies that help graduate students develop in each of these areas. It is no mistake that we have chosen to structure this volume in this way. We seek to create a more inclusive environment for graduate study. In first-generation students and their experiences, we find even more reason to bring this into reality with deliberate speed.

Notes

1 This lack of research was noted in Alicia Peaker and Katie Shives, "From First-Gen College Student to First-Gen Grad Student," *Inside Higher Ed*, *GradHacker*, December 12, 2013, https://www.insidehighered.com/blogs/gradhacker/first-gen -college-student-first-gen-grad-student.

2 Peaker and Shives, "From First-Gen College Student to First-Gen Grad Student."

3 Association of Public and Land-Grant Universities, "Public University Values," https://www.aplu.org/projects-and-initiatives/college-costs-tuition-and-financial-aid/publicuvalues/publicuvalues-resources/q3/employment-and-earnings.pdf.

4 Jess Waggoner, "Graduate Study for First Generation Students," *Inside Higher Ed, GradHacker*, December 8, 2013, https://www.insidehighered.com/blogs/gradhacker/graduate-study-first-generation-students. See also Auriel Fournier, "Family Ties and Grad School 'Why's,'" *Inside Higher Ed, GradHacker*, December 10, 2013, https://www.insidehighered.com/blogs/gradhacker/family-ties-and-grad-school-whys.

5 Waggoner, "Graduate Study for First Generation Students."

6 Sara Goldrick-Rab, *Paying the Price: College Costs, Financial Aid, and the Betrayal of the American Dream* (University of Chicago Press, 2017).

7 Waggoner, "Graduate Study for First Generation Students."

8 See Helen Pho, "Career Tips for First-Generation Grad Students," *Inside Higher Ed*, October 8, 2018, https://www.insidehighered.com/advice/2018/10/08/career-advice-first-generation-grad-students-opinion; Luendreo Barboza, "You're a First-Generation Graduate Student—How Do You Succeed?," *Cooper Square Review*, March 8, 2018, http://coopersquarereview.org/post/youre-a-first-generation-graduate-student-how-do-you-succeed/.

9 For more detail about graduate admissions, see Julie R. Posselt, *Inside Graduate Admissions: Merit, Diversity, and Faculty Gatekeeping* (Harvard University Press, 2016).

10 Princeton University, "Prospective Graduate Students Get a Peek Inside Princeton Ph.D. Programs" (October 10, 2018), https://www.princeton.edu/news/2018/10/10/prospective-graduate-students-get-peek-inside-princeton-phd-programs.

11 Office of Communications, "'60 Minutes' Features Princeton's Transformative Efforts to Increase Socioeconomic Diversity," Princeton University, April 29, 2018, https://www.princeton.edu/news/2018/04/29/60-minutes-features-princetons-transformative-efforts-increase-socioeconomic.

12 Kelly Field, "A Professor 'Who Looks Like Them,'" *Chronicle of Higher Education*, July 2, 2017, http://www.chronicle.com/article/A-Professor-Who-Looks-Like/240475.

13 Tiffany Pennamon, "HSI Pathways Program Aims to Increase Hispanic Representation in the Professoriate," *Diverse: Issues in Higher Education*, February 25, 2019, https://diverseeducation.com/article/139471/.

14 UW Graduate School, University of Washington, "First-Generation Graduate Students," http://grad.uw.edu/for-students-and-post-docs/core-programs/first-generation-graduate-students/.

15 University of Washington–Tacoma, "We Are First Generation," https://www.tacoma.uw.edu/news/we-are-first-generation.

16 University of Washington–Tacoma, "Jeff Cohen—We Are First Generation," https://www.tacoma.uw.edu/node/46396.

17 UW Graduate School, University of Washington, "David Eaton, Graduate School Dean," http://grad.uw.edu/student-alumni-profiles/dean-eaton/.

18 UW Graduate School, University of Washington, "What a Good Mentor Does," https://grad.uw.edu/for-students-and-post-docs/core-programs/mentoring/mentoring-guides-for-students/what-a-good-mentor-does/.

7

Building Professional Connections in Graduate School

• • • • • • • • • • • • • • • • • • • •

JOSEPH VUKOV

The term "networking" calls to mind an image that's distasteful to many graduate students and those who advise them: snappily dressed MBAs, name tags slung from their necks, moving in a frenetic pace to secure contacts before cocktail hour ends. That's probably not an attractive picture to you. It isn't to me. Networking for the twenty-first-century PhD student, however, usually isn't anything like this. For twenty-first-century PhD students, networking is, for the most part, *just talking*. Not pitching projects or deploying the newest corporate lingo or mastering the art of dropping resume lines into casual conversation. Really, networking is just talking.

But the reverse isn't true. Simply talking is not necessarily networking. You may talk regularly to your barista about the rotten Chicago weather, but that's not networking unless you use your conversations to build a professional connection. So networking is merely a matter of cataloging connections? No, it isn't that either. The sheer number of my contacts on LinkedIn has little to do with the strength of my professional network. This means, among other things, that advisors of graduate students cannot support their protégés merely by transferring contacts.

Professional networking is therefore not something the twenty-first-century PhD or those who support them can take for granted. Rather, twenty-first-century PhD students and those who support them must actively seek to build professional networks in graduate school. There are, of course, entire sections of your local bookstore dedicated to professional networking. But most of these manuals are geared toward the business world. And networking in the context of pursuing a PhD is not like it is in business contexts. The power suit, the million-dollar smile, the flashy business cards: these are more likely to inspire suspicion than confidence in many circles frequented by graduate students and their advisors. *And yet* we have good reason to think that creating and then strengthening a professional network is central to the professional life of a twenty-first-century PhD student and for those who seek to support them.

The truth is *networking works*. According to a recent survey by Performance-Based Hiring Learning Systems, 85 percent of jobs are found through networking. A recent NPR story, "A Successful Job Search: It's All about Networking," puts that number slightly lower at 70 percent. When percentages are that high, however, there's a sense in which the differences don't really matter. The lesson is the same. Securing a job after graduate school requires that twenty-first-century PhD students build an extensive and far-reaching professional network *while in graduate school*. The lesson is clear. If you are a graduate student, you need to know how to build such a network or, if you have one, how to strengthen it. If you are a faculty member or administrator who supports graduate students, you need to know how to facilitate the construction of your students' networks.

Not only does networking work, *networking matters* in that it is essential to building capacity in graduate students for collaboration and teamwork. While collaboration among scholars has been standard in STEM fields for decades, only recently has collaborative work become common among scholars outside STEM fields. Centers such as the Michigan Humanities Collaboratory have been founded to foster interdisciplinary collaborative work in the humanities. Foundations like the John Templeton Foundation fund research at the intersection of science and religion and often fund collaborative projects. My own home discipline of philosophy—long stereotyped as performed by a lone, bearded genius—has made a swing toward more coauthored projects. Collaborative work is no longer "side work" in the professional life of a twenty-first-century PhD student. It is paramount. But, of course, in order to collaborate effectively, PhD students first need a network of contacts with whom to collaborate. Networking matters because it supports collaboration.

Networking also matters because it supports the capacity to work in teams. While twenty-first-century PhD students build a variety of valuable skills— critical thinking, curriculum construction, project design and assessment, lab skills, and so on—developing teamwork skills can be either an afterthought or not fostered at all. That's a problem. Professionals in all contexts need to be able to work as teams, even if it is not as a primary role. And, of course, employers realize that. In the contemporary job market, being a "team player" is essential to being hired as a player at all. Building skills working with a team as a graduate student is therefore essential to success after graduate school. Like collaboration, however, it is impossible to develop teamwork skills sans a team. How to get one? Networking.

Networking *works*. And it *matters*.

Finally, networking is *actionable*. Building a professional network can seem a daunting task for twenty-first-century PhD students and those who seek to support them. But it needn't be that way. In what follows, I present actionable advice graduate students and their supporters can use to build or strengthen their professional networks. At the heart of this advice is two central contentions. The first is that academe already presents excellent opportunities for graduate students to build their professional networks. In fact, the opportunities for networking are arguably better within the academy than outside of it. Learning how to build a professional network in the context of a twenty-first-century PhD is therefore not so much a matter of creating opportunities for yourself or your advisees. It is rather a matter of recognizing opportunities that are already there.

The second central contention is that networking is not typically a matter of high-stakes informational interviewing, facilitated introductions, or planned networking events (though those have their place). Rather, networking is best done in small, low-stakes settings throughout the course of graduate school. Start early, and the twenty-first-century PhD student can build a strong network during their graduate school years. More importantly: they can develop the professional habits that will allow them to sustain that network after they've finished. Let's begin.

Don't (Always) Reach for the Stars

It can be tempting to think that the most valuable contacts for graduate students will be those who wield the greatest amount of influence. That graduate students should cultivate their professional network by establishing connections with the most well-known and well-connected scholars in their field, or with CEOs at companies where they'd like to work. That advisors of graduate students should introduce their protégés to the leaders of their respective fields. This mindset has led to many an awkward and unproductive conversation or email, by both graduate students and those who seek to support them. The mindset, however, is also misguided. For the twenty-first-century PhD student, the most valuable contacts will almost always be those at a similar stage of professional development as they are.

Of course, it can be satisfying for a graduate student to boast about having knocked back martinis with Professor Jones or spent a day exploring Santa Fe with CEO Smith. And there are times when these kinds of contacts are important for the twenty-first-century PhD student: a crucial letter of recommendation, a friendly face in the interview room, access to information about a new job. But when a PhD student finishes an article that still needs considerable editing, they won't (and *shouldn't*) be sending it to Professor Jones. And when that same graduate student is writing a cover letter, they won't (and *shouldn't*) be sending a draft to CEO Smith. No. Most of the time, they should be reaching out to professionals at a similar stage in their careers as they are.

If you are a graduate student, don't reach only for the stars as you build your professional network. When attending a conference, don't aim to meet the keynote speaker. Aim to meet the graduate student hosting the keynote speaker. When you are at a business lunch with an unfamiliar group, don't worry about getting to know whoever is sitting at the head of the table. Get to know whoever happens to be sitting next to you. When you are embarking on a new project, don't start building your team with the leaders in the field. Think first about which of your office neighbors might be interested in joining you.

Likewise, if you support graduate students as a faculty member or administrator and want to help your students develop their professional network, don't think first about the contacts at *your* stage of professional development. Think instead about how their work might best be supported at *their* stage of professional development. Forgo introducing them to your full professor coauthors; instead, introduce them to the newly minted PhD who helped you with the IRB application last year. When a graduate student is applying for a grant, don't reach out to the dean who has supported *your* development; instead, reach out to the newly hired grants officer in the dean's office. When a PhD student wants to transition from academia to the tech world, don't put them in touch with your college roommate who is now a manager at Google; instead, introduce them to your former PhD student who entered the tech world successfully.

Of course, sometimes it can be valuable for PhD students to meet (and even work with) the leaders in their field. And sometimes they will partner with professionals who are further along in their careers than they are. That's fine . . . good, even. Just don't make it the aim of networking as a graduate student. If graduate students are always looking at the stars as they build their networks, they won't notice the more obvious collaborators next to them on the ground.

Ask for Introductions

Imagine the following diagram: you are represented by a node, and your contacts are represented by a set of smaller nodes scattered around you. Some are close, some further away. A curved line connects the node representing you with each of those surrounding you. Imagining this? What I'm imagining looks like a chart at the back of an in-flight magazine, one that depicts all the routes your airline flies.

Now let's complicate things a bit. Imagine each of your contacts—each of the nodes surrounding you—as the center of *their own* networks. Scattered around each of them is a set of smaller nodes, each connecting back to your contacts. The diagram just got a lot larger, no? Here's the point. The first diagram you imagined is your network as it currently exists. The second diagram you imagined is your potential network.

How to access your potential network? Easy. Ask for introductions. If you are a graduate student, ask for introductions on your own behalf. If you support graduate students, ask for introductions on behalf of your graduate students. Ask for introductions over email, on LinkedIn, at staff meetings, and over the phone. The forum doesn't matter. Of course, you need a *reason* to ask for an introduction. No one should be asking for professional introductions simply to expand their network or that of others.

As you look to expand your network, it is crucial that you don't merely keep your current network in mind. Keep your *network's* network in mind as well. Sometimes, none of your own collaborators will fit the bill for a certain project, but your officemate's roommate from last year would be perfect. When that happens, ask to be introduced, either on your own behalf or on behalf of the graduate students you are looking to support.

Your contacts won't find this burdensome. What's more: their collaborators will appreciate the chance to be connected to someone new. You are reaching out to them, after all, about something you have good reason to think they'll find interesting.

Approach Conferences Strategically

Here's a familiar (even cliché) sight: the lonely graduate student, huddled over her drink and smartphone at a conference reception. She stays for an excruciating ten minutes before retreating to her hotel room to watch reruns on cable TV for the rest of the evening.

It's awkward seeing this person. It's worse being this person (I've been this person). But the worst part doesn't have to do with the awkwardness—it's the wasted opportunity. Conferences are excellent, even *ideal* opportunities for building professional networks, and a cocktail hour spent on the phone is a wasted hour.

So how to avoid this trap? Should graduate students down their cocktails, muster up some confidence, and begin working the room, armed with new-found social prowess and a pocketful of business cards? That can work, but many graduate students aren't particularly good at it. Moreover, many professionals are not particularly impressed with this style of networking.

So here's a better strategy: graduate students and those who support them should plan the conferences they attend ahead of time.

First, several weeks before each conference, PhD students and those who support them should study the program and make a list of attendees that may be valuable to meet or reconnect with: potential employers, friends they haven't seen for a while, contacts they've been wanting to make, scholars whose work they admire. Then, send some emails. Graduate students: feel free to reach out on your own. Networking ahead of conferences is standard practice, and no one will find it surprising to be contacted by an acquaintance, or even by someone they haven't met yet. Those who support graduate students: reach out on behalf of your students—introduce your graduate students to contacts you have, or those you'd like them to meet. Arrange a meeting at the conference reception, or for coffee or lunch.

Next, prepare some talking points for yourself, or for the graduate students you support. In this essay's introduction, I observed while not all talking is networking, all networking is talking. The upshot? If graduate students are to network effectively at conferences (and anywhere else for that matter), they will need to talk. To other people. But talk about *what*? Here are some strategies I have found work well with almost everyone.

Find a shared experience. If you work in the same profession, talk about developments at the local or national level. If you live in (or have visited) the same city, talk about your favorite restaurants, your least favorite bus routes, your insider tips on free days at the art museums. If you are attending the same conference, talk about the overdone chicken at the banquet or the stimulating keynote lecture. Conversation springs from common ground. You will be well served to find some.

Do some homework. If you or the graduate students you support have arranged to meet someone at a conference whom neither of you know, do some research on them beforehand. Not too much research. I'm not suggesting that you scour social media or perform an in-depth web search. But a little research goes a long way. If someone recently published a book or article, read it (or skim it). That will give you a shared experience and thus something to discuss. If someone works in a different city, you can ask for travel tips. If someone is employed by Company X, you can ask about what the company has been working on.

Prepare your elevator pitch. You typically shouldn't begin a conversation by pitching the projects you have been working on. But if you are networking effectively, people will inevitably ask about them. And you'd better be prepared to tell them in five minutes or less. The infamous elevator pitch. How to put one together? There's no precise formula, but here's one strategy: find a story or an anecdote that hooks your listener on your topic. Maybe a recent news item, a surprising fact, a historical tidbit, a baffling puzzle, a personal story. That's the first two minutes of your pitch. Then, explain how the hook raises a question or issue you are addressing in your projects. Maybe your research takes the surprising fact as its starting place; maybe the recent news item motivates the kind of questions that drives your dissertation. That's the third and fourth minutes of your elevator pitch. Finally, explain *as briefly as possible* how your project solves (or intervenes or clarifies) the tensions (or questions or issues) you've identified. That's the closing minute. This way of constructing an elevator pitch is by no means the only way. But I've found that this structure motivates a project and leaves your listener wanting to hear more. That's a good place to end.

All this planning ahead of time may seem overly methodical. Naysayers may think the approach to conferences I've outlined is, well, overly surgical. Aren't conferences supposed to be enjoyable?

Of course conferences are supposed to be enjoyable. But (perhaps unexpectedly) it is precisely by planning conferences ahead of time—from the people you or your graduate students meet to the subjects of conversation—that they can become enjoyable for graduate students. Graduate students who attend a conference that has been planned well can use it to build their network rather than presenting papers and then spending three lonely days attending talks alone. Rather than sipping cocktails in the corner, graduate students can be set up to have enjoyable and productive conversations throughout the conference.

Of course, networking at conferences shouldn't *end* with merely enjoyable conversations, at least not always. If you are a graduate student, you want your conversations at conferences to lead to professional topics: potential collaborations, job opportunities, new project ideas. But if you are regularly striking up conversations in a professional context, and if you follow the other strategies for networking that I outline here, this will happen naturally. Conversations in professional contexts inevitably turn to professional topics. My advice? Don't force the professional topics. If you spend an evening engrossed in conversation about the latest best seller, you can always follow up after the conference with a more professionally oriented email.

Send an Extra Email Every Day

Speaking of sending emails, here's an effective tip for increasing the strength of professional networks for graduate students: send an extra email every day. If you are like me, you already send dozens of emails a day: to students, to colleagues, to your credit card company, to your aunt in Albuquerque. You already know how to send emails.

So why not send one extra one, one that could do you or the graduate students you support some good? It doesn't matter where you send it. It could be to an old friend, a new contact, a potential collaborator, someone you met at the social last Friday. It also doesn't matter what the email is about: it could be about a *New Yorker* article you enjoyed, a project you've been planning, a lament about a recent political development.

Of course, sometimes your emails won't yield a reply. And sometimes they won't lead to anything of professional significance. But sometimes, a simple email will foster growth of your network in unexpected ways. I continue to be surprised how often a simple email can result in productive reply: "Good to hear from you! I was just starting work on a project yesterday, and we need someone else on board. You know of anyone who may work?" Often, you do: perhaps you; perhaps a graduate student you support.

Sending an extra email daily keeps your network alive. If you're a graduate student, that's good for you. If you support graduate students, that's good for you and the graduate students who are looking to you to help develop their networks. By keeping your network alive, you give it the opportunity to grow.

Professional socializing is part of a graduate student's job. Here's a common refrain among graduate students: "I can't attend the [PICK ONE: grad student social, lecture, career event, etc.] *because I've got too much work to do.*"

Newsflash: professional socializing is not a distraction from the work of a twenty-first-century PhD student. It is *part of* the twenty-first-century PhD student's work. One of the most important parts, in fact. PhD students simply won't build a professional network in front of their computers. Rather, they will build it at the socials, wine and cheese receptions, welcome back ceremonies, and Career Center resume workshops that make up a part of every graduate student's experience.

Once, I was invited to dinner with a prominent guest lecturer simply because I stayed until the end of his (lengthy and soporific) Q&A session. Another time, I met a future coauthor over mini hot dogs and mozzarella sticks at an end-of-the-year social. Neither of these meetings would have happened if I decided to polish a paragraph from my dissertation for the fifth time.

The lesson? Graduate students must resist the temptation to skip the social for an extra hour at the office. Spending that hour at the social is almost always going to be more productive. Whether you are a graduate student or an advisor of graduate students, it is therefore myopic to think that professional socializing is something that can be done after work or that it can be left out of professional advising. Part of the twenty-first-century PhD student's job is socializing, and both they and those who advise them would be remiss not to recognize this.

This advice, however, cuts two ways. If part of the twenty-first-century PhD student's job is socializing, then socializing is their job. Put differently: the social events graduate students attend are never *just* social events. They are also work events. That's not to say graduate students can't have fun (who said work can't be fun?!). It's rather to remind graduate students to maintain a professional mindset at social events they attend in their role as graduate students. Graduate students should take care about having that extra drink—or complaining about their dissertation advisor. When graduate students are socializing as graduate students, they are on the job just as much as when they are meeting with an undergraduate student or advisor back at the office.

So, the next time you or the students you advise are tempted to craft an abstract in lieu of the annual department party, remember that part of your job is attending the party Just remember this, too: attending the party is part of your job.

Cross Disciplines

The most *obvious* collaborators for twenty-first-century PhD students are their colleagues in neighboring cubicles. But these aren't always the *best* collaborators. Sometimes the best collaborators work on a different floor or in a different building or for a different institution altogether. Sometimes the best collaborators come from disciplines other than their own.

There are many benefits to interdisciplinary collaboration. Interdisciplinary collaboration helps graduate students see their work in a new light, teaches them how to pitch their projects to a diverse audience, and pushes them to expand their professional vision.

But how to cross disciplines? How to build connections outside the academy? How to help the graduate students you support find relevant collaborators in different disciplines within the academy, or with those outside academe? Truth is, it's not difficult. You *already* know scores of people outside your discipline and outside academe: your spouse's colleagues, the guy from biology you met at the university-wide kickoff event, the fellow Vikings fan you invite over to watch the game on Sundays, the neighbor with the grill that hosts barbeques throughout the summer. None of these people work in your discipline. Many of them work outside the academy. All of them are potential collaborators for you or the students you support.

The trick to crossing disciplines and building professional connections with people outside the academy, then, doesn't lie in meeting people outside your discipline or outside the academy. You already know people outside your discipline and outside the academy. The trick lies in seeing these people as part of your professional and not merely social network. Indeed, once you begin thinking about your professional network in more expansive terms, you'll be surprised at the places your professional interests overlap with people you already know. And you'll be surprised at the diverse opportunities for collaboration these areas of overlap provide.

Maintain a Professional Online Presence

Some professional development gurus will advise graduate students to maintain a wide-ranging online presence, to use it often, and to use it effectively. I'm open to these arguments but haven't yet been convinced by them. I'm not convinced there is any single online forum the twenty-first-century PhD student needs to maintain or that the forums graduate students do maintain need to be especially extensive. But there are two nearby pieces of advice I do find convincing.

First, graduate students need to maintain an online presence of *some* kind. If PhD students meet someone at a conference and don't pass along a business card (and you *do* have business cards, right?), how will their potential collaborators find them? Google. How can a graduate student convey professional information that doesn't fit into a resume? Include a link to a website or social media account at the top of the resume. How can graduate students impress a potential collaborator they met over the weekend? Direct them to an online portfolio. Graduate students must therefore seek out resources for crafting an online presence.

Some PhD students are digital natives and may already bring this ability to their professional skill set. But don't assume graduate students know how to craft an online presence. Graduate programs should work with other departments to organize workshops, bring in professionals to talk them through how to craft an online presence, and arrange for training in website construction. In my department, we look to other graduate students to facilitate this training, many of whom have experience in marketing, web design, and professional social media.

In addition to maintaining some kind of online presence, twenty-first-century PhD students must work to ensure that their online presence is professional. Thoroughly professional. How can graduate students maintain professionalism in online presence? Here's my advice: unless graduate students are especially adept at working with online platforms, they should keep their online presence sparse. If a graduate student maintains a website with nothing more than a CV, a brief description of their work, and their contact information, those who visit may not be impressed by their digital prowess. But it's also likely that they will find the information they need and that they will find it without having to wade through a mire of information that wasn't intended for them anyways.

Dress and Act the Part

Many graduate students believe that the superficial things—social mores, clothing choices, conversation style—don't matter, at least in the careers they are seeking. What does matter? Only the brilliance of one's ideas.

Well, maybe this should be true in certain parts of the professional world. But it isn't true, for better or worse. The professional persona of a graduate student matters, even in the most ivory tower contexts. When you have asked your PhD student to introduce a distinguished speaker, they should hold themselves with the same poise as the speaker they are introducing. When a newly minted PhD student is pitching a new project to a group of investors, the presentation must be given in the language and conversation style of the investors. The upshot? For graduate students to build an effective professional network in graduate school, they need to learn how to dress and act the part of a professional.

How do you encourage yourself or the graduate students you support to develop professionally in this way? Here's what worked for me: I began thinking about crafting a professional persona as a research project. My mind, like that of most twenty-first-century PhD students, is geared toward research. Research excites me. So once I approached this aspect of professionalism as a research program, it became less of a burden and more a source of curiosity. I found myself enjoying solving the mystery of "business casual." I began noticing the ways in which language use varies in different professional contexts. I become genuinely interested in analyzing the cadences of professional emails. The same, I believe, will work for you and the graduate students you support. Think about the "superficial" aspects of professionalism as an area of research, and they become immediately of interest to the graduate student mind.

Moreover, if you are like me, here is what you may discover: crafting a professional persona isn't a matter of layering a dishonest patina over one's true self or brilliant ideas. Rather, it's a matter of eliminating superficial distractions so that graduate students' ideas can shine through more brightly. The best professional persona is precisely one you *don't* notice: once PhD students have figured out how to dress and act the part of the professional, people stop noticing how they dress and act; instead, their conversation partners can pay attention to who they are and what they say.

Be Easy on Yourself

I'll share a secret with you: as a graduate student, I have attended conferences where I have followed very little of the advice I've given. I've failed to plan ahead. I didn't follow up with the people I met. I inelegantly trailed the keynote speaker, hoping for an impromptu conversation. I insisted on steering discussion to my own research and project ideas. As an advisor of graduate students, I have failed to advise hardworking PhD students to take time away from their thesis and attend departmental events; I have forgotten to connect my students with potential collaborators; I have congratulated them on being accepted at a conference without then helping them plan ahead to make the most of it.

And guess what? I survived. My network survived. My advisee's networks survived. I missed some opportunities to build my own network and the networks of the students I support, perhaps, but that's about it. Building a professional network—whether for yourself or on behalf of others—is a marathon, and it's a marathon in which you're going to have a couple rough miles.

So the next time you misstep in your efforts to build professional connections within the context of a twenty-first-century PhD, don't be too hard on yourself. Building professional connections is difficult work. Inevitably, you will falter at times and succeed at others. It's best to learn from both and dwell on neither.

In the pages above, I've suggested that building professional connections in the context of a twenty-first-century PhD does not typically involve high-stakes schmoozing. Becoming adept at networking in graduate school is not a matter of filling calendars or printing sleek business cards or finding the perfectly tailored power suit. Rather, it is a matter of developing a set of practically oriented habits and curating yourself as a professional.

According to Aristotle, habits are formed through repeated action. The more you perform brave actions, the more natural it becomes for you to act bravely; the more you perform temperate actions, the more natural it becomes for you to act temperately; and so on. Likewise: the more graduate students practice the tips I've presented here, the more they will find themselves developing the habits that are foundational to professional networking. On their own, these habits may seem insignificant. But taken together and over time, they can help twenty-first-century PhD students build a healthy professional network, one that will support them in graduate school and their life beyond.

8

Building Skill and Career Development Opportunities on Campus for Graduate Students and Postdocs

• • • • • • • • • • • • • • • • • • • •

MELISSA DALGLEISH

It was 2011, and I had become sure that I didn't want a tenure-track job. I started my PhD in the throes of the 2008 recession, and the tanking job market meant there were very few postings in my minuscule subfield—none near my home and family in Toronto, where I wanted to stay. But academic job scarcity wasn't the primary reason I no longer wanted a professorship. There were just too many aspects of the professoriate that didn't suit me—departmental politics made me uncomfortable, I didn't love teaching (and loathed grading), and I couldn't imagine going through the wildly onerous and fraught (interview on a hotel bed?) academic application and interview process.

This recognition—growing stronger as I got closer to my defense date— posed a problem. After all, I'd been training to become a professor since I started my master's degree, and I had no idea how to apply this training to another field. I'd have to find a job, but I didn't know what employers would be willing to pay me to do or what skills they were looking for. (That I felt this way despite having had previous successful careers in K–12 education and academic publishing tells you just how much I'd absorbed the "faculty or bust and you're good for nothing else" mindset.) I needed help getting from where I was (panic and despair) to where I needed to be: post-PhD employment that paid the bills and, ideally, would let me do meaningful, impactful work.

I looked around my department in vain for help. My graduate program—in what people thought and talked about, in what our professional development program offered—focused solely on academic careers. People who quit before they were finished and started work outside the academy and people who finished but still took nonacademic jobs were never heard from again. Certainly, faculty and administrators weren't keeping track of where they were going and what they were doing—or if they were, they certainly weren't sharing that information with us students. The prevailing feeling was that our Faculty of Graduate Studies (what in U.S. universities is typically called the graduate school) was good for little more than signing forms and creating rules—certainly not for helping people like me figure out what to do after the degree they were granting me. And everyone knew that the career center served only undergrads.

I'm exaggerating the lack of support, but that's how it felt at the time. I felt alone in my desperate search for some semblance of guidance about what to do with my life when everyone around me was telling me not only that the only thing I could possibly do was be a professor, but that becoming faculty was the only worthy career path. Everything else was giving up or selling out—and we'd be miserable to boot because there was no way we'd be able to find colleagues and work as smart and interesting as what we had.

Happily, things (as you'll read below) have gotten exponentially better at my university since that time, but that isn't the case everywhere. Today, the feelings I had when I embarked on my post-PhD career search are shared by many students and postdocs in graduate school cultures hostile to, or even just unwilling to acknowledge diverse post-degree career paths. This chapter, as you'll discover, is about what graduate faculty and administrators can do to change that.

Back to 2011. Not finding what I needed where I was, I went looking for support and information outside of my university. I found forums, books, and online communities for PhDs interested in pursuing non-faculty careers, including the website Versatile PhD, the book *So What Are You Going to Do with That?*, alt-ac Twitter, and more generally "quit lit."[1] I went from feeling like the only one in my situation to recognizing that I had a substantial and generous community, one that understood my struggles and could help me get where I wanted to go. I set my sights on a career in research administration and planned to kick off my job search in earnest as soon as I had a defense date.

I was going to be okay. But what about all of the other graduate students and postdocs at my institution who, like me, either didn't want or wouldn't be able to get a tenure-track job? What was my school doing to support them? Was it truly nothing, or was I just not able to find it?

It turns out it was a bit of both. And I found this out when, in the autumn, the Faculty of Graduate Studies at my university hired me—on the basis of the work I'd done to educate myself as a soon-to-be PhD job seeker—to research what was happening in the world of graduate professional and career development on campus and elsewhere. The dean and associate dean commissioned me to craft a white paper that would inaugurate what they hoped, should my white paper prove convincing enough of the feasibility and need, would become a new centralized Graduate and Postdoctoral Professional Skills (GPPS) program aimed at providing just the kind of support I'd been looking for but been unable to find. (Programs aimed at graduate and postdoctoral professional and career development are also referred to throughout this chapter as GPPS; they're also often labeled GPD, or graduate professional development.)

My job, which the faculty hired me to do in lieu of my usual teaching load, was to talk to everyone on campus who was providing professional or career development support to graduate students or postdocs—everyone from department chairs to student services to the library to the career center—and get a handle on many aspects:

- how much support actually existed;
- what gaps in support, accessibility, or comprehensiveness we could identify;
- what students and fellows wanted;
- opportunities for harmonization, centralization, and better communication;
- how we stacked up against other universities in Canada and around the world, and what we'd need to do to get to a level we'd be happy with.

I spent my days calling faculty, emailing with administrators, meeting with students and fellows, and researching online. And, it turns out, building a network and a skill set that would, in not very many months, lead me to the new post-PhD career I'd been hoping for.

In the course of my research, I found out that my university was actually doing quite a lot to support people like me, even before it had a formal, centralized GPPS program. Not knowing the efforts my institution was making was partly my fault—I hadn't been looking closely enough. Like many North American universities, my institution offered workshops, seminars, events, and experiences aimed at providing graduate students and postdocs with core research, teaching, and professional skills to support their successful transition into a variety of careers. On offer was everything from a dedicated graduate career counselor to workshops on social media, project management, clear-language communication, and many other career-oriented skills.

But my not having looked hard enough was only part of the problem. Most of these opportunities were very difficult to find, and many were accessible only by small parts of the graduate student population, meaning that support wasn't equally distributed and accessible across the organization. Both of these problems stemmed from the same, very common, source: career and professional development programming was dispersed across academic and administrative units. Events were poorly promoted, often overshadowed by undergraduate-aimed offerings. And they were on offer to a graduate student body that was often not on campus (we were all holed up at home reading for our comprehensives or writing up our research), hard to reach, and afraid of admitting to ourselves, our peers, and our professors that we were interested in, or at least curious about, something other than the professoriate.

When the white paper assignment—which read much like this chapter, which is handy for you—turned into a full-time administrative position with the Faculty of Graduate Studies, I was charged with launching that GPPS program—one that was centralized, visible, and comprehensive. My job, and my goal, was to ensure that every graduate student and postdoc at my university benefitted from our programming. This work led to a career: I now run a similar program for twelve hundred STEM graduate students and postdocs at a teaching-hospital-affiliated research institute and also consult with graduate faculty and administrators interested in building their own programs.

The End of the Apprenticeship Model

Universities need to do a better job helping their PhDs find that first non-faculty job and transition into meaningful, well-paying careers. They must provide graduate students and postdocs with the tools and skills they need to succeed in a broad range of careers. In a report on GPPS programs in Canada, Marilyn Rose notes that universities need to make sure graduate students are prepared in ways that "ensure the mobilization of their knowledge and skills and the realization of their potential in a variety of workplace settings—whether academic, for-profit or not-for-profit." Rose goes further: she calls PhD career preparation an "ethical imperative."[2]

I agree. And I'd add that training PhDs for diverse careers is also the pragmatic step to take. Professional and career development programs are exceptional recruitment and retention tools—you'll attract talented students. And once they graduate, they'll go out into a range of professional spheres, each confident in the knowledge that their PhD training equips them to be intellectual leaders, coveted employees, and valued ambassadors for their institutions and disciplines.

GPPS programs are proliferating because faculty and administrators have woken up to both the ethical imperative and the pragmatic value of this new approach to PhD training. Unwilling to reduce the number of graduate students they admit to their programs, graduate faculty and administrators are looking to GPPS programming as a partial remedy.

Maintaining the current graduate population—especially in fields like English and history—is ethical only if and when universities apprise prospective students of the academic placement rates for their programs and encourage incoming students to keep their options open throughout the PhD. But the shift has to be more than simply informational: graduate programs need to provide meaningful and accessible opportunities to develop skills that will serve PhDs in a range of careers. It's tough to encourage PhDs to enter programs with their eyes open. It's even more challenging to foster and sustain a willingness to learn not just about the academic subject they are passionate about but also transferable skills and research and the places they can put them to use. But no one ever said running a student-centered, ethical graduate program would be easy.

Professional Skills Are for All Professions—Including the Professoriate

Graduate school has long adopted an apprenticeship model, in most cases by default. Graduate school is, in this way of thinking, a period of training during which graduate students apprentice to the craft of becoming a professor. Yet studies show that graduate students are not being adequately trained for the skills required by the professoriate. A 2000 study by Nyquist and Woodford found widespread dissatisfaction among university faculty and administrators responsible for hiring new faculty with the skills and capacity of PhDs in the United States.[3] This is part of the reason why many new faculty find the transition into their first position so challenging—their PhD hasn't trained them for their job in the way they assumed it would have.

Students are receiving adequate training in essential skills. At most universities, the core work of being a graduate student doesn't even teach aspiring academics how to succeed in a faculty career, although that's ostensibly what it is training them for. Graduate school doesn't teach them how to budget their grants (or do business finance), supervise their lab staff (or become a hiring manager), run an undergraduate department (or coordinate business operations). The struggles of new faculty to situate themselves in their new roles (especially in the lab sciences where the transition from bench researcher to project manager is particularly jarring) is a major drain on their research productivity and overall well-being. Students need more training in pedagogical, supervision, and communication skills, all of which are crucial to succeeding as a professor or principal investigator. Yet many if not most of these skills are not exclusive to the professoriate.

Graduate students need to be doing more than just taking comprehensive exams and writing their dissertations. During graduate school, graduate students need to develop professional skills that will help them on *or* off the academic job market because professional skills are essential to any post-PhD pathway, including the tenure track: a study of over sixteen hundred academic job postings in English and the modern languages showed that over 75 percent listed skills typically associated with nonprofessorial careers.[4]

Despite the wishes of hiring committees and employers, core graduate studies curricula and activities still teach graduate students how to become subject-matter experts and skilled researchers, and not much else. As we've seen, this training isn't sufficient career preparation, even for a tenure-track post.

A useful way to think about the twenty-first-century PhD is as a fixed-contract job that pays graduate students to read, write, and research and affords opportunities to acquire a range of transferable skills that can be used in a faculty *or* a non-faculty job. The opportunities offered by GPPS programs help graduate students make the most of their time in graduate school and set themselves up for success in whatever career they choose once they graduate. Never again will they have access to such a wide range of free, tailored professional development opportunities—worth thousands of dollars. I would know, since most of my office's budget goes to paying for these programs, which we then offer to students and fellows for free.

It can seem daunting to establish or strengthen GPPS programming, but you need not reinvent the wheel. The ingredients and the directions are out there, if you know where to look. This chapter brings together the latest research and best practices on the subject and lays out the following:

- how GPPS programs work, how they are typically structured and offered, who runs them, and how to do an environmental scan of the GPPS programming happening on your campus;
- the skill areas that GPPS programs tend to cover, and how developing skills in those areas can help graduate students in their faculty or non-faculty careers;
- how to help graduate students identify the skills that are likely to be the most useful to them now and later, and how to decide what skill development opportunities to focus on;
- how to help your students design a personalized professional and career development curriculum that meets their needs and harmonizes with their core graduate school activities;
- strategies for creating, communicating, and assessing professional and career development programming for graduate students.

When you start researching GPPS, you discover that it is a vast, growing world of activity and research, with at least two professional groups dedicated to it—the Graduate Career Consortium (GCC) in the United States and the Graduate and Professional Development Network-Réseau pour le perfectionnnement aux études supérieures et postdoctorales (GPDN), of which I'm currently the president, in Canada.[5] It's also one with a long history; professional and career development programs for graduate students have existed since at least the 1970s. This chapter provides a place to start, a way into this world. I'm not aiming to be (nor is it possible to be) comprehensive.

Getting Started: Building and Optimizing GPPS Programs

Understanding What GPPS Entails

In her 2012 report on GPPS for the Canadian Association for Graduate Studies (the equivalent of the Council of Graduate Schools), Marilyn Rose gives a useful overview of GPPS in which she notes that professional skills refer to academic skills and transferable skills and other competencies that graduate students need in workplace settings of all kinds.[6]

Many GPPS programs now consciously avoid making a distinction between so-called "professional" and "transferable" skills, with the understanding that all skills taught in GPPS programs can be applied in a broad range careers, and that to silo skill types is to reinforce old career hierarchies. What has changed somewhat is the understanding of the core competencies that a good GPPS program needs to teach, ideally at both introductory and advanced levels. The 2017 update to Rose's report defines these competencies as:

- Career Building
- Health and Wellness
  - Physical & Mental Health
  - Personal & Business Finance
  - Reconciliation
  - Spirituality
- Innovation
- Leadership and Management
- Internet Tools
- Success in Graduate School
  - Communication & Writing
  - Ethics & Responsibilities
  - Research
  - Scholarship & Funding
  - Teaching

You may want to use these as a starting place for assessing or fleshing out GPPS programming in your department or on your campus. Or you may want to develop your own based on current research. Some useful places to turn to include the small but growing body of research into what employers (including academic departments) are looking for, research often highlighting key work-ready skills employers feel PhDs lack.

In Katina Rogers's study for the Scholarly Communications Institute, she asked nonacademic employers about the skills they wish PhD hires came prepared with and asked those same PhDs which skills they believed were most valuable to employers. The mismatch was significant: employers want better preparation in project management, technical skills, people management, leadership, administrative skills, collaboration, and interpersonal skills.[7]

A STEM-focused study by the Council of Graduate Schools noted that while employers held PhDs in high regard, they identified significant skill gaps, especially in "writing, speaking, and presentation including effective Power-Point[, c]ross-disciplinary and cross-cultural communication and teamwork [, and t]ime management and project management in an experiential context."[8] An Australian study came to similar conclusions. Comparing expectations of employers with what they saw from recent PhD graduates, the report concluded that employers' expectations were consistently not being met. Interestingly, this held true for university-sector employers, indicating that universities view many PhD graduates as not "work ready" for academia.[9]

Time and again researchers have noted the value of professional skills development for PhDs headed for faculty positions. Studies (like the one conducted by Rachael Pitt and Inger Mewburn) examine academic job postings to glean the crucial (and changing) skills required by university departments in their tenure-track hires. Pitt and Mewburn performed a text analysis of all academic job ads available at eight Australian universities on June 24, 2013; what they found was that in addition to subject matter expertise and teaching ability, academics are now also required to demonstrate substantial skills in academic administration, team building, people management, outreach, and multimedia content creation, among others.[10]

Beth Seltzer's study came to similar conclusions. She ranked the most often requested skills in the tenure-track job postings for English and modern languages listed by the MLA (the primary job board for PhDs in those fields) in 2016 (see table 8.1). She found that the most requested skills and expertise were not those we typically understand as professorial.[11] All of the skills from "professional/technical writing" and above beat out requests for expertise in British literature (12 percent) or American literature (13 percent), two of the areas most often hiring tenure-track faculty in North America. Professional skills are for all professions—including, increasingly, the professoriate.

Table 8.1

Percentage of MLA job listings seeking Alt-Ac skills, 2015–2016

	English jobs	Foreign language jobs
Advising	24%	22%
Administration	23%	25%
Curriculum development	23%	22%
Working with diverse populations	20%	16%
Public engagement	17%	12%
Digital writing/media	15%	5%
Digital scholarship	14%	6%
Professional/technical writing	14%	6%
Technology/online teaching	12%	16%
Assessment	8%	7%
English as a foreign language	8%	5%
Grant writing/fund-raising	7%	7%
K–12 connections	5%	3%
Editing/directing journal	5%	1%
Writing center work	5%	0%
Event organizing	2%	2%

Taking Stock of Existing Needs and Offerings

The first step toward optimizing GPPS programming for students and fellows is doing an environmental scan of existing campus activities that fall under that umbrella. That can sometimes be more challenging than it might seem. University websites are notorious for not being user-friendly, and in many places activities that fall under the GPPS umbrella aren't posted or centrally coordinated. You might have to go hunting to find out where skill and career development programming for graduate students is advertised and offered on your campus.

Depending on your institution, you might discover GPPS opportunities embedded in the core curriculum of graduate programs, as a credit course (i.e., curricular GPPS). In the Biochemistry and Immunology departments at the University of Toronto, this takes the form of the graduate credit course BCH2024H: Professional Development, which focuses on preparing for careers outside of academia.[12] At the University of Michigan, you might soon find one of the Public Humanities workshops, like "Editorial Work Within and Beyond Academia" or "Digital History," included as a credit course in a graduate program.[13] Or perhaps, like in many programs, there is a professional and career development unit embedded in a core methods course.

You might also find them offered as an additional professional development workshop program by graduate units, sometimes as a graduation requirement (i.e., co-curricular GPPS, along with all of the models below). In

York University's Graduate Program in English, this takes the form of the nine-part Professionalization Workshop Program, which all students must complete before they defend their dissertation.[14] Some graduate programs have placement officers who offer career development support and workshops. In other places, advising on this front is a more occasional and informal sort of thing—an alumni careers panel, or a professional development talk instead of a research presentation.

At some institutions, professional development programs are advertised (and often offered) by the School or Faculty of Graduate Studies or Career Center. At many universities, the Graduate School and/or the Career Center are the main governing and coordinating bodies of GPPS programs. Academics and administrators in those units should collaborate to determine, oversee, and coordinate

a   which skills the program should teach;

b   which workshops, seminars, courses, advising services, and experiential education opportunities should be on offer, sometimes in conversation with alumni, employers, or consultants;

c   which internal and external facilitators will deliver GPPS programming;

d   the extent to which facilitators need to tailor programming to specific disciplinary areas;

e   the distribution of resources and efforts to ensure that departments aren't offering competing programming instead of collaborating;

f   program promotion, budgeting scheduling, registration, and attendance tracking (which sometimes extends to issuing GPPS certificates or transcript notations);

g   a centralized schedule or curriculum of GPPS programs across campus;

h   facilitating or advising on graduate program reform intended to make the core work of the PhD more relevant to a variety of careers;

i   GPPS program development support, resources, or funding requests from graduate departments, faculty, or students.

Often, programming is provided and/or advertised by different administrative or educational units across campus. If your university doesn't centralize GPPS programming, all of the activities listed above might be currently conducted by independent campus units. These units, which may go by a variety of names, may include the teaching and learning center, the career center, the academic skills center, the knowledge translation/mobilization office, the research services office, the student wellness center/counseling office, and the library.

Programs that are structured this way are often a bit harder to access, as students and fellows have to search for opportunities in multiple places. At Ontario College of Art and Design, for example, a graduate student looking for thesis writing and career development support would have to separately go to the Writing and Learning Center and Career Development websites, whereas one at the University of Toronto could go straight to the Graduate Professional Skills program website and find both.

A key element of a professional skills environmental scan is figuring out what skills are being taught by the current programming on offer and which are missing. GPPS program frameworks, and centralized GPPS catalogs and websites, are often organized by skill or competency area. Which skills a GPPS program focuses on varies from institution to institution, but the core competency list above is a good place to start. Assessing which skills are currently being taught at your university should be a core part of any environmental scan. Identifying missing, underserved, or ineffectively taught competency areas is an excellent guide for program development. (Looking to assess current programming? There's a brief guide, along with further resources to check out, in the last section of this chapter.)

Organizing and advertising programming within a skills framework makes sense; it shows students the kinds of skills they should be developing for post-degree career flexibility. The University of California, Berkeley Graduate Division, for example, organizes their GPPS programming into writing and communication, teaching and mentoring, research and data analysis, leadership and management, career exploration and preparation, and professionalism skill areas.[15] York University lists professional development programming under the headings of career pathways and options, knowledge transfer strategies, transferable professional skills, writing success, and getting connected on campus and beyond.[16]

Collaboration is key. What if appropriate programs are not offered on your campus or are only offered to suit the needs of undergraduate students? It's likely that some of you find yourself in that situation. Some universities still work under the assumption that all of their PhDs will (or should) become professors, and so they shouldn't need support to become anything else. Others have been dominated by faculty and administrators who think that broadening skill sets with an aim toward post-PhD career flexibility is a waste of good research time, and so don't offer anything until almost the moment after students have defended their dissertation. But good GPPS programming should be timely and robust. If what students and fellows want and need doesn't exist, it's time to get building. Common program development strategies for GPPS include the following:

Reach out to the person offering the undergraduate version and ask if they have or can offer something tailored to graduate students. People are often willing to do this if they realize there's a need. We did this on my campus with writing instruction—all of the writing development courses were general or geared specifically to undergrads, so we asked a writing instructor who had done her PhD on dissertation writing to develop a new program. It became extremely popular and is now a core part of the GPPS communication competency.

Find the person or people on your campus responsible for overseeing and coordinating the work of other professional development units. See if they know who is (or isn't, but would be good at) teaching what you're seeking to learn.

A great example of this is the creation of a local branch of the Graduate Management Consulting Association (a student group that prepares graduate students for careers in management consulting through training and building connections with consulting firms) at my home university. Graduate students interested in management consulting came to the Faculty of Graduate Studies with a proposal for funding and coordinating the creation of a GMCA chapter. Having GMCA on campus to help graduate students build networks and skills in consulting was valuable, so we made it happen. (The folks who submitted the proposal are now successful management consultants, by the way.)

Find champions and funding—for faculty, administration, and students. Find partners who hold the purse strings and put in a program funding proposal. Talk to neighboring institutions about what their programs costs. While you're getting your program off the ground, look out for discretionary money held by your university's faculty or administrators specifically earmarked for professional development (or that could be used for it) that can fund course development or hire external facilitators to fill curricular gaps. This funding should be available not only to faculty and administrators, but also to graduate students and fellows, who often have the best sense of what programming is wanted and missing. After hearing from graduate students and postdocs that they weren't having luck finding teaching support resources geared to STEM researchers with little in-classroom experience, we provided funds to hire an external facilitator to teach a course on that subject. A number of the PhD students who requested that programming have moved onto teaching-intensive positions.

Note: if you're looking to create a centralized, organization-wide GPPS program, you should be budgeting for at least one full-time program manager, more if there aren't resources in place to support the communications, event management, and assessment work that goes into GPPS programming. Department-level programs can often get by on course releases and graduate assistants.

Identify the people on your campus who know what you want to learn and ask them to teach it. Do you know of a professor who is aces at academic social media? Chances are she'll be willing to run a workshop because it's a subject she cares about. (Dr. Dawn Bazely [@dawnbazely on Twitter] is a social media whiz of a biology professor at York University and has been my go-to person for social media talks.) Want to learn more about project management? Talk to the folks responsible for project management who work in administrative departments at your institution. Again, people generally like to be helpful, especially people who work in any kind of student service. Don't feel weird about asking. If you can, find a way to compensate them for their time.

Build partnerships with other institutions. Responsible for cultivating GPPS programming on your campus? You should join the GCC and connect with colleagues doing the same work. You'll learn about new developments and best practices in professional and career development. You'll build collaborations and share resources. If you're at a smaller college but not far from the nearest research university, it may be possible to leverage some of their programming for students and fellows. In Toronto, the larger, better-served programs open up spaces to students from other organizations. We've developed resource sharing agreements via collaborations supported by our national professional body and local interest groups. Other collaborative efforts at the national level in Canada include the myGradSkills online workshops. If you're affiliated with a research institute, make sure that you're aware of and know how to access programming at the institute and the affiliated university. There are also programs (if you're in Canada) like the Mitacs Step program that provide free workshops on specific university campuses to graduate students and postdocs from across a broad geographic area.

Provide program-level skill development opportunities. Many graduate programs have professionalization workshops on offer, but if yours doesn't, it is possible and advisable to create those opportunities. Students and fellows often have stronger relationships departments than with institutions, and program-specific offerings can be tailored to the disciplinary contexts and career trajectories of their students and fellows. Sometimes it is as easy as drafting a proposal to the departmental chair that outlines the benefits of integrating GPPS into their program. In others, it may require going through a lengthier governance process, especially if (and this is advisable) you're intending to make professional skills development a graduation requirement, which signals to students and fellows that their mentors consider professional skills development both important and supported.

A colleague of mine was able to do this building work in her history department while completing her PhD. After assessing what skill areas weren't being served, what careers alumni were moving into, and what was happening in comparable departments, she put together a convincing program proposal for the leadership of her department and offered to colead it with fellow students. She created the programming from scratch and was able to take advantage of its offerings herself. She turned the skills she'd developed in advocating for and helping to run her department's GPPS program into a post-PhD job managing a similar university-wide program.

Facilitating Learning

Provide students and fellows with opportunities to figure out what skills they need most. What skills will students and fellows need to succeed in their post-PhD careers? You've assessed and developed your GPPS program, and now you need to provide students and fellows with ways to do it for themselves, in specific reference to their personal strengths, graduate training, and career goals. A few ideas:

- Organize your GPPS programming within a skills framework and provide guidance on which programming to pursue and when in the degree it may be most valuable.
- Teach PhDs about how to do effective informational interviews with professionals in whose jobs (and the skills required to do them well) they're interested.
- Provide placement data for all alumni, not just the ones who become academics. The University of British Columbia does this very well, as does Stanford, and the University of Toronto will soon be releasing the results of its 10,000 PhDs data collection project.[17]
- Share information about self-assessment tools like those found in *So What Are You Going to Do with That?*, StrengthsFinder 2.0, the myIPD tool (for STEM students), and the new ImaginePhD tool for humanities and social science students.[18]
- Provide opportunities to learn about the skills needed to be a productive faculty member, not just the ones graduate students are usually exposed to. Do this with faculty panels, discussion groups, and job shadowing.
- Help students and fellows develop a personalized professional development plan. One of the challenges and benefits of cocurricular GPPS programming is their flexibility and separation from the core curriculum—courses, workshops, and internships can be pursued at nearly any point during a graduate degree or postdoc and can be fit around core academic work. (They also require students and fellows to pursue professional skill training in addition to an already demanding research practice and lab or teaching work.)

Once a GPPS program becomes sufficiently robust, it can be difficult for students and fellows to choose what to do and when. One key role of GPPS administrators is to provide guidance and tools. Once students and fellows have had opportunities to assess the kinds of skills they might need in the career paths they might pursue, they should have opportunities to design a personalized professional and career development curriculum that meets their needs and harmonizes with their core graduate school activities. This is most effective when students and fellows are provided with a framework in which they can see and plan what they need to do in an academic and professional/career context simultaneously. This can be built into graduate handbooks and GPPS websites, communicated via formal and informal advising, or disseminated through tools like the program-specific GradMaps created by Queen's University, which lay out what students in each graduate program need to do in each year of their degree in five realms: achieving academic goals, maximizing research impact, building skills and experience, engaging with their community, and launching their careers.[19]

Developing professional skills and career plans takes time. You and your colleagues should of course encourage graduate students to invest this time. To allow students to build their professional skills while not detracting from their graduate work, where possible, skill development opportunities should be integrated into core graduate and postdoctoral work.

Program Assessment

It isn't enough just to have a GPPS program—you need to know that it's doing what you want it to. Assessing GPPS programming is notoriously difficult, and at present there aren't really good models for doing it well. There is much, however, to learn from the best practices of program assessment in other realms and a clear pathway forward to implementing effective assessment practices. At the very least, those responsible for GPPS program development and planning at your institution should be clear on the following:

- Set clear goals for the program: Retention? Student satisfaction? Alumni satisfaction? Employers who are happy with the skills and competency of their new hires who come out of your graduate programs? Higher post-PhD salaries? Higher post-PhD job satisfaction? Note that the goal of your program should not be to improve PhD employment rates. PhDs already have the highest labor market participation rate of any educational category—nearly all PhDs already get jobs—so GPPS programming can't take credit for that.[20] It could, if you can figure out a way to measure this, take credit for making it easier to get those jobs, or making it possible to get better ones.
- Units and methods of measure: These should be both direct and indirect, that is, you'll want to balance measuring the easy to

measure, fuzzy things (program uptake, attendance, student self- or program perception) with the more difficult to measure, empirical things (a measurable increase in a specific skill before and after a GPPS intervention, a measurable decrease in the time to first post-PhD position, a measurable increase in post-PhD salaries or job satisfaction).

- How findings will inform program development: assessment is useful only if what you find changes what you do. What's your plan for future improvement? Do you have contingencies in place if you've begun moving in one direction while assessment is ongoing and your results tell you to move in entirely another?
- Timelines and responsibility: How often will assessment happen? Whose job is it? And who is resourcing it?

I've been incredibly brief here; for a much more thorough overview of GPPS program assessment and recommendations on how to do it well, see the 2017 GPDN report on the subject.[21]

Limitations and Disadvantages of GPPS Programs—and Their Alternatives

GPPS is not a panacea for the ills of graduate education. In some ways, they can become an additional burden to already heavy-laden PhD students. Cocurricular GPPS programming requires students and fellows to pursue training and skill development opportunities on top of demanding research and teaching requirements. The separation of programming from core graduate activities can suggest that they are inessential, optional, not supported by supervisors and departments. Programs can focus on broad coverage of skill domains at the expense of in-depth skill development.

Coordinating university-wide GPPS programs is a complex undertaking that requires immense amounts of coordination, collaboration, and negotiation between academic and administrative units. Because of the lack of robust assessment practices, it is difficult to assess the wholesale effectiveness of GPPS programming, although we have suggestive evidence and anecdotal accounts from students.

Make Sure Help Is Right at Hand—and That Students and Fellows Know That Part of Their Job Is to Take It

Universities are doing ever more to provide graduate students and postdocs with the support and training they need to succeed in and out of the academy. Despite some of the current drawbacks of GPPS programs, they have major advantages too: they're usually free, fit into a flexible schedule, are taught by expert facilitators, and provide opportunities for students and fellows to broaden their networks beyond their departments, the university, and the academy.

Now it's up to you to make sure that students have the time and support to take advantage of what your campus offers during their graduate school and postdoc years.

Notes

1 For more information, see the Versatile PhD, "Helping Graduate Students and PhDs Envision, Prepare for, and Excel in Non-Academic Careers since 1999," https://versatilephd.com/; Susan Basalla and Maggie Debelius, *"So What Are You Going to Do with That?" Finding Careers Outside Academia*, 3rd ed. (University of Chicago Press, 2014); Sydni Dunn, "Why So Many Academics Quit and Tell," *ChronicleVitae*, December 12, 2013, https://chroniclevitae.com/news/216-why-so-many-academics-quit-and-tell.

2 Marilyn Rose, "Graduate Student Professional Development: A Survey with Recommendations" (Canadian Association for Graduate Studies and Social Sciences and Humanities Research Council of Canada, September 2012), http://www.cags.ca/documents/publications/working/Report%20on%20Graduate%20Student%20Professional%20Development%20%20-%20A%20survey%20with%20recommendations%20FINAL%20Eng.OCT%202012.pdf.

3 Jody D. Nyquist and Bettina J. Woodford, "Re-envisioning the Ph.D.: What Concerns Do We Have?" (Pew Charitable Trusts, 2000), https://depts.washington.edu/envision/resources/ConcernsBrief.pdf.

4 Details of the MLA study quoted in Scott Jaschik, "The Ph.D. Skill Mismatch," *Inside Higher Ed*, January 5, 2018, https://www.insidehighered.com/news/2018/01/05/study-shows-academic-job-searches-languages-value-alt-ac-skills?utm_source=Inside+Higher+Ed&utm_campaign=db1d03ed99-DNU20180105&utm_medium=email&utm_term=0_1fcbc04421-db1d03ed99-198627041&mc_cid=db1d03ed99&mc_eid=8446eda839. It would have been simpler here to say "required in alt-ac jobs," but I purposefully chose not to. While alt-ac is a handy term for non-faculty careers, it's both misleading and unhelpful. Given that more than 50 percent of PhDs go into careers outside the professoriate—far more if we include the people who begin but do not finish a PhD—there's nothing "alt" about non-faculty jobs. Framing these jobs as alternative to academic ones also frames academic careers as the primary goal, which contributes to the feeling among graduate students exploring a range of careers that they're doing the wrong thing or that non-faculty careers are lesser in some way. Neither is true. While we've yet to come up with a satisfactory alternative to alt-ac ("non-faculty" also falls into the trap of giving academic jobs primacy), I try to avoid using it and advise that you do too. Just call them careers and jobs, full stop.

5 For more information on these organizations, see GPDN-RPESP (n.d.), https://cags.ca/gpdn/about-us/; Graduate Career Consortium, "Home—Graduate Career Consortium" (n.d.), https://gradcareerconsortium.org/.

6 For Rose, the umbrella category of professional skills "includes academic skills developed while undertaking the courses and research that characterize

disciplinary areas of study. Such skills include both those related to the conduct of research and related scholarly work and those connected to teaching through work as teaching assistants or, in the case of some doctoral students, as course instructors. The second kind of professional skills with which this study is concerned has to do with the acquisition of transferable competencies of a broader nature, ranging from interpersonal and leadership skills to career search and career advancement strategies. These have to do, in general, with a student's ability to present himself or herself professionally and to integrate quickly into complex workplace environments after graduation." Rose, "Graduate Student Professional Development."

7   Katina Rogers, "Outside the Pipeline: From Anecdote to Data" (n.d.), https://katinarogers.com/2012/11/05/outside-the-pipeline-from-anecdote-to-data/.

8   Daniel Denecke, Keonna Feaster, and Katherine Stone, "Professional Development: Shaping Effective Programs for STEM Graduate Students" (Council of Graduate Schools, 2017), https://cgsnet.org/ckfinder/userfiles/files/CGS_ProfDev_STEMGrads16_web.pdf. A new tool you might want to explore (and share with students and fellows) was recently created by *Science* Careers, based on just this kind of research. It allows people to assess the match (or mismatch, in many cases) between the skills provided by PhD training and the skills necessary to succeed in a variety of careers (including academic ones), based on data collected from more than 3,800 science and engineering PhDs. For more information, see Maggie Kuo and Jia You, "Explore the Skills That Can Open Career Doors after Your Doctoral Training," *Science*, November 27, 2017, https://www.sciencemag.org/careers/2017/11/explore-skills-can-open-career-doors-after-your-doctoral-training.

9   Rachael Pitt, "Australian Employers' Expectations and Perceptions of PhD Graduates in the Workplace," in *Proceedings of the 2012 Quality in Postgraduate Research Conference*, ed. Margaret Kiley (2012), 233–234, http://www.qpr.edu.au/Proceedings/QPR_Proceedings_2012.pdf.

10 Rachael Pitt and Inger Mewburn, "Academic Superheroes? A Critical Analysis of Academic Job Descriptions," *Journal of Higher Education Policy and Management* 38, no. 1 (January 26, 2016): 88–101, https://doi.org/10.1080/1360080X.2015.1126896.

11 Beth Seltzer, "One Hundred Job Ads from the Humanities Ecosystem—Profession," *MLA Profession*, Fall 2018, https://profession.mla.org/one-hundred-job-ads-from-the-humanities-ecosystem/.

12 University of Toronto, "Biochemistry, University of Toronto—BCH 2024H" (n.d.), http://biochemistry.utoronto.ca/courses/bch2024h-professional-development-2/.

13 Rackham Graduate School, University of Michigan, "Rackham Program in Public Scholarship" (n.d.), https://rackham.umich.edu/professional-development/program-in-public-scholarship/.

14 Faculty of Graduate Studies, York University, "Degree Requirements | Current Students | English | Faculty of Graduate Studies | York University | English" (n.d.), http://english.gradstudies.yorku.ca/current-students/degree-requirements/.

15 University of California, Berkeley Graduate Division, "Professional Development Guide" (n.d.), https://grad.berkeley.edu/professional-development/guide/.

16 Faculty of Graduate Studies, York University, "Graduate & Postdoctoral Professional Skills (GPPS)" (n.d.), http://gradstudies.yorku.ca/current-students

/enhancing-your-experience/graduate-postdoctoral-professional-skills/#squelch -taas-tab-content-0-0.

17 University of British Columbia, "PhD Outcome Tracking" (n.d.), http://outcomes .grad.ubc.ca/explore.html; Institutional Research & Decision Support, Stanford University, "PhD Jobs" (n.d.), https://irds.stanford.edu/phd-jobs; School of Graduate Studies, University of Toronto, "10,000 PhDs Project" (n.d.), https:// www.sgs.utoronto.ca/about/10000-phds-project-overview/.

18 Basalla and Debelius, *"So What Are You Going to Do with That?"*; Gallup Clifton Strengths, "StrengthsFinder 2.0" (n.d.), https://www.gallupstrengthscenter.com /home/en-us/strengthsfinder?utm_source=strengthsfinder&utm_campaign =coming_soon&utm_medium=redirect; My IDP Science Careers (n.d.), http://myidp.sciencecareers.org/; ImaginePhD, "Welcome" (n.d.), https://www .imaginephd.com/.

19 Career Services, Queen's University, "Grad Maps" (n.d.), https://careers.queensu .ca/gradmaps.

20 Jessica Edge and Daniel Munro, "Inside and Outside the Academy: Valuing and Preparing PhDs for Careers" (Conference Board of Canada, November 24, 2015), https://www.conferenceboard.ca/(X(1)S(worzlymvnfqnfropi1z5ztvc))/e-library /abstract.aspx?did=7564&AspxAutoDetectCookieSupport=1.

21 Canadian Association for Graduate Studies, "Graduate Professional Development Program" (n.d.), http://www.ca.cags.ca/gdps/index.php.

9

Expanding Horizons and Diversifying Skills

••••••••••••••••••••••

Transforming Graduate Curriculum

KAREN S. WILSON AND

STEPHEN ARON

Not all PhDs in the humanities do or should become professors. Obvious as that statement may seem today, most graduate students and their faculty mentors would have deemed it heretical a few years ago. Some still do. The idea of careers outside the professoriate was not discussed, at least not in polite academic society. That remains true at many institutions, where a code of silence keeps conversations from happening and graduate training from evolving away from an exclusive focus on "making" professors. But times are changing, as more academics grapple with the realities of the declining number of tenure-track professorial positions and the possibilities opened by the diverse careers of humanities PhDs.

Armed with the understanding that around one-third of its PhDs are engaged in nonprofessorial careers, the UCLA Department of History has addressed this reality in a variety of ways over the past few years. One effort in particular leveraged the familiar structures of a PhD program, widespread knowledge of the shrinking academic job market, and the growing awareness of the varied career paths of its own PhDs. A hybrid graduate seminar/workshop recommended itself as it could foster career exploration by students, while enhancing their in-demand skills and expanding their understanding of the diverse applicability of their graduate training. It would allow the department to move forward while recognizing—and understanding better—the inherent challenges of introducing, sustaining, and institutionalizing cultural change. The course, which we cotaught twice, disrupted some departmental cultural norms, increased student networks inside and outside the university, and unleashed student self-awareness and creativity. Although we intended the course to expand networks, we did not plan for or anticipate the immediate effects on the students.

In this chapter, we share how those effects happened and why, despite our limited evidence, we think they are worth fostering in the efforts to transform graduate curriculum across all disciplines. Indeed, we believe the course we designed and taught on "The Many Professions of History" could be readily expanded into one on "The Many Professions of Humanists." That seminar and our collective efforts to prepare graduate students would, in fact, benefit from the adoption of a multidisciplinary framework and the embrace of an "all in this together" attitude.

Background

For some forty years, there has been an ongoing characterization of the academic job market, especially in the humanities and social sciences, as being in "crisis," with a steady decline in tenured faculty positions. Periodically, various academics and university departments offered some coordinated responses, primarily aimed at diverting freshly minted PhDs to other job sectors. In unintended ways, these usually short-lived efforts reinforced the idea that the problem was one of mismatched supply and demand and PhDs could be "placed" in other sectors with evident and continuing growth.[1]

As the gap between the number of newly earned humanities PhDs and the number of available tenure-track positions continued to widen, perhaps made even more starkly evident by the Great Recession of 2008 and its lingering effects, a number of new efforts made it clear that the "crisis" was not temporary but rather a condition, the new normal at least for the foreseeable future. One set of efforts came from the American Historical Association (AHA), initiated by an article published in October 2011 titled "No More Plan B." Coauthored by then AHA president Anthony Grafton and executive director James Grossman, the article raised a profound challenge to academic business as usual. In particular, Grafton and Grossman called attention to the irony of the professional embrace in recent years of new approaches and new technologies in the study of history with the simultaneous ignoring of the realities of academic employment and the narrowing of graduate training.[2]

As intended, the article provoked widespread reactions, conversations, and, significantly, actions. Most relevant to our story here, the AHA began collecting data on history PhDs careers, compiling information about job outcomes and from focus groups of historians outside of the academy and their employers. One resulting report, "The Many Careers of History PhDs: A Study of Job Outcomes, Spring 2013," provided a snapshot of the diversity of employment pursued by advanced degree holders. The conversations with employers yielded insights about various career opportunities and about the skills that were required to succeed beyond the professoriate. Most particularly, an understanding emerged that graduate training needed to teach students to communicate in a variety of media to a variety of audiences, to collaborate with people with diverse backgrounds, training, and perspectives, to develop quantitative and digital literacy, and to acquire the intellectual self-confidence that would enable students to adapt their skills to a range of situations. These efforts to understand what historians did post-PhD fueled the development of the AHA's Career Diversity Initiative in 2014.[3]

The UCLA Department of History had labored for several years to expand the public presence and mission of the department in ways that model and point to nonacademic career prospects for new PhDs. From developing close relationships with local museums and history-oriented media companies to offering a seminar on history and museums to creating a timely public discussion series titled "Why History Matters," various members of the department leadership and faculty endeavored to demonstrate the roles historians and their fellow humanists can play in the public square. Further, the department introduced a two-quarter professional development seminar to orient graduate students to the nuts and bolts of job search and success. When the AHA invited proposals for its Mellon Foundation–funded pilot on career diversity programming, the department saw it as the necessary next step to concentrate, systematize, and professionalize the various efforts to expand career prospects for PhDs. The UCLA Department of History served as one of four pilot projects (the others being history departments at Columbia University, the University of Chicago, and the University of New Mexico), working to pioneer new approaches to graduate education as well as to explore new platforms from which to launch our graduates.

Course Description, Objectives, and Iterations

Serving as the chair of the department and the graduate career officer, respectively, authors Aron and Wilson shared primary responsibility for implementing the AHA's Career Diversity Initiative. We designed "The Many Professions of History" as a one-quarter graduate course (ten weeks) that was a cross between a traditional seminar and a practicum. As stated in the course description, the primary focus was on exploring and demonstrating the ways in which the skills of historians are transferable to an array of professions and exercised in diverse ways and roles. Most of the weekly meetings featured guest speakers holding PhDs or related advanced degrees, drawn from realms ranging from museums to politics to entertainment. Assigned readings and viewings covered debates about the role of historians and other humanists in contemporary society, emerging ways of presenting and teaching history, and past and future uses of history.

In a departure from the seminar tradition, we assigned students to work on projects unrelated to their own research in collaboration with other members of the class. The projects included a historical evaluation of recent work by the UCLA Labor Center, a contribution to an institutional history project, and an assignment to create a public history assignment for undergraduate students. The goal of these projects was to move students outside the carrel, classroom, and archives to diversify and enlarge their experience with the practice of their discipline. The team-based projects pushed students to practice key skills in conjunction with their peers, simulating a common workplace situation while simultaneously creating an uncommon graduate student course experience.

As noted above, collaboration is one of the skills that the AHA's research identified as crucial to broadening career horizons. Accordingly, we made teamwork central to "The Many Professions of History" course. Likewise did the other key skills identified by the AHA—effective oral and written communication with a variety of audiences, basic digital and quantitative literacy, and enhanced intellectual self-confidence through practice and assessment—figure prominently in the learning objectives and assignments for the course. Increasing students' connections to humanities PhDs working outside the professoriate was an unstated, but equally important, goal.

In both iterations of the course, the weekly three-hour class meetings typically allotted time for discussion of assigned readings and viewings, exercises designed to facilitate the work and review the progress of teams, and extended interactions with guest speakers. Predominately alumni of the department, the speakers came from a variety of sectors and roles in which they applied their training. Among them were the director of education of a national museum, the producer/head of research for the popular television program *Who Do You Think You Are?*, an independent scholar/consultant, and the founder/head of an innovative public secondary school. Given the late afternoon starting time for the class and to ensure sufficient time to cover all the agenda items as well as to induce guests to brave Los Angeles traffic, dinner was provided each week and conversations with guests and/or about projects continued over the meal with only a brief break. The guest speaker segment usually consisted of the speakers summarizing their career path and current professional responsibilities in response to questions from the instructors, then providing more details in response to questions from the students. Overall, students engaged well with the guests, who appreciated the opportunity to share their stories and encourage the individual and project work of the students as well as their career considerations.

In both versions of the course, students completed pre- and post-course assessments of their competencies and confidence in their skills and surveys about their post-PhD career goals. They also did peer assessments of their team members at the conclusion of the course. Although the sample is small (ten students completed all instruments), the results of the assessments and surveys provided a baseline for understanding what elements of the course were effective. They not only offered feedback about how well the course had addressed the stated learning objectives but also allowed students to be reflective about their experiences, abilities, and career goals. For example, one learning objective was to facilitate student exploration and understanding of different professional applications of PhD training. By the end of each course, 50 percent of the enrolled students changed their stated professional goal, indicating an expanded perspective on their employment options. In surveying students on their experiences working in teams, we found significant agreement that overall they found teamwork to be a positive and empowering process, suggesting that the course had fostered effective collaboration, another learning objective.

The course debuted in January 2016 with eight enrolled students, three women and five men. Most were in their second or third year in the program, in the process of preparing or having just finished writing their dissertation prospectus. Students hailed from a wide range of geographic and chronological specialties.

In this initial iteration, we organized the students into two teams with applied history projects, that is, projects with a defined research question, a set of deliverables, and a client beyond the course instructors. Ensuring students from different fields worked together (a rare opportunity in a large department) was the primary criterion for team assignments. The projects had been solicited through departmental connections, including a faculty member not associated with the course and a recent alumna working as an independent consultant.

One team took on a challenge from the UCLA Labor Center Minimum Wage Project, which asked for assistance in documenting its role in a 2015 local campaign for a higher minimum wage and analyzing its significance to the success of the endeavor. The second team was given the Hillcrest Country Club (HCC) Project, which required it to chart and assess how the outside world has perceived the club through its nearly one-hundred-year history. The Minimum Wage Project tested a widely held assumption about the influence of the

Labor Center, while the HCC Project contributed an external perspective to a centennial history commissioned by the club's leadership. Each team had ten weeks to complete the project and deliver (1) a poster presentation at a department-sponsored career diversity conference, (2) an oral summary of findings and analyses to the class, and (3) a written detailed report to be delivered to the instructors and external clients.

With minimal guidelines, each team developed a research strategy, divided the labor among the members, and scheduled the necessary tasks to meet deliverable deadlines. The Minimum Wage Project team consulted with a History Department faculty member and an independent researcher to develop a focused research question ("What was the impact of the work of the UCLA Labor Center on the passage of a minimum wage law in Los Angeles?") and a comprehensive set of primary and secondary sources, opting to drill down on the local history while setting it in a national context. The team made use of published histories of minimum wage campaigns and policies, searchable newspaper accounts of recent efforts, academic research reports, and quantitative analyses of local and national trends in setting minimum wages. Two of the team members took the lead on the bulk of the research and analysis, while the third member wrote the final report and oversaw the creation of the poster. The HCC Project team consulted with the independent historian contracted by the country club to create a centennial history to clarify that there would be no access to the club's members or resources, requiring a research question that could be addressed by external sources only ("How has the outside world perceived Hillcrest Country Club over the past century?"). The team turned to popular publications, including newspapers, and their visual and textual representations of HCC for answers. The team members met weekly in person to share their individual findings and eventually craft a coherent analysis of the changing perspectives of the club.

None of the students in the first iteration had done a poster presentation before. Most found it challenging to distill substantial research and analysis into a visually effective offering. Some of the students had never worked with certain kinds of primary sources and so had to be tutored by their teammates in how to interrogate them properly. In knowing that their "product" would be seen and discussed by a wide variety of people, the students worked diligently to address these and other challenges professionally and creatively, producing attractive posters and informative reports. In both cases, the teams chose to minimize the text on the posters, offering eye-catching graphs and charts in the case of the minimum wage project and a simulated advertisement featuring the club's changing architecture and place on the Los Angeles social landscape in the case of the HCC project. Presenting the posters at a national conference hosted by the UCLA History Department provided the teams with immediate feedback from academic and nonacademic historians, an experience that students reported as gratifying as well as useful in helping them to understand where they had succeeded and failed in conveying their findings. Both teams were invited to present their posters at the 2017 AHA annual meeting.

A second iteration of "The Many Professions of History" occurred in the Winter Quarter of 2017. Six students initially enrolled in the course, again representing a wide range of fields of specialization. The gender ratio reversed in this second offering, with four women and two men enrolled. A series of unrelated circumstances reduced the enrollment to four students early in the quarter, making only one team possible. The continuing students were a master's student in Latin American studies applying to PhD programs, a first-year doctoral student in the Ancient history field, a second-year student in Chinese history, and a PhD candidate finishing his dissertation in Southeast Asian history.

The project for the second iteration again required the team members to work outside their fields of expertise and to be creative in responding to a broad assignment. This time, students were asked to design a potential research project and application model for undergraduate students working on "Project 1919." Inspired by UCLA's upcoming centennial, Project 1919 was a multifaceted, course-based public history venture initiated by the History Department to develop and make widely accessible the many histories of the university. In essence, the graduate students piloted a possible project that undergraduates could later do in teams in a one-quarter undergraduate course on the history of student protests at UCLA.

For the graduate trial run, the students in "The Many Professions of History" course were given examples of a few notable protests on campus and asked to choose one on which to focus. The students decided to research a 1993 hunger strike provoked by the UCLA chancellor's refusal to elevate the interdisciplinary Chicano/Chicana studies program to academic department status. Over the course of the quarter, the team had to (1) present and defend their choice and their research plan, (2) pitch their design for engaging the campus community and beyond in the history of a specific protest, and (3) submit a written research summary and project concept overview to the instructors.[4]

The students in the second iteration struggled first with an unfocused research agenda and then with an overly ambitious one. They eventually organized around the community engagement requirement and conceptualized a mobile app that could serve as an educational tool as well as a memory collector related to specific sites of protest events on campus. With limited technological expertise, but deep enthusiasm for connecting place, memories, and history, the team offered a creative way to crowdsource information while simultaneously expanding historical understanding.

Although the two versions of "The Many Professions of History" that we taught were tailored to the History Department at UCLA, the course's design lends itself to ready modifications for adoption elsewhere. Certainly, the local histories on which we focused and the local networks we tapped can be replicated in other history departments. For the most part as well, the skills that the AHA identified as necessary for history PhDs to succeed beyond the professoriate and that we built into "The Many Professions of History" are not unique to our discipline. Across the humanities and social sciences, doctoral students would do well to learn to work collaboratively, to build capacity as communicators in a variety of media and to a variety of audiences, to develop their quantitative and digital literacies, and to become more self-confident about their abilities (and about the wider range of careers for which their doctoral training has prepared them).

Disrupting Culture through Familiarity and "Forced" Collaboration

In capitalizing on certain aspects of departmental culture while defying others, "The Many Professions of History" placed students in a recognizable, yet challenging, environment. Offered as a formal graduate-level course, it fit the departmental culture that privileges transferring knowledge through structured faculty-organized classes and rewards learning with unit hours toward a required minimum for a degree. Thus did the course provide a safe and department/university-endorsed opportunity for grad students to engage in professional development (though that is a term and process rarely connected to humanities PhD programs until recently). With the additional endorsement of being cotaught by the department chair, the course had legitimacy within the History Department not present in any offerings by the university's Graduate Career Services, the AHA, or any of the other burgeoning resources for PhD students facing the realities of the academic job market or interested in pursuing career objectives beyond the professoriate.

The guest speakers recruited for each iteration of the course further reinforced how it fit in with a culture that honors the master scholar/practitioner. Of the twelve guest speakers, all but four were PhDs: two were ABDs in history, one holds an MA in history, and one, a master visual designer and adjunct instructor, holds a BA. They were considered appropriately credentialed by the instructors and the enrolled students, able to speak authoritatively and practically to aspiring PhDs. For example, one formerly tenured professor at a public research university spoke in great detail about how she came to the decision to leave academia for family reasons and with much frankness about the challenges of being an independent scholar today. Students asked about the adjustments that were required professionally and personally, offering clear evidence that these were of concern. Another formerly tenured professor who moved into public history and later university-community relations listened to a team pitch their project with great enthusiasm, then brought the team members to a new awareness with a simple question—"Have you asked the stakeholders in this historical event what they think of your project?" Their answer was "no." That question and answer proved to be an important insight for those students who were considering public history as a potential career path: engaging with the living made history an interactive process. This realization caused the team to redesign its project, shifting from a passive "history happened here" app to an ambitious, innovative place-triggered memory-capturing app. Immediate engagement was a primary goal of having guest speakers, and, in most cases, the goal was achieved.

By design, the course intended to disrupt the cult of the individual that remains prevalent in the humanities and social sciences despite the growing examples and necessity of collaboration, in teaching (team-based learning, online curriculum development) and in research (pick any digital humanities project). The pedagogical approach of the course facilitated students learning by experience the meaning and methods of collaboration. Each student collaborated in a team on an assigned project unrelated to any individual student or faculty research interests. Students had to prepare and complete the course assignments through combining efforts with those of other students. While working as a team was challenging to most of the enrolled students, the "forced" collaboration displaced the idea of atomized individualism as the only legitimate or productive approach to academic-level research, analysis, interpretation, and presentation in the humanities. Collaboration as a conscious, deliberate strategy could no longer be ignored or feared, as was the more common case.

Some student teams were more successful at collaborating than others, but all students had to engage with their team to produce a final project for which all participants shared the same grade. The team members did not know each other well before their assignments and that necessitated a level of trust as well as risk taking. Some students were more adept at leadership, and some were more inclined to follow. Regular check-ins with the teams in class helped identify areas where the instructors could intervene in team dynamics or provide more guidance in the process of moving projects along efficiently. In the practice of "working well with others," students had the opportunity to understand their own strengths and weaknesses as communicators, planners, researchers, thinkers, writers, and producers. They received immediate and ongoing feedback from their peers over the span of the projects, facilitating an authentic team experience as well as collaborative learning.

From its title to its concluding dinner, the course sparked conversations about careers and drew into the open discussions that too often have taken place only in the shadows of humanities departments (or not at all). Guest speakers in particular were asked by the instructors to be specific and honest about their career paths and their daily work routines. We wanted the guests to explain how their graduate training helped and hindered their ability to find their way in a variety of workplaces and to do their diverse jobs. For example, students heard from one speaker about his multiple miserable years as an adjunct before securing a tenure-track job only to discover that university administration was the more rewarding path. Another speaker shared that because she embraced the emerging digital humanities as a graduate student, she was able to create her own job post-PhD—a job that did not exist until she designed it. Face-to-face with humanists in various professions, students enquired about the rewards and challenges of real-life, in-process careers. They traded speculations, assumptions, and fantasies for actual experiences related to them by people with whom they shared intellectual values and practical concerns.

Benefits and Effects

"The Many Professions of History" proffered five significant benefits to the enrolled students. First, it provided hands-on practice with highly valued skills broadly required by twenty-first-century employers and for successful careers outside and inside the academy. Second, the course exposed students to an array of career possibilities utilizing those skills. Third, it expanded each student's professional network beyond the department. Fourth, it demanded students use interpersonal skills and intellectual abilities in nonacademic, externally defined ways. And fifth, "The Many Professions of History" allowed students to experience confidence-building creativity and productivity, an unanticipated, though highly desirable, effect.

As summarized above, a primary learning objective of the course from its initial inception focused on creating and improving competencies in key skills that would serve PhD students well whatever their career trajectory. At the first meeting of the course, students self-assessed their levels of competency in each of the five areas. Since the team project assignments were designed to enable practice in these skills, we expected to see improvement over the ten-week quarter. Post-course self- and peer evaluations documented that our expectations were met. Of the students, 70 percent rated two or more of their competencies in key skill areas higher at the end of the course compared to the beginning. Confidence levels rose nearly 30 percent over the quarter in both classes. Being able to apply their skills in structured and supportive circumstances prepared students for the contemporary workplace.

To help them better understand the value of the competencies they were acquiring and practicing in the course and the PhD program, students heard from historians using them every day in careers ranging from museum curator to television producer to independent consultant to academic administrator, among others. While inviting guest speakers, particularly alumni as most were, is common in career development programming, incorporating them into the course created an extended "informational interview" that was low-stakes for the students. They could actively participate or simply witness a lively conversation about each individual's work, career, and choices. In a convenient and informative manner, the professional paths open to students grew more diverse as simultaneously their professional networks expanded with each passing week of the course.

Requiring students to work on projects not of their own choosing was a deliberate effort to move them out of their comfort zone. And it did. Some students attempted to shape the assignment to align with their research interests. However, the projects and specified deliverables did not lend themselves to such efforts. Further thwarting such attempts was the fact that most of the students are engaged with fields, geographies, and/or eras very removed from the assigned topics. Out of necessity the student teams had to rely on their common training in historical research methods and analysis, rather than any subject-specific expertise, to complete their projects. The privileging of general disciplinary skills initially provoked some anxiety, yet it proved to be critical not only to well-distributed tasks within a team since there was no expert to lead the way, but also to building confidence in those general skills.

Increased student self-confidence in their skills, over singular subject expertise, frankly was an objective that had no obvious path to achievement. In a sense, we just trusted that students would rise to the challenges of the course and more confidence would ensue. Simply put, that is what happened. However, that expanded confidence also unleashed student creativity and productivity, which probably should not be surprising, but it was. In both iterations of the course, after some initial tentativeness and confusion, students adjusted to the course pace and expectations. At that point, the teams picked up the speed of their progress and the quality of their work, delivering coherent plans and designs on time. Collaboration became a resource, rather than an impediment to getting things done. In the end, each team produced a public presentation of their research that demonstrated their skills as scholars, as communicators, and as creative contributors to interpretation and understanding. Asked to make posters, give brief oral presentations intended for nonacademics, and write reports for project clients—unlike any other graduate course assignment they had had before—the student teams showed their willingness and ability to apply their skills in new ways and for new purposes. More than any other outcome, this result proved the value of the course for students. In ten weeks they had opened their minds to the unfamiliar and successfully met several new challenges, including holding each other accountable for the completion of the project.

The benefits realized by most of the enrolled students had some significant effects, on both the students and the department. Based on pre- and post-course surveys, half the students changed their originally stated career ambitions, while half retained their goals. Most of the students are still in the PhD program, although two have left the academic career track, one immediately after taking the course and one after graduating from the program. The first students to enroll in the course initially did not share that fact with their advisors, fearful that participating in the course would mark them as not to be taken seriously as scholars. By the end of the quarter, they all were able to tell their advisors and their peers about their participation. As a consequence, none of the students in the second iteration withheld news of their enrollment from their advisors. Although a very modest step, the demise of the secrecy represented a clear cultural change in the department—doctoral students pursuing and contemplating careers outside the academy are not failures or slackers.

While the course had a clear immediate impact, it is too soon to know if it will have more long-term effects. The course is not sustainable as designed with low enrollment. The small set of data produced by the two iterations is encouraging but not sufficient to suggest how to make the course more attractive to more students. Most of the department's faculty members were not aware of the existence of the course until some national press attention caused them to take note. Making more students and more faculty members aware of the positive benefits and effects of the course will have to be addressed before another iteration can occur.

Conclusion

According to student assessments, the explicit learning objectives of "The Many Professions of History" were achieved. Competencies improved, confidence rose, and diverse career options were explored. In the instructors' assessments, the implicit goal of increasing graduate students' networks was met as well. Moreover, the experience of the course over two iterations has fueled discussions about how the department can better facilitate collaborative projects, perhaps with graduate students supervising teams of undergraduates, and better foster clear and unambiguous support, even encouragement, for those doctoral candidates willing and interested in exploring various career paths while in the program. The comparatively low enrollment in both iterations, however, has raised questions about whether a dedicated graduate course is sustainable as an approach to cultural change.

For two cohorts of students, the primary objectives of the department's career diversity initiative were achieved—knowledgeable, self-confident, practiced historians with career options. The experiences and outcomes discussed above offer ample evidence that our course approach is an effective strategy for expanding the horizons and diversifying the skills of PhD students. The course iterations unleashed student self-awareness and creativity—unanticipated outcomes that reinforce the hybrid method as feasible and adaptable for navigating reimagined advanced degree programs.

Still, in the History Department at UCLA, we face the challenge of how to sustain the career diversity initiative now that funding from the Mellon grant has ended. As noted, we also must figure out how to sustain a course whose enrollments touched only a fraction of the doctoral students in the program.

One answer to the challenge of low enrollment would be to make the course (or courses like it) mandatory. But that may yet prove too much of a change for many departments to undertake. Many faculty members, particularly at elite research universities, still believe that all, or almost all, doctoral students are destined for tenure-track positions. That view persists even in the face of statistics that demonstrate the contrary. So getting faculty buy-in to make a course such as "The Many Professions of History" required probably won't fly.

An alternative approach would be to open the course's content and enrollment to a wider group of students. We can easily imagine working with colleagues outside the History Department to turn "The Many Professions of History" into "The Many Professions of Humanists (and Social Scientists Too)." We very much hope that some will take this chapter as an invitation to join us in that project.

Notes

1 Among the responses in the 1980s, for example, were an annual "Career Opportunities Institute," intensive training in the basics of management conducted by the University of Virginia for PhDs in the humanities, social sciences, and physical sciences who wanted to enter business and government; a call for a curriculum in applied history focused on public policy; and an event to educate business leaders on the many uses and features of a corporate history program that would employ historians. "Career Opportunities Institute: University of Virginia," *Public Historian* 3, no. 3 (1981): 137–138, https://doi.org/10.2307/3377745; Peter N. Stearns and Joel A. Tarr, "Curriculum in Applied History: Toward the Future," *Public Historian* 9, no. 3 (1987): 111–125, https://doi.org/10.2307/3377191; Barbara McGuirl and Gordon L. Olson, "Business History Has a Future," *Public Historian* 3, no. 3 (July 1, 1981): 153–159, https://doi.org/10.2307/3377752.

2 Anthony T. Grafton and Jim Grossman, "No More Plan B: A Very Modest Proposal for Graduate Programs in History," *Perspectives on History*, October 2011, https://www.historians.org/publications-and-directories/perspectives-on-history /october-2011/no-more-plan-b.

3 To access the initial job outcomes report, see more information on the data that the AHA has accumulated and to access articles and resource related to the initiative, visit the section of the AHA's website devoted to Career Diversity. See American Historical Association, "Career Diversity for Historians" (n.d.), https://www .historians.org/jobs-and-professional-development/career-diversity-for-historians.

4 For the syllabus for the 2017 iteration, see Stephen Aron and Karen Wilson, "The Many Professions of History (UCLA)" (American Historical Association, n.d.), https://www.historians.org/jobs-and-professional-development/career-diversity -for-historians/career-diversity-resources/career-diversity-faculty-resources/the -many-professions-of-history-(ucla).

10

Reimagining Graduate Pedagogy to Account for Career Diversity

● ●

VERNITA BURRELL

How are PhDs in the humanities prepared to share their knowledge with others? What kinds of knowledge should be shared by PhDs, and in what kinds of contexts? I ask these broad questions advisedly: most PhDs trained today will not end up working at the kinds of institutions that produced them.

Because we've come to understand the pedagogical portion of PhD training as primarily concerned with preparing PhDs to teach undergraduates, such training hasn't engaged with many of the fundamental questions about how to connect the knowledge generated during the PhD with knowledge dissemination during and following graduate training. This volume wrestles with many of these foundational questions: What is a PhD for? Who is a PhD for? In what different ways can and should the knowledge created during the PhD be shared?

I begin this chapter by asking another, similar question: who are the imagined audiences that we are training PhDs to engage? By "we," I mean graduate administrators, graduate faculty members, current humanities PhD students, and humanities PhDs deploying their training in an array of contexts. When we think about pedagogical training as a part of the PhD experience, all too often we're not thinking about an array of contexts in which pedagogy—or, more broadly, the sharing of knowledge with nonspecialists—happens for the vast majority of humanities PhDs after they leave their graduate programs.

At the research-intensive institutions that produce the preponderance of humanities PhDs, pedagogical training has as its spoken or unspoken audience undergraduate students in the four-year college classroom. In fact, as shown in Robert Townsend's data included in this volume, most humanities PhDs do not end up teaching students enrolled in four-year colleges. For most humanities PhDs, the college classroom won't be the space in which they use their degree, and PhDs who remain in the academy will encounter a range of learners in an array of contexts, and rarely will these audiences be a homogenous group of well-prepared four-year college students. Teaching at a community college or at a K–12 institution or at a national park are all potential and realistic outcomes for a range of humanities PhDs.

Data (including the varied and vibrant outcomes for humanities PhDs this volume highlights and champions) need to inform a reimagination of pedagogical training for humanities PhDs. Graduate program administrators and faculty need to recognize the need for a wider, more fundamental type of preparation. The range of outcomes for humanities PhDs—and the need for PhDs in a range of sectors beyond higher education—call for flexible, broadly applicable pedagogical training.

Take, for instance, the path I always knew I wanted to pursue: teaching at a community college. This is an area of education that sees enrollments that surpass those of what are often—now perhaps misguidedly—called traditional four-year institutions.[1] And teaching and working at a community college involves different kinds of preparation, different goals for each learner, and a range of outcomes that may or may not include a bachelor's degree.

In this chapter, I argue that in order to reimagine graduate education—and to prepare graduate students for a wide range of careers—we must reimagine the ways we incorporate pedagogy into graduate training. If we are to prepare graduate students for a range of careers, we would do well to begin by overhauling our pedagogical training. Rather than train PhD students in the humanities to teach at the kinds of institutions that produced them, we need to refocus much of our attention on training them to engage a range of audiences—within and beyond academia. There needs to be more emphasis on how to engage diverse audiences of all kinds, and this needs to permeate our pedagogical training from the start. Such work begins by checking our assumptions.

Don't Assume You Know Who Is in Your Grad Seminars and Don't Assume You Know Where They Are Going

I was nearing the end of my PhD program when I told my faculty advisors about my dream to be a community college teacher. They could not have been more effusive in their support. Encouraged, I began sharing the news more widely.

Until, that is, another faculty member I told responded like I had slapped his grandmother. Why, this faculty member wondered with a degree of unveiled disgust, would I *want* to teach at a community college? That's not what PhD students from our program are supposed to do—he implied with his response—or if they do, they aren't supposed to want to do it. If they had to do so to survive, fine. But to aspire to this? Almost unthinkable.

In most PhD programs and for a very long time, we've admitted PhD students who we think will end up at institutions that are more or less the same as the ones that train them. We admit students, in other words, who will make up the professoriate of the future, and by "professoriate" we mean those who will teach at institutions similar to those in which they are being trained. (All too often, I should note here, there is a tendency to completely elide community college professors when we think of the professoriate. This is a problem, and it needs to change.)

A reimagined PhD requires committing to a renovation of our pedagogical training and ensuring that our graduate programs prepare graduate students for the audiences they will engage, not the students we'd prefer they would teach. As PhD students, faculty and administrators, and PhDs working in a variety of contexts, we all need to keep evaluating and adjusting our pedagogical strategies, as well as the way we're communicating with audiences of all kinds.

Don't assume that just because your scholarly work deals with race, for example, that this alone helps you consider the practical steps a good pedagogue should take when advising first-generation, low-income students, and/or students from groups historically underrepresented in undergraduate and graduate populations.

My fear is that in many doctoral programs that include pedagogical training diversity is a term that is bandied about, but rarely does this include an attention to the nitty-gritty: what practical steps do my BIPOC (Black, indigenous, and people of color) students need our department to take, and what practical steps will they need to take when they are teaching, professing, or applying their PhD in a myriad of different contexts?

It bears emphasizing here that just because you've adapted your pedagogy to fit the needs of well-prepared doctoral students, don't presume that this preparation will translate to other demographics, particularly to undergraduates at community colleges.

You have to be open-minded enough to ask questions. You have to be open-minded enough to admit that you need to learn and grow alongside your graduate students. Particularly if you are trying to teach a different culture from that which you are accustomed to teaching, or a different culture from the one in which you were trained.

Teach to the lived experience of your students, whether they are in your graduate seminars or in your community college classrooms. This applies to both those who are teaching and training graduate students and those of us who teach in community colleges. I regularly remind my students that my experiences are not theirs and vice versa. The lesson here, I think, is that no matter where you end up teaching, you always have to approach it with humility. In short, don't assume you have the answers when it comes to preparing graduate students for a range of options. Ask. Listen. Adapt. Repeat.

Effective Graduate Pedagogical Training: Individualized, Integrated, and Adaptable

Pedagogical training for PhD students in the humanities should not be experienced the same way by each student. It needs to connect to the diverse interests of current graduate students, reflect accurately the historic and recent outcomes for PhDs at your institution (at both the departmental and institutional levels), and connect to career and professional development workshops that can and should at times overlap with pedagogy seminars.

There are no universal solutions to revamping our graduate pedagogy programs. But there are individualized, local solutions, and these solutions begin simply by asking the graduate students in each program: what are your goals?

Before engaging graduate students in our graduate pedagogy training, it would behoove graduate administrators and faculty to survey the graduate students with questions like: Why are you pursuing a PhD? Do you want to teach? If so, what do you want to teach? Are you married to teaching your field? (If you are an early modernist, are you only interested in that field? Or would you be open to teaching composition and rhetoric?) What kinds of audiences and students would you like to reach?

Such surveying—alongside data transparency about departmental outcomes—is vital: it allows graduate students to make informed decisions about how they'd like to prepare and the ways they can navigate a particular pedagogical training sequence. If a graduate student indicates a desire to prepare to teach at a range of institutions, they can proceed through the pedagogical training in ways that are different from the student who really doesn't see teaching at a college or university in their future.

My small PhD cohort's outcomes include a poet who largely has eschewed the tenure track in favor of politically engaged work and public-facing writing, an academic administrator who works with graduate students on professional development, and a museum curator and educator. Each of us now teach in different ways, yet we each produced a nearly identical teaching portfolio at the conclusion of our pedagogical training. That needn't be the case. Students can progress through even a shared, synchronous pedagogical training program with different assignments and can thus produce different kinds of portfolios.

Pedagogical training in graduate school can be—rather than a monolithic preparation for university-level instruction—deconstructed into a series of discrete skills: pedagogy need not be about only the college classroom, nor even classrooms writ large. Pedagogy seminars can equip graduate students with broadly applicable skills, like teaching and sharing information with technology, public speaking, and so on—that can be applied in a range of contexts, including a variety of academic contexts. A broad base of skills that can be applied in a variety of contexts within and beyond the academy is much preferable to spending undue amounts of time on hyperspecific skills like crafting a syllabus. This last exercise—much prized in some programs—has limited value, as community colleges often have prescriptive templates that vary little, and syllabi at K–12 institutions are markedly different in form and content. In short, unless the exercise of crafting a document like a syllabus is flexible, it can end up being a waste of time for the majority of graduate students.

Yet while there needs to be the recognition that while we can expand pedagogy and deconstruct it into a variety of modules, these modules aren't for everyone, particularly those who might be interested, say, in careers in museums or the public humanities. Surveying graduate students before a pedagogical training sequence will help them begin to compose a list of careers they're interested in and can help determine what kinds of jobs they'll end up applying for and the kinds of portfolios they'll need. Then, the graduate students can take a look at the kinds of jobs that exist and how many jobs are currently posted. Push them toward a range of possible outcomes and show them the materials that they'll need to produce and the kinds of teaching—or public engagement—they'll need to do to be successful applicants and practitioners.

If they lean toward community college or K–12 teaching or museum education, then set up individualized tracks, connections to alumni, and ways for them to develop skills that prepare them for that track or related tracks. Incorporate a range of alumni voices—whether through synchronous participation or by having graduate students connect with them in informational interviews—into your pedagogical training, as well as faculty who have an open mind about teaching at a community college or working beyond academia.

Connect your adjustments to pedagogical training to the graduate student, not to an overall, comprehensive curriculum that everyone goes through in the same way. To sum up: think using a modular mindset, not a coverage mindset. Everyone would go through the same kind of training but would have variations of key assignments that would help them prepare for a range of careers.

Keywords: Reflection and Assessment

Wrestling with fundamental questions about the relationship between our content expertise and our pedagogical training should be an integral part of how we craft graduate pedagogy seminars and curricula. The outcome (i.e., what your department decides to put together in terms of pedagogical training) can and should look different: each institution has particular strengths, resources, and contacts—including alumni from a range of careers—that can inform their particular approach to pedagogical training.

Each year, a standard practice in graduate programs should be to survey recent alums about the pedagogy training they received and asking them how well it prepared them for their first outcome. Alumni who are more established in their careers should also be surveyed to incorporate longitudinal outcomes.

But surveying and reflection need to begin with the graduate students who are in the program now. Solid pedagogical training is about the graduate students in the room and connects with their particular strengths, goals, and commitments. It's all about the students. Ask them what they need, taking care to give them the time and the space to reflect early and often in their graduate training.

What would have made a difference for me during my PhD program would have been structured opportunities and endorsed spaces in which to reflect on the kind of PhD I was—and the kind of PhD I wanted to be.

In particular, we need to give BIPOC PhD students the room to discuss and process the toxicity that pervades the academic spaces they've inhabited for years as undergraduates and allow them the time to reflect on an additional range of topics that now confront them as graduate students—including whether particular aspects of the academic life are for them, navigating barriers in academia, and avoiding burnout due to being called on for service to departments and schools that often do not reward this labor.

These spaces for reflection are not merely about helping BIPOC students cope with a toxic environment. Graduate programs must attend to the issues that arise in these conversations and work to create local solutions, not merely committees or statements of support.

Creating spaces for reflection fused to action needs to also lead to a reevaluation of the language we use to describe student populations. We need to shrug off, once and for all, many of the labels we've inherited, and which we still sometimes apply to students. For example, as someone who started a PhD a bit later than my peers, I was at times called a "nontraditional" PhD student. Now I teach so-called nontraditional students at a community college. Labels matter. And as labels go, nontraditional is terrible. Those yoked with it are othered from the beginning, allowed to join an institution but from the beginning cast as somehow separate and apart from the traditional core of students. What's more, when we invoke terms like "nontraditional," we're ignoring national, local, and institutional demographics.

But here's the thing: in both undergraduate classrooms and graduate seminars, there are no traditional students, only an imagined traditional student who can, if we're not careful, become a kind of ideal. Having even the faintest shadow of an imagined ideal student in our minds—whether in a departmental admissions office or in the college classroom—inhibits our ability to deliver effective graduate training and undergraduate education. And the imagined ideal student keeps us from equipping PhDs who will end up working beyond the academy: it is very rare indeed to encounter a group of people that are as alike in age or background as those admitted to Harvard or Yale, for example. If we train our graduate students only to teach to this supposed traditional audience, we forget that these audiences are anything but traditional.

As a Black woman teaching during my doctoral preparation at Fordham University, I taught BIPOC students who were the high achievers in their high schools and saw firsthand how they had to navigate an institution that was primarily white and geared for white students. In addition to navigating a new learning environment, these students had to forge relationships and adjust their affects to merge into this primarily white institution.

This adjustment is true for many BIPOC graduate students as well. And so spaces for reflection within graduate pedagogical training are vital. If there are no spaces for reflection, PhD students may not connect why they are doing what they are doing to their pedagogical practices, may not find the support systems they need and so everyone—including the students they are teaching—can be negatively impacted.

At the macro level, practical, concrete strategies need to include a focus on assessing not just our graduate students but also (and more importantly) our graduate programs—especially the ways we prepare PhDs to teach. A central focus of assessing our pedagogical training needs to evaluate the ways this training prepares PhDs to work and teach in a variety of contexts. When was the last time your graduate program assessed its pedagogy program?

I was lucky: my doctoral program included relatively robust pedagogical preparation, especially compared with other institutions. But I wonder, at times, about the ways the training was assessed. Without a clear set of desired outcomes, how do we know whether our teaching programs work? By what metrics are we judging their success? Who are our PhDs prepared to teach?

While there are a growing number of programs that prepare future faculty, my hunch is that we've got a lot of work to do, particularly when we remember that these programs must prepare PhDs to teach and engage with a wide range of students and audiences. I know this is doable; we just haven't spent the requisite amount of time thinking about it.

Actionable strategies are a sign of good pedagogical training. If you look back at your pedagogical training and cannot recall concrete strategies, this is a problem. If you're crafting pedagogical training for doctoral students at this moment, and you're attending only to the theoretical, this is a problem. And it is a problem if you're teaching graduate students, undergraduates, or just about any population.

My own experience has been that simple mantras are helpful to remind me of fundamental truths about teaching, as even concrete strategies that you've learned can fade from memory if unused. My mantras include "You are not the most important person in your classroom: the students are" and "Make it about the students, and their writing and ideas." Mantras like these remind me to embrace the death of my own self-importance: great teaching needs to be rooted in healthy humility. This is true, I think, of all classrooms, perhaps especially the graduate seminar.

Student-Centric Classrooms: Don't Accommodate the Hidden Curriculum, Abolish It

The thing that really struck me about transitioning from my PhD program to East Los Angeles Community College was how quickly I realized that everything I'd prepared—drawing lessons I'd taken from my doctoral program's pedagogical training seminars as well as my previous college teaching experience—was not appropriate. It took me thirty minutes. After thirty minutes with my students, I realized I had to adjust reading selections and recalibrate the pace of my lessons. More importantly, I had to adjust my assumptions about what my students were prepared to do, what they needed to learn in my classroom, and why they needed to do it. I junked textbooks, and my assumptions. Every class is different: and so for each class, I teach the students in front of me. The materials may be the same, but the ends and the goals of each class are like an amoeba.

By now I hope it is clear: the graduate pedagogy seminar in the humanities should be as student-centered as we can make it. The more diverse the students—and the broader their interests—the more we'll need to recalibrate and tailor.

In East Los Angeles—for a host of reasons—my classrooms are diverse in many ways, including when it comes to the students' reasons and motivations for being in the classroom. Students returning to school after a while are often the most excited and most apprehensive at the same time. Their apprehension is usually unwarranted: they dive into class, and once they are comfortable and realize that I don't speak Martian, they embrace the routine and are fine. My younger students often fear saying the imperfect thing, and so many of them avoid saying anything. I combat both of these apprehensions with a key, primary message: don't be afraid of me or of making mistakes. Don't be afraid of putting yourself out there. Idea balloons need to be floated, and to encourage them to speak and try out ideas—especially to do so in office hours—I bribe them with chocolate.

While most family members I've met—wives, husbands, children—are proud of their family members who are in my classroom, I have also taught young women who are looked down upon or berated by their family members for enrolling in college. There's not much I can do here, other than be a sympathetic ear. I have come close, at times, to encouraging such students to study surreptitiously. Sometimes all they need is someone to listen to their concerns. I usually end up saying some variant of "I can't tell you what to say to your husband/father/uncle," as I work to convince them that they needn't drop out because of pressure from family members. It's most often young women, but not always. Young men who have come out to their family, for example, find the community college a safe place. And so often it feels as though I—their English professor—am the person they feel comfortable sharing this with.

The first week of my course is now a quasi-boot camp for doing well in college. Among many other important practical steps, I hammer down the idea of coming to see me during my office hours. I walk students to my office. I explain to them the precise steps for how to connect with me. I break down the classroom protocol on a granular basis, answering questions like "how do I know what to read by October 15?" or "what should I look for while I'm reading?"

My materials are chosen to help my students read and write (and thereby think) critically. I work with them to integrate the same kinds of ideas I taught while a PhD student at Fordham—rhetorical devices and logical argumentation—but in this context I am conscientiously putting these tools into a dialogue with their world. Which means we talk about the Zoot Suit Riots, or recognizing modes of oppression that may otherwise be cloaked by language itself. We interrogate both history and their daily lives through the lens of language. Grammar and sentence structure matter—but we're working on clear ideas and connecting ideas from one mind to another. How can my students convey what it is they want to say but haven't been encouraged to say? How can I get them to recognize that their voice matters?

I want my students to have confidence in their own thoughts and in their own conclusions. And that's where being open to new ideas and interpretations becomes important to me, and to them. I show them that I can be convinced of a new reading of a text I've taught them, so long as they can back their arguments up with evidence that fits the kinds of cases they are building.

I think it is clear that this kind of approach can—and must—hold true in the graduate seminar, where all too often we treat graduate students as if they've been groomed for graduate school and that they'll take up a job similar to the one the professor at the head of the table has. This need not be the case. We can and must make the graduate seminar about the graduate students in the room, and that begins by having local and precise plans for doing so.

The Time Is Now

The times call us, more than ever before, to an inclusive, wide-ranging approach to our pedagogical training for PhDs. As I write this, a global pandemic is wreaking havoc on my students: roughly half of them did their work on campus because of a lack of resources at home. I worry about how they'll be able to progress without access to the internet, to printers, to the library, to in-person resources on my campus. And I'll need to continue to adjust the way I do things to meet their needs and their shifting goals.

If I had a magic wand when it comes to training graduate students, I would make every PhD aware that there are no cookie-cutter students or audiences, and there are no paths that are better than others. The goals of education and knowledge acquisition are varied. I would ensure that PhDs know how diverse the populations are that appear in classrooms across the country. I would make sure PhDs know that most college students—and most audiences—are reading averse. (This is true at Fordham, where many students I taught couldn't recall what they read in high school.) My wand would make all PhDs aware that teaching—or reaching an audience of any kinds—requires flexibility, empathy, and humility. The willingness to learn and adapt is more important for the teacher, even more so than it is for the student.

The effects of a global pandemic have made even more visible the heartrending educational inequality that pervades the United States and is rooted in systemic racism. And so our work as teachers, mentors, advisors, and administrators of graduate programs matters ever more than ever. Our assumptions about who is in our classrooms and our beliefs about what kinds of outcomes count need to change.

To this day, I'm still living out my credo of teaching the students in front of me in each classroom, not the students I imagined I would have, nor the students my graduate training prepared me for.

How much better would it be if we reconfigured pedagogical training in humanities PhD programs to put flexibility—and graduate students—front and center?

Note

1 The Community College Research Center at Columbia University's Teachers College notes that—when Integrated Postsecondary Education Data System (IPEDS) data are correctly analyzed—roughly 2.5 million more undergraduate students are enrolled at community colleges than are enrolled at four-year institutions. https://ccrc.tc.columbia.edu/easyblog/shifting-sectors-community -colleges-undercounting.html.

11

Preparing for a Digital
Humanities Career

· ·

WILL FENTON

One of the key strengths of the digital humanities may be its definitional malleability. Beneath banners of "digital scholarship," "digital humanities," and "digital innovation," humanists interweave disparate fields, disciplines, and institutions. There's something heartening, even hopeful, about the patchwork quality of the digital humanities (DH). At a moment of real scarcity across humanities disciplines, DH presents one thread of opportunity.

A little over a year ago, I profiled five rising stars in the digital humanities. Although new luminaries have since brightened the field, the state of DH remains much the same. "Digital humanities work increasingly extends across institutional types and institutional spaces," explained Matthew K. Gold, creator of the *Debates in the Digital Humanities* series. "It includes scholars working in libraries and alt-ac roles ... emblematic of the next wave of digital humanities research, teaching, and participatory action." Marissa Parham, whom I also profiled, added that the field could change practices within the academy. "There's a lot of talk amongst DH-ers about this moment as an opportunity to change how we engage, disseminate and produce academic work, from our work as teachers to our work as cultivators of institutional practices and norms," said Parham.[1]

In this chapter, I consider how one specific group—doctoral students—can use the digital humanities to thrive—or, at the least, to expand their career possibilities. Given my own close vantage point (having recently defended a dissertation in literary studies), I am acutely aware of the difficult market facing recent humanities PhDs. But I'm also guardedly hopeful. Recent graduates can leverage digital expertise to pursue rewarding careers inside, across, and beyond academe. The collaborative work that DH requires will, in the long term, strengthen ties between universities, nonprofits, libraries, and a constellation of cultural heritage institutions.

This chapter unfolds in three acts. Following a brief note on methodology, I begin with an overview of the digital humanities job market, circa January 2019. Reading across job ads from the MLA Job Information List (JIL), *Inside Higher Ed*, and Digital Humanities Now, I consider how the digital humanities enable PhDs to fashion career trajectories they might not have seriously considered ten years ago, including roles at galleries, libraries, archives, and museums. In the second act, I turn to my experience at such institutions, highlighting how digital projects enabled me to acquire new skills, connect with new partners, and cultivate new professional networks. Finally, I close with concrete steps drawn from both my global assessment of the DH job market and my experiences at Philadelphia cultural heritage institutions. I address three core audiences: current graduate students, faculty, and program-level administrators. These audiences are rarely addressed concurrently, and yet, if we are to both support graduate students today and imagine a more diverse and sustainable conception of humanities careers, both graduate students and program administrators need to take up this challenge together. I hope that this chapter and others in this volume underscore the common cause shared by students, faculty, and administrators.

Methodology

What does the DH job market look like? It depends on where you look. Given the diversity of roles associated with the digital humanities, applicants may need to expand their search beyond the usual job boards, such as the MLA JIL. Let me be clear, I focused on the MLA JIL because my field is literary studies; however, the kinds of digital humanities job postings that I found on the JIL are widely applicable across humanities disciplines. For example, a cursory look at the H-Net job postings aligned quite closely with those on MLA, and many of the same jobs were cross-listed. It's also important to remember that, given the prevalence of contract, postdoctoral, and grant-funded positions, not all opportunities will be posted in the fall. The digital humanities job market is not so different from the humanities job market: many jobs are contingent and appear later in the spring calendar, demanding both economic and geographic flexibility from applicants.

To provide a snapshot of the DH job market as of January 2019, I searched the JIL as well as *Inside Higher Ed* Careers (IHE) and Digital Humanities Now

(DHNOW).[2] I chose these three platforms in order to identify roles that required DH skills and expertise both within specific humanities departments (JIL), across university administrative structures (IHE), and across various university-adjacent cultural heritage institutions (DHNOW). My aspiration for this survey is a representative rather than a comprehensive view of the DH job market at the outset of academic year 2019–2020.

While I experimented with various filters, I opted to use keyword searches ("digital humanities," "digital scholarship," and "dh") in order to retrieve the greatest number of possible opportunities.[3] Where jobs were cross-posted, I selected the most detailed synopsis for each job.

The DH Job Market

As of January 2019, I identified 111 positions that called for at least some degree of digital humanities expertise.

A small but significant fraction of positions (thirteen jobs) were devoted explicitly to research, teaching, and service of the digital humanities. For example, the University of South California posted a fellowship in humanities in a digital world postdoctoral research. The University of Chicago called for a senior lecturer and academic director of digital studies. And Stonehill College posted an ad for an assistant director of the Digital Innovation Lab, specialist in digital pedagogy and scholarship.

Such "digital-first" positions would likely not have existed ten years ago, and they present new opportunities—for the right applicant. Notably, all three of these opportunities exist outside of traditional academic fields, under the auspices of a fledgling department (the USC Digital Humanities department), program (the Digital Studies program at the University of Chicago), or lab (Stonehill's Collaboratory for Innovative Design).

Nascence presents both opportunity and risk. On one hand, such positions allow an enterprising applicant to shape new programs. For example, applicants for the job at Chicago are told that if they land the position they will "take a leading role in building the Digital Studies program." That a twelve-month (renewable) hire is being asked to build a long-term, sustainable program speaks to kinds of systematic challenges facing new hires as well as new DH programs. These programs are no panacea for the labor troubles of academic humanities; they reproduce the same precarious employment model that undermines established humanities programs and departments.

Moreover, the very thing that makes these roles possible—location outside of existing programs and departments—also renders them precarious. Of the twelve postdoctoral fellowships listed in January 2019, two-thirds of those roles (eight) were situated in programs and departments founded in the past decade. None of the three aforementioned jobs were tenured or tenure-track, and

Table 11.1
Digital humanities job postings, January 2019

	Information technology	Computer science	Language and literature	History	Cultural studies	Humanities	Liberal arts
Faculty	3	3	34	9	9	4	4
Limited term	1		8	3	2	1	2
Tenured or tenure track	2	3	26	6	7	3	2
Administrative	6	0	0	1	1	2	0
Contingent				1	1	1	
Staff	6					1	
Total	9	3	34	10	10	6	4

SOURCE: Job listings on the Modern Language Association Job Information List, *Inside Higher Ed* Careers, Digital Humanities Now as of January 2019.

contract terms range from one to three years. Such terms may not be deal breakers for some applicants, especially given that many PhDs are pursuing postdocs as a rite of passage, but they also aren't a panacea to the woes of the academic job market.

Instead, the majority of results looked like traditional humanities teaching jobs with both subject area specializations and preferences for digital skill sets.[4] Four out of five positions (eighty-three) required or requested a PhD in hand. While a dozen of those roles might be out of reach for humanities-trained graduate students (three positions were listed in computer science and another nine in information technology), language and literature continues to shape the field (thirty-four positions), followed by other complementary fields of study, such as history (ten), cultural studies (ten), and humanities and the liberal arts more broadly (nine).

Notably, more than half of the roles represented in table 11.1 (forty-nine) are tenured or tenure-track faculty positions. That number compares quite favorably to the industry writ large, where only one-quarter of jobs qualify for tenure.[5] While one cannot stake a causal claim—i.e., that DH expertise enables applicants to land better jobs—the most coveted teaching jobs increasingly require, among other things, digital skill sets, ranging from experience in digital history to familiarity with specific learning management systems such as Blackboard.[6]

More often than not, those digital skill sets are vague or undefined. This, perhaps, lends some nuance to a point made by Lindsay Thomas at the 2019 MLA Annual Convention: Although digital humanities and digital scholarship job postings may be growing more specialized, DH-inflected humanities teaching jobs remain stubbornly generalist.[7] At George Mason University, an assistant professor of folklore and narrative posting called for a "record of innovative and dynamic teaching and a desire to develop folklore educational strategies for the 21st century." The keyword "innovation" appears in more than a dozen of the listings, variously referring to pedagogy, habits of mind, research, departments, programs, and even institutions. (The appendage "twenty-first century" is no less common and no more specific.)

Hiring committees often measure innovation through teaching. Northern Michigan University posted a job for assistant professor of composition and rhetoric in which the hiring committee associates the "ability to demonstrate commitment to innovative and effective pedagogies" with "experience with integrating technology, digital resources, and learning management systems into one's pedagogy." In a posting for an assistant professor of early modern literature at Central Washington University, digital humanities is listed as one preferred qualification in a litany of other secondary interests. More important was "expertise in online teaching," which is identified as a *minimum* qualification.

Many institutions prioritized online education experience. A hiring committee at Pennsylvania State University sought an assistant professor of digital humanities with a rhetoric and composition background and "experience in developing traditional, hybrid, and web-based courses." That many institutions associate online teaching and learning with the digital humanities underscores how expansively departments are thinking about the field of the digital humanities.

While applying computational tools and methods to pedagogy will satisfy committees seeking someone—anyone—who can "do DH," many departments also want a candidate who can bring those skills to bear in research and service.

Alongside web-enabled teaching, the aforementioned Penn State posting also requested a candidate with "demonstrated evidence of scholarly publication or research potential in digital literacies and/or multimodal rhetoric." At Messiah College, the hiring committee sought an assistant professor who could "contribute to programming in the digital humanities" (in addition to running a writing center). In the case of the University of Colorado, Colorado Springs, the hiring committee sought an expert in critical theory with "additional expertise in (and evidence of professional commitment to) either Victorian British literature or Digital Humanities for a tenure-track position." The hiring committee measures that evidence of professional commitment in two forms: teaching experience as well as a "promising research agenda."

As an increasing number of programs use DH credentials to brand themselves digitally "woke," a growing share of hiring committees expect evidence of such commitments woven throughout candidates' teaching, service, and research.

Postdoctoral fellowships often have the clearest and most concrete descriptions of the kinds of DH skills coveted by hiring committees.[8] Perhaps this owes to the fact that postdocs are contractual and often conceived to solve a particular problem(s). Bucknell University posted a humanities postdoctoral fellowship that included minimum qualifications that were more prescriptive than most faculty positions: "The successful candidate will have a PhD in a humanities field, a concentration in DH (or equivalent), and experience with: database creation and management; coding in Python, JavaScript, and other applicable programming languages; and web application and GUI design." Bucknell is well established in the field—the university offers a minor in DH and regularly hosts major conferences and institutes. Perhaps it is unsurprising, then, that this department has a clearly defined set of priorities for their prospective fellow.

In other instances, external funding necessitates clarity of purpose. That is, postdoctoral fellowships often serve as a means to achieve particular institutional priorities. For example, the digital humanities postdoctoral fellowship at Williams College, funded by the Andrew W. Mellon Foundation, seeks a candidate who will pursue "digital humanities scholarship and methodologies within a museum context, with access to collections and involvement in exhibitions and public programs." Qualifications include experience in the application of methods such as visualization, text mining, text encoding, and network analysis; the capacity to work in interdisciplinary environments; and proven aptitude in scholarly communication. In addition, the position requests "demonstrated digital project management experience," "deep familiarity with museum collection databases," and "undergraduate teaching experience" as preferred qualifications.

The GLAM Alternative

By pairing teaching and scholarly communication with commitments to public programming, access, and discovery, the field of digital humanities creates continuities between universities and cultural heritage institutions. Questioning how the DH job market extends beyond the walls of the university enables applicants to uncover new opportunities to apply humanistic training. Put another way, recent graduates with DH expertise can pursue rewarding careers outside of faculty positions.

One-fifth (twenty) of the DH positions that I identified were housed in libraries. Some of those roles were quite compelling in their own right. For example, the British Library recently posted a curator of digital publications. While that role is a fixed-term contract, the position offers tremendous promise at a venerable institution in a desirable city. Meanwhile, California State University, Fresno sought a director of library technology and collection management. The wide salary range on that position ($44,712–$153,204) suggests that the hiring committee was open to a range of candidates.

Similar to pursuing a job in academe, seeking a career at a gallery, library, archive, or museum—a so-called "GLAM" institution—requires specialized experience, expertise, and professional networks. There are no shortcuts. While a PhD is a valuable and recognized credential in academic-adjacent institution, it is not a golden ticket. Moreover, there are still many institutions that require an MLS. In fact, seven of the twenty library jobs required or requested the credential.[9]

The more consequential challenge is, not unlike higher education, GLAM institutions tend to hire from within their tribe. Practically, a recent PhD has spent five (or more) years entering a tribe in which the logical culmination of that experience is a tenure-track teaching job. The skills graduate students master, the jargon they learn, and the networks they cultivate are largely adapted to that path. Choosing another path means entering another community, learning its norms and customs, and earning the trust, respect, and goodwill of its members.

This is a challenging but not daunting task. Applicants with a DH background already speak the lingua franca. There's significant technical and experiential overlap, whether it's called digital humanities or digital scholarship. For the Digital Library Federation (DLF) 2018 Forum, Paige Morgan created an interactive study of requested skills and expertise associated with recent (2010–2018) DH and DS library positions.[10] Notably, the top six skills requested in 2018 were, in order of frequency, *scholarly communication* (i.e., research trends and practices of scholarly communication); *institutional repositories* (familiarity with existing repositories); *preservation* (appraisal, selection, acquisition, de-accession, arrangement, preservation, and description); *open access* (best practices and copyright management); *data visualization* (collaborative workspaces and access to expertise); and *project development and management* (project management expertise and familiarity with project management software).

Even without DH experience, PhD students have already achieved some degree of expertise in three of those clusters. Graduate students are well versed in the tools of the trade (scholarly communication), comfortable navigating a host online resources and databases (institutional repositories), and practiced in shepherding a large project—the dissertation—from conception to completion (a form of product development, not to be confused with project development). The remaining skills can be acquired through DH projects with partners outside of one's department.

A second point to make is that even if an applicant isn't interested in a career at a GLAM institution, the related skills lend themselves to other forms of academic employment. In a recent study for MLA *Profession*, Beth Seltzer considered one hundred job ads, half of which were traditional faculty roles and half of which are commonly called "humanities careers," such as professional roles in university administration, nonprofits, and libraries.[11] Reading across those postings, Seltzer identified some thirteen "transferable skills" several of which (digital scholarship, educational technology, program development, and educational technology) dovetail with preferences identified by Morgan. Other transferable skills, most especially grant writing and public engagement, are sewn into both the operations and missions of GLAM institutions. That is, pursuing experience at cultural heritage institution will serve applicants well whether or not they pursue a career in the field.

In the next section, I touch upon my own experience entering the GLAM tribe. Drawing lessons from my own experience, I consider how applicants may use the digital humanities to connect with new partners, develop new expertise, and cultivate new networks that lend themselves to a diverse range of career paths.

From Fellowship to Employment

There was no template for my career path. My current role, director of research and public programs, didn't exist two years ago when I started at the Library Company of Philadelphia.

My path started with a research fellowship. In 2016, I landed a long-term research fellowship from the Library Company. I was a fourth-year PhD writing a dissertation about Quakers at a Jesuit university. Suffice it to say, I needed to travel for my research. I moved to Philadelphia to make as much headway as I could on my project, and I resolved to stay, if I could, in the Quaker City.

In the process of researching and writing my first dissertation chapter, on the fiction of Charles Brockden Brown, I lost myself in what was supposed to be the backdrop of the chapter. Researching the 1763 Paxton massacres and subsequent print debate, a little-known incident outside of the Philadelphia early American studies community, I contracted an incurable case of pamphlet fever.

The Paxton incident began in the Paxtang township, just outside of what is today the capital of Pennsylvania. In December 1763, backcountry vigilantes murdered twenty unarmed Susquehannock Indians. A month later, hundreds of these "Paxton Boys" marched toward Philadelphia to menace refugee Indians under the protection of the government. The marchers were stopped six miles north of Philadelphia by a delegation led by Benjamin Franklin. But this was just the beginning of the war for public opinion. Supporters and critics of the Paxton Boys spent the next year battling in print, in a pamphlet war that was not so different from the Twitter wars of today.

A number of scholars had written on the incident, but nearly everyone cited John Raine Dunbar's sixty-year-old edition.[12] *The Paxton Papers* collected the full-texts of twenty-eight pamphlets that Dunbar deemed most extraordinary. However, as I worked through the vast print collections at the Library

Company, I realized that there were many other pamphlets and still many more editions that didn't make the cut. Full text also failed to convey the rich materiality of the debate. Some pamphlets included engravings, and others repackaged and reframed earlier arguments. I also had no idea how to work with the printed materials that circulated contemporaneously. Certainly, someone had to do something with the political cartoons and broadsides that would have been posted all over the city's taverns and coffeehouses. These ancillary materials came to preoccupy my own research, and it seemed only right that I show my work and make those materials available to other scholars.

After speaking with librarian Jim Green, who happened to share my interest in the print debate, I concocted the wild idea that we ought to digitize all of the Paxton holdings available at the Library Company and the neighboring Historical Society of Pennsylvania. When I look back at this period, I'm struck by my own boldness. Here I was, one researcher among many, asking two preeminent Philadelphia cultural heritage institutions to digitize hundreds of pages of materials at their own expense. If I didn't have the support of Green, I suspect I would have been politely but promptly waved away. I also benefited from fortuitous timing: both institutions were taking on interns, which they were willing to assign to the task, if I could define it.

I spent several months working with the Green to identify materials and collect metadata in a shared database. This was no small thing, given that the Library Company and Historical Society of Pennsylvania both have their own catalogs structured to address their own institutional needs. It also required many value judgments, which could be made only on the ground. If both institutions had the same edition of the same pamphlet, which would we digitize, and why? There were also seemingly endless technical considerations. Both institutions had their own scanning equipment, conventions, and DAM (digital asset management) systems. I spent many hours—time I could have invested in my dissertation—working with technologists at both institutions, drafting best practices, learning about long-term preservation plans, and crafting a memorandum of understanding that stipulated the roles and responsibilities for all parties.

Digitization was the easy part. The interns finished their task in less than six weeks, after which it was my responsibility to make those materials discoverable.

This is the part of DH that isn't saleable, but it couldn't be more essential—and more collaborative. I worked with more than a dozen staff members across the institutions. I found myself regularly corresponding with staff at the Alliance for Networking Visual Culture (USC), who had created the open-source online publishing platform Scalar (https://scalar.me/anvc), which I used to make the Paxton materials discoverable.[13] Configuring our instance of Scalar to achieve the ends stipulated in our memorandum of understanding required customization. Not only did we want a custom URL, but in order to ensure long-term preservation, the Library Company needed to host digital assets. The process compelled me both to navigate both institutions' bureaucracies and to learn the ins and outs of Scalar.

That project, *Digital Paxton* (http://digitalpaxton.org), launched in April 2017, but the work had only just begun.[14] To share it with scholars, I presented at a McNeil Center for Early American Studies seminar and curated a modest exhibition of Paxton materials at the Library Company of Philadelphia.[15] I do not doubt that the publicity I received with the project launch helped me to secure a second long-term fellowship, this time at the American Philosophical Society.

I was admittedly overextended during that fellowship. I was sprinting to finish my dissertation, publish journal articles, and apply for jobs (mainly postdoctoral fellowships). The terms of the fellowship also required I take responsibility for a secondary project: I was asked to canvass diaries from across the collections and to work with the Center for Digital Scholarship to create an online research guide. Over the next year, I examined more than 1,700 volumes across 115 manuscript collections spanning 340 years (1671–2011). In addition to writing diary notes for each of the 115 collections, I collected keywords, subject headings (keyed to the Library of Congress), and thousands of points of GIS-mappable location information. While the Center for Digital Scholarship performed the technical heavy lifting, I took every opportunity to learn about how the institution structured data and built an HTML project.[16] As with *Digital Paxton*, I had the opportunity to formally launch the *APS Diary Research Guide* at a public event, the institution's monthly Lunch at the Library seminar.[17]

In scouring the manuscript collections for diaries, I also found a tremendous quantity of material related to my Paxton project. Thanks to the goodwill that I had earned through my work on the diary research guide, staff generously digitized those materials for *Digital Paxton*. In fact, at present, the American Philosophical Society is the third largest contributor to the project, having digitized fifty-seven different items, including correspondence, sermons, pamphlets, and even indigenous passports. The support of the American Philosophical Society helped me to advance the project in two key ways. First, it compelled me to broaden my inquiry into the Paxton incident to include treaty minutes, diaries, letters, and other forms of printed materials. Second, with the imprimatur of the three major Philadelphia institutions, I had more success convincing other institutions to contribute to the project.

Today, *Digital Paxton* features materials from some two dozen research libraries, archives, and cultural heritage institutions as well as contextual and interpretive materials from educators, historians, art historians, and literary scholars. Without the networks and institutional ballast of the partnerships

I formed during my fellowships, there's simply no way the project could have matured. As my pet project, *Digital Paxton*'s acceptance aligned with my own in the GLAM community, and I certainly hope the project embodies the care and collaborative spirit that I bring to scholarship.

With the growing scale and sophistication of *Digital Paxton*, I began to think more actively about the silences and erasures of the materials we have digitized. The tension I have continually faced is how to tell the story of a colonial massacre, mediated through colonial documents, in a manner that doesn't simply reproduce colonial biases, assumptions, and erasures. With *Digital Paxton*, I may have reached the limits of a digital collection, scholarly edition, and teaching platform.

But what if we could imagine a perspective on the Paxton massacre that, given the genocide of the Susquehannock, could not be retrieved? That is, what if, instead of telling a story about the Paxton vigilantes, we sought to tell a story about the Conestoga, their fortitude, and their formative role in the history of colonial Pennsylvania?

To take up that challenge, I coauthored a major grant application with the Library Company. *Redrawing History: Indigenous Perspectives on Colonial America* (https://librarycompany.org/redrawing-history), which was ultimately funded by The Pew Center for Arts & Heritage (2018–2020), comprised of three public-facing components: an educational graphic novel, a national educators' seminar, and an exhibition, accompanied by a series of programs.[18]

If *Digital Paxton* enabled me to reimagine my dissertation as I was writing it, *Redrawing History* challenged me to envision its afterlife, to collaborate with new stakeholders who will reinterpret the project for nonspecialists.

The grant has also made my current position both conceptually and materially possible. In coauthoring on the grant, I had an opportunity to articulate my values of public-facing scholarly innovation through a specific case study. The generous funding that we received enabled the Library Company not only to execute the project but to defray some of the costs associated with my own staff position. My hope is that *Redrawing History* serves as a proof of concept on which we can build through subsequent collaborations with the institution's extensive network of patrons, research fellows, and community members.

At the moment, I'm privileged to have a quite rewarding career. I get to live and work in a city I adore, contribute to an institution that was dispensable to my research, and collaborate with luminaries both inside and outside the academy. Alongside my role as creative director of the *Redrawing History* project, I've developed a continuing education series with topics as wide ranging and timely as political caricature, Afrofuturism, and Benjamin Franklin's immigration politics and creating a virtual commons for current and former research fellows.[19] If this is what a humanities career can look like, we should welcome that future.

Of course, my experience isn't necessarily reproducible. Nothing about my career path was certain, nor the landmarks easily discernible, save in hindsight. There are, however, some values that may serve other humanities PhDs irrespective of whether they secure a perch inside or outside the academy. Those include curiosity, humility, and receptivity to new ways of knowing and a commitment to work with and learn from colleagues.

Contrary to the traditional university rewards systems, which fetishizes the monograph, most work outside the academy—and arguably within it—is collaborative, or, at the least, coalitional. Because digital humanities projects demand cooperative skills, cooperative labor, and cooperative acknowledgment, they should rightfully be regarded as both a product (connective tissue between intra- and extra-university institutions) and a practice (a means of developing those competencies and forging those alliances).

Call(s) to Action

I close here with actionable steps that synthesize findings from both macro (DH job market) and micro levels (my own experience). I speak variously to three core audiences: current graduate students, faculty (most especially those in advisory roles), and program-level administrators (namely department chairs, directors of graduate study, and directors of placement and professional development).

Graduate Students

Even if you want to pursue a humanities career, the actions you can take will be informed by your enrollment status. That is, what you can do as a first-year PhD is quite different from what you can reasonably pursue if you're currently submitting materials for the job market.

No matter where you are in your graduate experience, you ought to take some comfort that you've already done a lot right to get where you are. At the risk of sounding too hopeful, you have valuable specialized skills that include expertise in both major fields and subfields. Despite all of the changes to the academic job market, this kind of fine-grain expertise is valued and valuable. You already have experience in teaching, research, and service—skills coveted by universities and compatible with other forms of employment. Moreover, the barriers to entering the digital humanities are remarkably low. If you want to eavesdrop on the field's major debates, they're almost always unfolding in public via Twitter and Slack and through regional consortia (e.g., Philly DH in my case).

If you're a late-stage PhD student, exercise self-care and look for shortcuts to build some kind of DH portfolio. This could be as simple as reading the latest edition of *Debates in the Digital Humanities* to gain some sense of the state of the field.[20] You can also look for a low-bandwidth means to translate some of your research into a digital form. That might look like an Omeka gallery with a Neatline timeline or WordPress site with CommentPress theme.[21] The point is to show that you can do more than yack—even if you can't quite hack, to paraphrase a popular DH debate.[22] While there's a practical way to become a digital humanist overnight, many hiring committees don't have a clear sense of what they want (as evidenced by my earlier survey). Many departments want their new hires to figure out the field, and as long as you can demonstrate that you're conversant in the debates, you ought to clear that hurdle.

If you're reading this chapter earlier in your graduate career, look for ways to pursue a DH project or, at the very least, introduce digital tools and methods into your dissertation research. Perhaps you want to start a text-mining project, a visualization of correspondence, or a digital edition of an overlooked work(s). Follow your interests—not what you think interests the market. As with your dissertation topic, you deserve to choose a project that you're invested in and not something that will appease an amorphous hiring committee.

Pursuing a DH project doesn't mean you need to code. Certainly, you might learn to along the way. However, if there's a suitable platform for your project (as in the case of Scalar and *Digital Paxton*), use it, but take the time to survey options and weigh their limitations and affordances. That is, as with a lit review in a dissertation chapter, find out what's out there and think carefully about your goals and methodology. If the right tool or platform doesn't exist, you might be able to partner with someone who can help solve that problem. Look to your university library or, if your university has one, digital humanities lab. Talk to other graduate students, including—and especially—those outside your department. For example, I was an early Americanist, but I found that medievalists asked wonderfully rich questions of my records' materiality.

The more counsel you solicit, and the more widely you solicit it, the better informed your choices and the more likely you are to find new partners. When you exhaust the resources at your university—and I say "when" rather than "if," given the limits of institutional resources—consider the moment of exhaustion an invitation to seek new partners. I've benefited immeasurably from external research fellowships; however, I'm the first to admit that I wrote a stubbornly archival dissertation. That might not be the case for your project. Follow the counsel of your advisors, and, as important, follow your instincts. If you're going to invest in a DH project, it ought to ignite your passion.

Finally, it's worth noting that the stakes to pursuing a DH project aren't that high. You're a graduate student. This is a learning process, and you will make mistakes. Fortunately, everyone knows that you're an apprentice. If there was ever a time to be bold and to try something that might almost certainly fail, it's now.

Faculty

I have great sympathy for faculty trying to support or advise graduate students today. You have deep experience supporting students who pursue traditional tenure-track teaching jobs; you've built your career and your professional networks around that world. I also acknowledge how much you've sacrificed to sustain this field and the discipline more widely. It is this spirit of commonweal that will enable the humanities to endure the current crisis. But make no mistake, this is a crisis, and you're on the frontlines.

With the collapse of hiring at public universities, recent cohorts of humanities PhDs need somewhere to go. At the 2019 Association of American Historians Convention, fellow contributor Robert Townsend noted that, at present, more than half of humanities PhDs (56 percent) find employment teaching at the postsecondary level—a considerably higher percentage than in other fields.[23] Put another way, we've already found homes for the majority of humanities PhDs, despite an anemic academic job market. Now we need to find rewarding employment for the considerable minority of PhDs who are still struggling.

One answer is to incentivize the acquisition and acknowledgment of skills compatible with other professions. To frame graduate education in terms of skills that are compatible with—rather than transferable to—other careers is to highlight continuities between university departments and partners at nonprofits, libraries, and cultural heritage institutions.[24]

Thinking actively about the skills PhDs acquire in a graduate school does not require that we jettison our shared commitment to humanistic study or the creation of new knowledge. Rather, it presents an opportunity to think critically about how PhDs demonstrate mastery over subject matter, develop research projects, and communicate the value of work to individuals outside of their field. I see the integration of digital humanities projects as one means to catalyze long-overdue adaptation. Practically, this means encouraging students to think seriously about planning digital projects, applying for external grants and fellowships, and conducting informational interviews early in their graduate careers.

If you're an advisor, you exercise considerable influence over what your students deem success or failure. Initiate conversations about what kinds of digital projects graduate students might pursue to enrich their dissertation research, how they might create them, and whom they might consult. You don't have to have all of the answers. As Molly Des Jardin recently posited, highlighting the range of DH activity will only help your students feel more comfortable entering the field.[25] Putting students in touch with colleagues at other institutions and other kinds of institutions is exceedingly valuable. The earlier students think about taking on a digital humanities project, the more they can accomplish, and the more they'll have to show at the end of their graduate experience.

Administrators

If you're a chair or director of graduate studies the first thing you can do—and at virtually no expense—is to reconnect with your alumni. Former students can serve as models for current students as well as ambassadors to new institutions. Find out what your alumni are doing, especially those who went silent after they failed to secure a tenure-track teaching position. Invite them back to campus. Promote their achievements on your department's social media and website. Connect current students with alumni. Recognizing and elevating different types of career trajectories is crucial to destigmatizing nonteaching careers and inculcating graduate students with some sense of agency over their futures.

As you question what your program might look in five years, consider how the structures of your department might advance the skills aggregated by Seltzer and Morgan. This might begin with early and active integration of DH training. What that training looks like will probably depend upon the strengths and priorities of your department; however, I would be inclined to support Julia Flanders's claim that DH training include work with metadata, informatics, information design, and project management; as Alison Booth has noted, such training is, all too often, too little and too late.[26] In addition to providing students with valuable technical skills, Booth noted, the collaborative nature of the digital humanities counters prevailing norms of solo authorship. That is, DH training might not only aid the career prospects of graduate students but also prove salubrious for the rewards systems within your academic departments.

Each of the constitutive components of a PhD could be refined to enable students to pursue a range of humanities careers: a comps minor field could be devoted to a DH survey to introduce graduate students to computational tools, methods, and practices; a graduate teaching requirement could be cross-listed with another department to encourage graduate students to collaborate and coteach with peers outside their department; the dissertation could include at least one public-facing component to be assessed by a committee member(s) outside the university; and by offering startup grants or limited matching funds, departments could encourage students to apply for external funding. Irrespective of whether you find these prescriptions persuasive or actionable, I encourage you to experiment using your departmental structures. Your students will almost certainly welcome a period of trial and error.

Allow me to close with a word to the last point, which might be objectionable to some students, faculty, and administrators. I understand that grant writing, in particular, is often considered an onerous task that distracts from the very kind of work we entered this profession to pursue. Certainly, I would much rather write about Charles Brockden Brown than draft a memorandum of understanding. Moreover, I have trepidations about institutions that rely upon term-limited grants to develop sustainable projects. That said, at an individual level, I've found grant writing to be incalculably clarifying. Grant writing has challenged me to think specifically about my audiences, how I propose to reach them, and why I believe my research is urgent.

As a recent PhD, I know how difficult it is to write a dissertation, teach, publish, attend conferences, cultivate professional networks, and conduct a job search. Given the daunting list of things we're told that we need to succeed, there's little time or incentive to consider public engagement. Nevertheless, my experience with *Digital Paxton* and *Redrawing History* enriched my research, broadened my professional networks, and enabled me to share my work with new audiences.

There's no way I could have translated *Digital Paxton* from a labor of love into a public resource without the support of a vast network of interdisciplinary experts. That includes librarians, archivists, and technologists who have helped me to digitize, catalog, and ingest records. Equally important has been the counsel of historians, whose aid I have solicited to curate an exhibition, whose scholarship I have edited for the project's critical apparatus, and whose lessons I have sought as teaching resources. Also importantly, this project has opened new opportunities for me to share my research, including venues as wide ranging as *American Quarterly* and the *Journal of Interactive Technology and Pedagogy* as well as the *Philadelphia Inquirer*, NEH *HUMANITIES* magazine, and NPR *Code Switch*.

In the context of anemic public funding, shrinking enrollments, and deep-seated skepticism of humanistic inquiry, I am convinced that pursuing other modes of engagement, such as digital projects, can enable graduate students to reimagine both the stakes and forms of scholarly work. The reward is the process: collaboration is necessarily coalitional, and with each new effort we enlist support of new stakeholders and engender goodwill with future allies.

Notes

1. William Fenton, "The Rising Stars of the Digital Humanities," *Inside Higher Ed*, August 2, 2017, https://www.insidehighered.com/digital-learning/article/2017/08/02/rising-stars-digital-humanities.
2. Modern Language Association, "Job List" (n.d.), https://www.mla.org/Resources/Career/Job-List; Inside Higher Ed Careers (n.d.), https://careers.insidehighered.com/; Digital Humanities Now (n.d.), http://digitalhumanitiesnow.org/.
3. It is worth noting that "digital scholarship" is often employed rather than "digital humanities" at research libraries, archives, and cultural heritage institutions. I am strategically avoiding definitional debates as I see significant continuities between these terms, which I'll explore with greater care in the section titled "The GLAM Alternative."
4. My results aligned with Jonathan Kramnick's assessment of the English job market: namely that while subfields remain stable, the generalist category has all

but vanished. See Kramnick, "What We Hire in Now: English by the Grim Numbers," *Chronicle of Higher Education*, December 9, 2018, https://www .chronicle.com/article/What-We-Hire-in-Now-English/245255.

5 A recent analysis of federal data by the American Association of University Professors found that 73 percent of all faculty positions are off the tenure track. For more information, see American Association of University Professors, "Data Snapshot: Contingent Faculty in US Higher Ed " (n.d.), https://www.aaup.org /news/data-snapshot-contingent-faculty-us-higher-ed#.XXlzIihKgdU.

6 Notably, many of the positions seek candidates with the ability to perform additional administrative work, such as editing a journal, running a writing center, or launching some kind of digital humanities program, lab, or center.

7 This isn't an ideal situation for institutions or for applicants. Paige Morgan and Helene Williams canvassed 150 job ads and noted a "lack of clarity around library-based DH/DS support roles" For more information, see Lindsay Thomas, "'The Irrational Sense of Having Done One's Job Well': Professionalization, Graduate Education, and DH" (Chicago, 2019); Paige C. Morgan and Helene Williams, "When Does a New Role Cease to Be New? Situating the Work Of Library-Based Digital Humanities/Scholarship Support Positions" (2018), https://scholarlyrepository.miami.edu/librarypapers/4/.

8 Notably, that are a lot more DH/DS postdoctoral fellowships than my January survey may suggest. Many of these fellowships are posted throughout the spring via organizations such as CLIR, which places dozens of PhDs each year. CLIR, "CLIR Postdoctoral Fellowship Program" (n.d.), https://www.clir.org/initiatives -partnerships/postdoc/.

9 Applicants would do well to distinguish between positions that prefer and require the MLS. Where there is a preference, there is flexibility. Inquire with the hiring committee. Some institutions support new staff as they pursue the credential.

10 Paige C. Morgan, "Requested Skills & Expertise, DH/DS Library Positions, 2010–2018. Mouse over for More Info, or Sort by Skills or Years. Created for DLF Forum 2018 " (Tableau Software, October 15, 2018), https://public.tableau.com /views/RequestedskillsexpertiseDHDSlibrarypositions2010-2018/Requestedskill sandexpertiseDHDSfrontfacinglibrarypositions2010-2018?:embed=y&:display _count=yes&:origin=viz_share_link.

11 Beth Seltzer, "One Hundred Job Ads from the Humanities Ecosystem—Profession," *MLA Profession*, Fall 2018, https://profession.mla.org/one-hundred-job-ads-from -the-humanities-ecosystem/.

12 John Raine Dunbar, *The Paxton Papers* (M. Nijhoff, 1957).

13 For more information, see Alliance for Networking Visual Culture, "About Scalar," https://scalar.me/anvc/scalar/.

14 For more information, see Digital Paxton, "Digital Paxton: Digital Collection, Critical Edition, and Teaching Platform " (n.d.), http://digitalpaxton.org/works /digital-paxton/index.

15 Of the two launch events, the exhibition was decidedly the more challenging. While my graduate training had prepared me to give an academic talk, I had never been asked to curate an exhibition. I found the skills of composition, juxtaposition, and economy (particularly in label text) elusive, especially after spending so much time working on the maximalist exercise of dissertation writing.

16 In fact, we later partnered to create a digital gallery pertaining to a serendipitous discovery that I made during my work on the diary research guide.

"Americanization: Then and Now" contextualizes a naturalization pamphlet that I found folded into the spine of a 1908 European travel journal maintained by plant geneticist George Harrison Shull (1874–1954). As I read it, this pamphlet isn't only an idiosyncrasy of the Shull Papers but also a window into pro-assimilation propaganda that circulated in the months after the First World War. See American Philosophical Society Library, "Americanization: Then and Now " (n.d.), https://diglib.amphilsoc.org/labs/americanization/index.html.

17 Will Fenton, "Guide to Diaries Held at the American Philosophical Society " (American Philosophical Society, n.d.), https://search.amphilsoc.org/diaries /search.

18 For more information, see Library Company of Philadelphia, "Redrawing History" (n.d.), https://librarycompany.org/redrawing-history/.

19 For more information, see Library Company of Philadelphia, "Seminars " (n.d.), https://librarycompany.org/seminars/; Library Company of Philadelphia, "Fellows Commons " (n.d.), https://librarycompany.org/academic-programs /fellowscommons/.

20 Matthew K. Gold and Lauren F. Klein, eds., *Debates in the Digital Humanities 2019* (University of Minnesota Press, 2019).

21 For more information, see Omeka (n.d.), https://omeka.org/; Neatline (n.d.), https://neatline.org/; CommentPress, "Welcome to CommentPress," https:// futureofthebook.org/commentpress/.

22 Bethany Nowviskie, "On the Origin of 'Hack' and 'Yack,'" *Bethany Nowviskie*, January 8, 2014, http://nowviskie.org/2014/on-the-origin-of-hack-and-yack/.

23 Robert Townsend quoted in Emma Pettit, "What the Numbers Can Tell Us about Humanities Ph.D. Careers," *Chronicle of Higher Education*, January 6, 2019, https://www.chronicle.com/article/What-the-Numbers-Can-Tell-Us/245417.

24 I prefer the term "compatible" to "transferable" skills in order to communicate respect for both existing disciplines and the digital humanities. In her paper at the 2019 MLA Convention, Susan Schreibman critiqued the association of "transfer-able" skills with the digital humanities, arguing that it ultimately devalues technical expertise.

25 Molly Des Jardin, "Teaching 'East Asian DH'" (2019), http://dx.doi.org/10.17613 /xcs8-7x30.

26 Alison Booth, "Digital Future of Graduate Study in the Humanities (Roundtable Remarks)" (2019).

12

Skill-Building and Thinking about Career Diversity for Graduate Students

ALEXANDRA M. LORD

Dissertation. Comprehensive exams. Teaching assistantships. Research.

Graduate school can be an all-encompassing experience. Add in the fact that it takes on average between six to nine years to complete a PhD and it is easy to forget the world outside the academy. Yet graduate school experiences can open doors in and outside the academy. Doctoral and master's programs are not, however, vocational programs like law or medical schools. As a result, graduate students must be extremely assertive in planning for their careers while in graduate school. Similarly, faculty and administrators must aggressively work to counter the lingering stigma against careers beyond the academy by providing students with clear support to explore diverse careers.

Both academic and employers beyond the academy seek many of the same skills: the ability to conduct research, to analyze data, and to communicate effectively. While there are some differences between the skills these employers prioritize—employers beyond academe, for example, emphasize the idea of collaboration more than academic employers—the similarities between academic and careers beyond the academy ensure that a well-trained graduate student can be highly competitive in both types of job markets.

Ideally, graduate students should always see themselves as preparing for both academic and a diverse range of careers beyond the academy. Obviously, preparing for both types of careers will ensure that students develop the widest skill set. But there are other benefits in preparing for a range of careers. Graduate school, which stretches over nearly a decade, can be a period of intense change. The first-year graduate student, who is willing to move across the country for an academic position, may, for example, find it difficult to move with a young family when they complete the program years later. In short, preparing for a diverse range of careers enables students to find careers that fit their personal and professional ambitions—even as those goals change in unexpected ways over time.

Although information about academic careers has always been fairly easy to find in most universities, information about careers beyond the tenure track tends to be less available. In recent years, a new emphasis on career diversity has led some universities to develop and provide information about diverse careers, but that information still tends to be limited. Fortunately, while career diversity initiatives may be new at many universities, there is nothing new about doctoral students leaving the academy. The poor academic job market, which stretches back at least fifty years, means that every university has a pool of alumni who have forged a career beyond the tenure track. Developing and maintaining relationships with graduate alumni working beyond academe can provide universities with the broad network their students will need to explore a range of careers. Encouraging and promoting these relationships also creates a culture that enables students to ask questions about diverse careers while enabling students and faculty to see a range of outcomes on a par with academic job outcomes.

Career planning should begin with a clear understanding that graduate training results in the acquisition of diverse skills. At a basic level, this training entails acquiring skills and tools that enable individuals to continually grow, both professionally and intellectually. Along with the acquisition of content knowledge, one of the primary goals of graduate school is to teach students new ways to analyze and solve problems—a skill that is always valued by employers in and outside the academy.

One of the most important skills students learn in graduate school is the ability to initiate and complete projects independently. This emphasis on independence, as well as the unstructured workday common in academia, provides students with the freedom and flexibility to investigate and even try out a range of careers during their graduate career. And, of course, the more careers a student explores, the more informed the decisions he or she will make when preparing for a career.

Faculty sometimes hesitate to encourage students to explore diverse careers, seeing internships and other positions as distracting students from their research. But exploring different careers can improve and even help jump-start a student's dissertation or thesis. An internship in an archive can, for example, not only give a student unparalleled access to a specific archive but also encourage him or her to learn how archives are organized, a crucial skill for many scholars. Similarly, a research position at a public relations firm can expose students to different methods of gathering and assessing statistical data. Internships or similar positions that prioritize the acquisition and use of research skills enable students to acquire skills and knowledge that can lead to the speedy completion of a dissertation or thesis.

Best of all, teaching students to learn about diverse careers can prevent career disillusionment down the road by ensuring that students fully understand the nature of specific careers. In the long run, this approach can not only decrease faculty turnover for universities but also ensure that graduates of doctoral and master's programs are more committed to their employers, whether this is a university, a nonprofit, a corporation, or a government entity. On an individual level, this approach helps ensure that graduates find the job that truly works for them, both professionally and personally.

Inside and Outside the Ivory Tower

Because academic culture places a strong emphasis on independence, research, analysis, and communication, it is easy to fall into the trap of seeing academia as the only place that offers a career rooted in the "life of the mind." The nomadic and unstructured nature of academic work, which makes it difficult to develop and maintain networks outside of academia, can exacerbate this belief. By stepping outside the academy, even if only briefly, students can see that academia is simply one of many places where independence, research, analysis, and strong communication skills are valued.

Temporary or part-time positions, such as summer internships and fellowships, can introduce students to diverse careers which prioritize "the life of the mind." Working as a predoctoral fellow, a summer employee, or an intern at a government agency such as the National Institutes of Health or the Smithsonian Institution exposes students to the work culture in a government laboratory or a museum. There, students can discover not only the kinds of projects and work people in these institutions do on a daily basis but also how the federal government operates and the types of resources and issues that shape federal employment. In some fields, this can have substantial benefits on a student's work. A fellowship in a museum may encourage a student to think more broadly about material culture or to better understand the complexities, both political and intellectual, in creating a museum exhibit. These work experiences may also expand a student's professional network. For scientists, even a temporary summer position at a place like the National Institutes of Health may provide insight that will improve their grant writing skills. Most importantly, positions of this type provide students with new skills such as the ability to write a briefing paper or a museum label. On the job market, the more varied a student's skills, the more varied his or her options.

Working part-time or during the summer as a researcher at a consulting firm provides an opportunity to learn how research is conducted and used in the for-profit sector. As for-profit firms often respond quickly to issues as they arise, corporate work often involves direct engagement with ongoing issues. This may be extremely appealing to students who wish to see an immediate impact for their work. This work also tends to entail higher pay than that of a teaching assistantship, research fellowship, or internship at a government or nonprofit institution—an important consideration for almost all graduate students. Finally, this approach has the added benefit of enabling students to see and understand that corporate America also values research and intellectual rigor. This is especially important for students and faculty who may have spent their entire careers in academia and who may be unfamiliar with corporate culture. Obviously, this kind of experience is crucial for those who want comprehensive information about career options, but it is also crucial for those who remain in the academy. Faculty who have held internships themselves can provide better guidance to students and provide them with an understanding of career options in and outside of the corporate world. Equally importantly, as universities face deep cuts, academics who have honed their communication skills in a corporate environment will be able to use those same skills to communicate more effectively the value of a liberal arts education to parents, administrators, and even potential donors.

Stepping out of the academy encourages students and, indirectly, faculty to understand the value and importance of becoming a public intellectual. For decades, universities, whether rightly or wrongly, have come under attack for being isolated ivory towers. Strong connections between academics and those outside academia can improve understanding of academic work and even foster better venues for this work. In short, recognizing that workplaces ranging from a government lab to a think tank allow one to pursue the "life of the mind" is not only crucial for students—it can benefit universities in the long run.

In the United States, where an estimated 50 to 70 percent of job offers are the result of networking, job applicants in every sector always need to have a broad social and professional network. Small activities can help students establish footholds within and beyond academe. This may entail asking editorial staff at an academic journal about their jobs when publishing an article or volunteering to review polling data for a political campaign. Simply put, the more varied a student's experiences, the more aware he or she will be of the range of professions and opportunities both in and outside the academy.

Finding Resources

For decades, students and faculty have responded to the academic job crisis by requesting career workshops and pushing universities to create and implement career-planning programs. In some universities, this agitation has led to the hiring of dedicated graduate career counselors. In others, it has led to the establishment of dedicated funds for career workshops. But even in universities that did not respond directly to students' demands for improved career programs, there are ongoing conversations about career diversity. Organizations such as the National Endowment for the Humanities and the American Council of Learned Societies have developed grants and programming that encourage universities to provide students with better and more information about their career options. Overall, opportunities in this area have exploded with more workshops and more fellowship programs,[1] enabling students and departments alike to take a more creative and more comprehensive approach to career planning. In institutions that lack these kinds of dedicated programs and offices, activities may be on a smaller scale. In those instances, students and faculty should work together to organize lectures with speakers, especially alumni, who can assist graduate students in thinking broadly about careers. Required attendance at these workshops and lectures will broaden students' and faculty's understanding of employment opportunities and networks while also connecting students and faculty with people outside of the academy.

As part of this process, departments, career offices, and universities should promote the stories of alumni who have followed diverse career paths on their websites or in other promotional material. Whether they choose to acknowledge it or not, every university has alumni who have successfully transitioned to careers outside the academy. As programs such as Beyond the Professoriate demonstrate, many of these alumni are eager to reconnect with their academic colleagues and to share their stories with the next generation of graduate students. For alumni who left the academy in the early 2000s, when discussions about career diversity were more muted than they are today, the chance to tell their stories has an especially strong appeal. Best of all, these older alumni are now in positions that enable them to provide information about not only the arc of a career over time but also how to best apply for a job (at this point in their careers, many of these alumni make hiring decisions for their employers).

While growing numbers of universities provide workshops and other opportunities to learn about career diversity, students must do investigative research on their own, if only to see which departments provide career workshops and career counseling. Many research universities now have a career services office specifically dedicated to assisting doctoral and master's students in their job searches. These offices typically provide workshops to assist students in learning how to determine the type of career they want, where to look for a job, and even how to apply for specific types of jobs. Often career services offices host workshops with guest speakers; attending these workshops can be a great way to learn about a range of different professions. Even better, an office like this can help students to broaden their network, especially if they take the time to introduce themselves directly to guest speakers and fellow students who may come from other departments.

Not all universities have a career services office specifically for graduate students. At these institutions, faculty should organize lectures with local speakers, especially local alumni, who can assist graduate students in thinking broadly about careers. Working to bring one or two local speakers each year not only broadens a student's understanding of career options but also enriches his or her professional networks. Career workshops and lectures directed at undergraduates can also provide both networking opportunities and, at a more basic level, simple yet valuable career advice, even for graduate students.

In addition to workshops directly sponsored by a university or department, a growing number of academic and professional conferences have embraced the idea of career diversity. Professional organizations such as the National Council on Public History or the American Geophysical Union routinely bring together practitioners and academic professionals. Students and faculty members who attend these meetings can engage with practitioners in a diverse range of professions. Scholarly organizations, like the Modern Language Association (MLA) and the American Historical Association (AHA), also often provide workshops or panels on career diversity at their annual conferences. Outside of these conferences, faculty and students should also prioritize attendance at in-person events such as the proseminars on career diversity sponsored by the MLA or the growing number of webinars scholarly organizations are now hosting. Workshops, career diversity panels, and webinars also provide outstanding opportunities for networking. When a National Park Service biologist or a senior associate researcher at the Pew Charitable Trusts speaks about his or her career path at a workshop, initiating a conversation with him or her about different careers at either the event itself or after the event becomes an easy opportunity for networking.

Most disciplinary associations, such as the American Anthropological Association, the American Philosophical Association, and MLA, host a "Career Resources" section on their websites. Many of these organizations also publish a "disciplinary journal" focused on the profession. These journals routinely include articles that explore careers in and outside the academy. Articles cover topics as varied as teaching, grant writing, the tenure process, trends in academic hiring, and even how to interview for an academic job. Along with professional organizations' disciplinary journals, publications, such as the *Chronicle of Higher Education* and *Inside Higher Ed*, discuss the academic job market across multiple disciplines and diverse types of educational institutions. These journals detail not only the process of applying for an academic job but also the tenure and promotion process, information that assists students in understanding what an academic career will entail.

Because these journals and organizations tend to be dominated by academics, they can be less helpful in providing advice about the job markets beyond the academy. Although they do provide some information about careers outside the academy, these journals and organizations focus on the idea of leaving academia—as opposed to the nature of the work done beyond the academy. While the process of leaving academia can be difficult for many people, this emphasis on leaving academia has meant that students seeking information about the world beyond academia have needed to look elsewhere for information.

Since 2000, a growing number of organizations have started to provide more detailed information about career diversity. The largest of these is Versatile PhD, an online forum with over fifty thousand individual members from all over the world. VPhD allows students to meet and speak with people in different fields, career counselors, and graduate students in different disciplines. Access to VPhD's premium context is on a subscription basis. Students and faculty at nonsubscribing universities can, however, still participate in ongoing discussions. Many large cities and/or university towns also have in-person VPhD meet-up groups. Within the online forum discussions run the gamut from questions about salary to questions about how job candidates with a PhD can be competitive for a specific type of job.

The site hosts a series of weeklong "career discussions" throughout the year. These discussions highlight specific professions, such as careers in technical writing or careers in market research. Anyone can pose questions to people who work in the field. Careful monitoring of the site ensures that the tone is always positive and helpful. Because anonymity is central to the site, and because it is a closed forum that is strongly protected from online searchers, members often ask deeply personal questions—everything from detailed queries about specific work cultures to requests for assistance with job applications.

VPhD's origins date back to the late 1990s, a clear indication that students have long been seeking better advice about careers. Since then, opportunities for students to learn about career diversity have grown. Among the many new programs is the Graduate Career Consortium's free assessment program called ImaginePhD (www.ImaginePhD.com). The program helps students at three distinct phases in their graduate careers (early stage, mid stage, and late stage or completed PhD). ImaginePhD encourages students to identify skills and values that can help them to discover and learn about potential careers that may reflect their interests. It also provides basic steps to enable them to plot a path to these careers. Graduate programs interested in promoting a conversation about career diversity should encourage students to use sites such as ImaginePhD and VPhD throughout a student's graduate career.

Beyond the academy, professional organizations also provide information about careers that are especially suited to people with doctorates and master's degrees. For example, the American Alliance of Museums posts job advertisements as well as information about careers in museums on their website, while the Council on Foundations provides information, more broadly, about careers in nonprofit organizations. Because careers beyond the academy are so broad ranging, no one site lists all of the organizations associated with this range of careers. Consequently, students and departments should look for organizations that serve as clearinghouses for information about diverse fields. As is true with everything on the internet, sites should be vetted with a university's career services center or those who work in the field to determine both the site's reputation in the field and its overall accuracy.

Students tend to postpone researching careers or even thinking about career diversity, leaving this to the end of a graduate program but seeking information about potential careers should begin in a student's first year. The information gleaned from attending career workshops, reading disciplinary publications, and participating in online communities about jobs should inform the decisions students make about coursework, the paid work they do during their graduate career, and the way in which they approach their research and dissertation. Learning about careers while in graduate school is one of the best ways to get the most out of a graduate education. So while students often say that they are too busy to do this kind of research while they are in graduate school, the truth is this kind of research will always save time in the long run—and it will ensure that their job search goes more smoothly.

What Do Employers Want?

Knowing what employers seek in job applicants enables students to make informed choices about courses and opportunities, which can make them competitive for a range of jobs. Reading job ads throughout graduate school—not simply when one is on the market—provides students with the information they need to acquire skills associated with different careers before they look for a job. Because job descriptions fluctuate to reflect new trends in academic scholarship and mainstream culture, students and faculty who constantly read job advertisements can also anticipate hiring trends and how these trends might shape future job ads. For example, studying job ads in the early 2000s would have revealed a growing emphasis on digital scholarship. Students who saw this trend emerge early on in their graduate careers were able to acquire the skills associated with digital scholarship just as the field exploded. Similarly, understanding the cyclical nature of job markets—the season for posting and filling positions—is also crucial. Learning that most organizations beyond the academy move more quickly in terms of completing hires—with jobs being advertised and filled in a matter of weeks—than the academic job market is crucial in determining when and how to apply for different types of jobs. This knowledge allows departments and students to better coordinate the completion of dissertations, job searches, and start dates for potential jobs.

At a very basic level, employers seek three things in their professional staff: education, experience, and collegiality. Graduate school provides the opportunity to acquire all three of these qualifications. More narrowly, it also provides students with experience in public speaking, time management, and project planning, all skills that are valued outside the academy. Because collaboration is less common in the humanities, students in these disciplines should initiate and pursue collaborative as well as independent projects. Faculty can assist with this by prioritizing collaborative research projects within the classroom. Obviously, no one collaborative project can demonstrate a job applicant's collegiality. However, job applicants who can point to a successful history of working on collaborative projects tend to have an edge in demonstrating their ability to work with others.

Informational Interviews

Informational interviews or informational conversations should be a fundamental element of every graduate education. An informational interview is simply an opportunity to speak with individuals in a specific field and to learn more about the field overall. Typically, an informational interview provides an opportunity to discover how and where jobs in a specific field are advertised; the skills demanded by specific professions; the type of work required, both on a daily and on a long-term basis; and the best way to prepare a job application for a specific field (every profession has its own quirks in terms of job application formats). The more informational interviews one does, the more informed the career decisions one makes.

Outside of academia, informational interviews are extremely common. Although informational interviews in the academy are uncommon, this means not that informational interviews within the academy should not be done, rather that these should be approached in a less formal manner. Students can initiate an interview by sending a person in the field a brief email asking to speak with him or her about his or her work. This could involve contacting faculty or recent alumni who have taken positions at a small liberal arts college or a different type of educational institution and then asking directed questions about the nature of the work. Outside of academia, these interviews are common practice, which means that most people are very receptive to participating in an informational interview. Often interviewees agree to do these because they see it as a way of "paying it forward" for interviews they themselves did as a job applicant.

Scholarly organizations have created spaces to encourage graduate students to conduct informational interviews. In 2015 the AHA launched Career Contacts, which "has arranged hundreds of informational interviews between current PhD students (junior contacts) and history PhDs (senior contacts) who have built careers beyond the professoriate . . . in a variety of fields, including academic administration, non-profit management, public policy, archives and libraries, K–12 teaching, as well as a range of positions in the federal government and private industry."[2]

Students should also understand that much of the work that professors do, whether it is serving as an external reviewer for a tenure and promotion committee or dealing with a student disciplinary hearing, may not be visible to them while they are in graduate school. Even the most sophisticated graduate students may be unaware of the nuances inherent in faculty work. Faculty at research universities, for example, face pressures to publish that those who teach at a community college do not face, while faculty at community colleges face extraordinary pressures related to their teaching. Expectations for teaching loads tend to differ between small liberal arts colleges, regional universities, and leading research institutions. The differences in responsibilities and opportunities between instructors, adjuncts, associate professors, and assistant professors vary dramatically depending on the nature of the institution and even the position. Job applicants who are aware of these differences not only make more informed decisions about the type of job they want but also are able to construct better applications for these positions.

Informal and formal informational interviews can be conducted over the phone or in person. Doing these in person helps establish a more personal connection between the interviewer and interviewee. However, because traveling to do an informational interview can be extremely costly, informational interviews are commonly conducted by phone. Most interviews run about thirty minutes. Interviewees expect their interviewers to have done basic research about a profession and to have developed some focused questions beforehand. Typical questions may explore the structure of a typical workday, the potential for different types of career advancement, or, more simply, the nature of work products. While not every interview subject will ask to see or review a resume, having one on hand is crucial.

Universities and departments should encourage graduate students to do one or two of these interviews during their graduate career. The skills needed to conduct these types of interviews are not dissimilar to those used by historians, sociologists, anthropologists, and other scholars who routinely conduct interviews as part of their research. This includes doing research beforehand, listening carefully, and assessing responses in context. Interviewers should never assume that because their interview subject loves his or her job, they will love this job too. Different people want and need different things from their career, and information learned during the course of an informational interview should always be weighed against an individual's personal professional ambitions.

As with any job search, thank-you notes after an interview are de rigueur. There is no rigid format for these thank-you notes; they can be a handwritten card sent via the mail or an email. What is important is that the thank-you note is sent in a timely manner (within a week of the interview). Sending a thank-you note is not simply good manners. It also further strengthens a student's connection with the interview subject. The stronger the connection, the more likely this person will follow up with the student in the future. Finally, the more informational interviews a student does, the broader his or her professional networks becomes.

Along with these formal ways of learning about careers, students and faculty should take advantage of any and all informal opportunities to learn about different careers. Being aware of others' careers and how those careers change over time will help students to see and understand how employees learn new skills on the job as well as what employers want from their employees. In short, the more people students and faculty know and the more familiar they are with their careers, the more they will understand what employers want and how employees themselves change and grow over the course of their careers.

Research Skills

If there is one skill employers know that a graduate program teaches, it is the ability to conduct research. Graduate school offers multiple opportunities to engage in diverse research projects. The most notable of these projects is obviously a dissertation or master's thesis, but graduate programs also require more routine research papers and articles. Job applicants and interviewees should be prepared to discuss their research projects, outcomes, and process with both academic and lay audiences.

Outside the academy, long-term research projects are often understood as "deliverable products," projects with a clearly defined outcome and due date. A "deliverable product" may be a research paper completed for a class, a dissertation prospectus, an annotated bibliography or any similar research product. Encouraging faculty and students to see these kind of projects as "deliverables" helps employers beyond the academy to understand that graduate programs require the completion of a variety of different research projects in a timely manner as opposed to just one (i.e., a dissertation or master's thesis). This approach also helps these employers understand the multiple steps involved in completing a dissertation or even coursework.

All employers—within and beyond academe—not only want evidence of an applicant's ability to research but also want to understand how these projects progress. Successful job applicants should be able to set and meet clear milestones on long-term projects. Within academia, junior faculty who possess this skill will easily navigate academic processes such as tenure and promotion. Outside of academia, where time is money, the ability to complete a long-term project in a timely manner is central to job retention. Over a graduate career, students should learn to scope out a project and to establish and meet concrete deadlines. Universities that ensure that there are real consequences for students who fail to meet deadlines do the best job of preparing students for a variety of job markets. Writing groups and even apps can help students establish and meet deadlines, but so too can simple steps such as setting deadlines with one's advisor.

Universities that prioritize research assistantships for students provide them with opportunities to play diverse roles in the development and completion of research projects. At universities where these positions are less common, students should seek opportunities to participate in a collaborative research project as employers want employees who can successfully demonstrate experience in conducting collaborative research. Collaborative research projects can take a variety of forms, including something as simple as editing a fellow student's work.

Written Communication Skills

While writing is at the forefront of all doctoral and most master's degree programs, most graduate programs emphasize a specific writing style. For students who opt for a career in academia, learning to produce work in this style is crucial. But as universities seek to make a broader argument for the value of a liberal arts education, future faculty will also need to master and use different writing styles. Outside the academy, the ability to write in a variety of styles is and always has been fundamental as employers typically interact with different audiences—colleagues, supervisors, museum visitors, clients, and a variety of other stakeholders.

Most programs have clear incentives and reward systems that encourage students to produce a peer-reviewed article or two during the course of their graduate careers. Unfortunately, few graduate programs provide these kinds of incentives and rewards to encourage students to learn to write in diverse styles.

Classes should include projects that promote diverse writing styles. For example, teaching students to write museum text for a difficult scientific concept or encouraging historians to draft a position paper for a federal agency can stretch their writing abilities. Students whose coursework does not include this type of project must look outside the classroom to expand their writing skills. Writing for a blog, even one with limited circulation, or a departmental newsletter can introduce students to different types of writing while also honing their writing skills. This work may also lead to writing for publications with larger circulations. Writing for institutions, such as museums, that have their own blogs is preferable to writing for a small blog, as institutional blogs are more likely to provide editorial feedback. Because this type of writing is unfamiliar to many academics, universities and departments should establish clear and comprehensive methods of evaluation that encourage students to develop this type of skill. This may entail something as simple as assessing how the blog is viewed by those within the field.

Departments should encourage students to choose writing projects that demonstrate versatility in terms of content and intended audience. Over the course of a graduate career, graduate students should develop a writing portfolio that demonstrates a range of writing styles.

Oral Communication Skills

As most graduate programs require students to teach and to present their research at conferences, graduate school fosters extraordinarily strong oral communication skills. Even those who feel shy or who struggle with public speaking when they enter a graduate program become comfortable with public speaking over the course of their graduate career. Within the academy, this skill is so common that it is easy to forget how rare and how valued a skill this is outside the academy.

As is true with writing, there are multiple forms of public speaking. Interacting with students, presenting a paper at a conference, and speaking at an evening event at a public library all differ radically. Finding opportunities to teach and to present at conferences is easy and straightforward as these activities are typically required of graduate students. Finding opportunities to speak to the general public can be less straightforward. A good network, as well as participation in activities that take graduate students beyond their department and institution, will provide opportunities to speak to different types of organizations and to gain insight into the expectations of different audiences. Knowing a librarian who oversees public events may open doors for speaking engagements while also allowing students to ask frank questions about the background knowledge library patrons typically bring to a public talk.

Academia's growing emphasis on service learning and outreach means that more and more universities seek to hire faculty members with experience working with the general public. Whenever possible, departments should encourage students to develop this kind of skill. In those instances where departments do not provide guidance or incentives to assist students in acquiring this skill, students themselves should seek out opportunities to speak and work with the general public.

Paid and Unpaid Work

Graduate students typically hold teaching assistantships or research assistantships during their graduate careers. For most students, teaching assistantships provide their first exposure to teaching, and as such these positions help students determine if they enjoy this kind of work. Research assistantships obviously improve research skills and provide students with an opportunity to collaborate on a research project. This latter skill is especially valued outside the academy, but it is also important for those who become faculty members. Students should keep in mind, however, that research and teaching assistantships are typically constructed to meet the needs of the university—not the needs of students.

Whenever possible, students should avoid performing the same job over and over, semester after semester. Students rarely benefit from teaching an introductory survey course more than twice. At the very least, students should focus on teaching different courses, but obtaining varied work experiences should also be prioritized. Students should have the opportunity to take advantage of both a research assistantship and a teaching assistantship. This will make them more well-rounded candidates for the job market.

Universities that are serious about providing their students with myriad opportunities to grow intellectually and professionally should avoid tying stipends and tuition waivers directly or solely to teaching or research assistantships. Similarly, they should avoid forbidding students from taking paid internships or jobs outside of the university. This latter practice handicaps students financially as well as professionally.

Students who opt to find paying work outside the university should take a long-term view and think carefully about the kinds of skills an external paying job can provide. An office job in a university may, for example, provide crucial administrative experience. It can also broaden a student's network, a fundamental step for those who are interested in a career in academic administration. Similarly, finding a paying job, even an entry-level position, at a local institution such as an art gallery or a marketing research firm can broaden networks and enable students to learn about diverse workplace cultures.

Unpaid work is more problematic. Yet it can offer benefits for those who can afford it. A good internship not only builds skills but also provides insight into the day-to-day nature of specific careers. Internships have the most value when they are paid.[3] Whenever possible, universities should avoid indirectly charging students who take internships (this sometimes occurs when an internship is linked to a class and tuition). Ideally, universities should help students to find and take paid internships. On those occasions when a paid internship becomes impossible, students and faculty should weigh the advantages and disadvantages of the internship and make decisions on a case-by-case basis. If possible, departments and universities should provide financial incentives for students who take unpaid internships, whether the incentive is a small stipend to assist with travel costs or, more simply, a tuition waiver. Students who take internships, especially those that are not paid, should complete a focused project, such as developing a specific and clearly defined social media campaign with a set outcome. This project can then be listed on a resume or curriculum vitae (CV). Most institutions that host unpaid interns are aware that projects for unpaid interns should have an educational component. However, some of these institutions place the burden for ensuring that the project has an educational component on the students, which means that they must be extremely proactive in setting up and completing these types of internships.

Along with structured internships, students should serve on committees, whether in their department, university, or even professional organization. Universities should encourage students to do this and include graduate student positions on university committees (these need not be voting members of a committee). This not only helps the institutions understand the perspective of its graduate students but gives the student valuable experience. A graduate student who serves on an academic hiring committee, for example, gains insight into academic hiring. Students who actively take leadership positions in graduate student unions, committees, and other student organizations reap similar benefits. Potential employers value this kind of work as it demonstrates a commitment to the profession as well as evidence of collegiality.

Building a CV or Resume

Because graduate programs take, on average, six to nine years to complete, it is easy to lose track of the different projects completed over the course of a graduate career—yet this information is crucial for any job search. Ideally, students should maintain and frequently update their CV throughout their graduate careers. Departments can assist students in maintaining CVs or, even more simply, encouraging students to track their activities by underscoring the importance of continually tracking this kind of information, beginning when a student enters a graduate program. This enables faculty and students to see and track progress over time. It also allows tracking of projects that are easy to forget over a period of several years—and yet are important for employers to know.

Creating a World of Opportunities

Some students enter graduate school with an open mind regarding their career options. Others begin their graduate career convinced that they want an academic career. However, these views are always subject to change. A student may begin graduate school convinced that the only career he or she wants is an academic one—only to discover a few years later that an academic career has lost its appeal. Further complicating this is the poor academic job market. Over the last fifty years, the production of PhDs has consistently outstripped the number of academic jobs. Within this environment, universities that care about their students must prepare them for a range of professions

While it is tempting to see graduate school as an oasis separate from the humdrum world of jobs and paychecks, this view limits not only one's professional opportunities but also one's intellectual growth. Obviously, students who see graduate school as an opportunity to build and expand on their qualifications will be more prepared for the academic and nonacademic job markets than those who do not. But students who see and use the skills they acquire in graduate school in diverse settings tend to approach problems with an especially broad and open mind—a skill that can serve one well, regardless of one's chosen profession.

Notes

1   See, for example, workshops on a range of careers hosted by organizations such as the Association for Jewish Studies and predoctoral fellowships at museums such as the Metropolitan Museum of Art.

2   American Historical Association, "AHA Career Contacts" (n.d.), https://www .historians.org/jobs-and-professional-development/career-diversity-for-historians /career-diversity-resources/aha-career-contacts.

3   A 2015 survey by the National Association of Colleges and Employers indicates that paid interns have an advantage over unpaid interns in finding jobs. See NACE Staff, "Paid Interns/Co-Ops See Greater Offer Rates and Salary Offers Than Their Unpaid Classmates " (National Association of Colleges and Employees, March 23, 2016), https://www.naceweb.org/job-market/internships/paid -interns-co-ops-see-greater-offer-rates-and-salary-offers-than-their-unpaid -classmates/.

Afterword

· ·

From Action to Collective Action

PAULA CHAMBERS

Graduate education is indeed officially a "mess" and needs to change in profound ways.[1] What makes this moment different is that the conversation is now unfolding against a backdrop of social, economic, and political volatility here in the United States and around the globe. The academic job market, already bad, will likely get worse as a result of the COVID-19 pandemic: decreased undergraduate enrollments and reduced federal and state funding are crushing university budgets,[2] exacerbating the problems called out here and elsewhere.[3] I would like to think that the protests against police brutality—happening a mile away from me as I write this—will ultimately help transform higher education by reducing racism in the academy and making PhD cohorts more diverse, but it's too soon to tell.

Even before this volatile time, graduate education was already getting side-eye in a changing culture. In April 2014, I attended a regional meeting of the Council of Graduate Schools at which its then- president Debra Stewart spoke of rising public demand for "accountability" on the part of colleges and universities. She said, forebodingly, of that demand, "*It's coming* to doctoral education." Recent developments have sped up the timetable. Now it's on our doorsteps. And because we have not yet successfully convinced the public that the humanities matter, or that doctoral education matters, it's coming first for *us*—the graduate students, faculty, and administrators who are directly involved in humanities doctoral education, plus other stakeholders. Whatever the calamity du jour, we can probably count on none of it being particularly positive for doctoral education in the humanities—unless we seize this potentially transformative moment and finally make the changes that have long been needed.

I write as one of those "other stakeholders." In 1999, while dissertating in rhetoric and composition at Ohio State, I decided I would actually *prefer* a career beyond academia. Looking around for resources to guide me, I found none—so I created one. I founded a listserv called WRK4US (pronounced "work for us") in order to create a safe, shame-free space where humanities PhD students including myself could discuss a diverse range of careers. WRK4US the listserv became Versatile PhD the web-based business in 2010. My mission in founding Versatile PhD was twofold: (1) to help humanities graduate students and early-career PhDs envision, prepare for and excel in a range of careers, and (2) to change academic culture. I wanted to end the taboo against careers beyond the academy for humanities PhDs and make career diversity a central value in doctoral education. Responding to demand from students and clients, a STEM discussion forum was added in 2011, and in 2013, STEM premium content was added, at which point Versatile PhD (VPhD) officially served all of the arts and sciences disciplines. But its roots and mine are in the humanities.

A socially positive business, VPhD operated on an institutional subscription model: free content was available to anyone, but universities paid an annual fee so that their doctoral students (and postdocs, where possible) could access the premium content. The premium content consisted of detailed, high-quality, first-person career narratives written by PhDs and CK who had successfully transitioned into careers beyond academia, and deep discussions of specific career paths featuring multiple PhDs who had followed those paths. When I sold VPhD in 2018,[4] over eighty research universities were subscribed, and the community had nearly 100,000 members, making it the largest online community of PhD career-changers at the time.

VPhD had to be a business, not a nonprofit, because in my judgment as a professional grant writer (grant writing had been my first job after completing my PhD in 2000), there weren't enough funders to sustain it. Moreover, the few funders that existed would not have supported the project, ironically because I was not affiliated with an institution. Perhaps as a result, VPhD is often not mentioned in historical surveys of doctoral education reform efforts. Perhaps being a business disqualifies it as a reform effort. I would like to debate that. My purpose *was* reform, and I did my reform work from the only structural niche available to me, as a self-funded, socially positive vendor to the academy. Regardless, my purpose here is to share salient observations that could only be seen from my unique vantage point, and issue calls to action based on those observations.

The exact nature of my work is worth describing because it illustrates the experience in which my observations are grounded. The main things I did were to

1 create and maintain a safe space where doctoral students in the humanities (and later, STEM) could learn about careers beyond the academy and get support from others like themselves;
2 edit and publish hundreds of thick, rich, first-person career narratives written by and for humanities (and later, STEM) PhDs;
3 advocate with decision makers at research universities to get them to literally "buy in" to career diversity by subscribing; and
4 present talks and workshops in person at client institutions, to various audiences including graduate students, faculty, staff, and administrators.

In the WRK4US era, when the listserv was just my ten hour a week hobby, my work was 80 percent community organizing and 20 percent publishing. When VPhD debuted, it became my full-time job, and my work was more like 30 percent community organizing, 30 percent sales and retentions, 30 percent publishing, and 10 percent travel and presenting.[5]

Items 2 and 3 are where the most useful observations are found.

Observations While Wearing My Editor/Publisher Hat

Between 1999 and 2018, I developmentally edited and published the career stories of some 650-plus post-academic PhDs, about half in humanities and qualitative social science, half in STEM. This work began in the WRK4US era, when I recruited twenty humanities PhDs a year on average to serve as "guest speakers" (panelists) on the listserv—220 in all. Drawing on my rhetoric and composition skill set, I gave them clear guidelines for how to write their self-introductions and detailed, supportive feedback to make the self-introductions as useful and accessible as possible to the audience. That same work intensified at VPhD: higher volume, higher standards, heavy deadline pressure. Now I needed thirty-five panelists per year, plus on average about forty more PhD career-changers per year to write Hiring Success Stories and Career Autobiographies, two written genres that I created and codified with clear guidelines. The Hiring Success Story genre in particular required a high degree of editorial attention because of the rather extreme level of detail I wanted in the narrative—a concrete, chronological description of everything they did to get their first job outside the academy. I worked very closely with Hiring Success Story authors to craft the concrete, detailed, nothing-is-obvious narratives that I knew would be most helpful to graduate students. In working with these courageous career-changers on their drafts, I was in many cases the first person who was fascinated and excited by the career transitions they had undergone; who told them they were not failures but, in fact, spectacular successes; and who praised them for their impressive achievement. It was very affirming for them that I valued their stories enough to invite them to write, and then that I paid such close attention to their journey, reading between the lines, asking more questions, praising specific moves they wisely made. The revision process even teased out achievements that the author had not previously recognized. A psychotherapist might say that I "witnessed" their experience. Many authors told me that writing their stories in such detail and to such positive response had been cathartic and healing for them.

Managing the discussion forums also had a healing quality: my role there was to create a safe space and provide a much-needed elixir of empathy, information and hope. It was the same in my oral presentations on university campuses. I was tremendously satisfied by the healing aspect of my work.

I found these authors and panelists by spending literally hundreds of hours a year searching LinkedIn for PhDs who had made some sort of impressive leap directly out of the academy.[6] With no specific names to work with (universities did not track nonacademic placements, and even if they did, the Family Educational Rights and Privacy Act [FERPA] would have prevented them from sharing that data with me), I would search for PhDs who matched whatever unconventional criteria I was looking for at the time, such as humanities PhDs working in technology, or STEM PhDs working museums.

Paging through profile after profile, certain ones would give me an almost physical sensation in my body: a buzz in my bone marrow, a palpable excitement about the leap this person had made. In some cases, their leap was impressive for its boldness or weirdness; for example, a philosopher who went into software development (wow) or a classicist who went into finance (say what?). In other cases, the leap was not so much bold or weird as just impressively well executed, like a literature PhD who became a language arts teacher at a prestigious independent school or a history PhD managing digital education at a historical museum.

These hundreds of stories soaked into my consciousness, peopling my views with specific individuals, each with their own voice, talents, problems, and strategies for overcoming. I was dazzled by the beauty, the bravery, the resourcefulness of these PhD career changers. You may have felt a buzzing in your own bones at times while reading this book. A versatile humanist is

- someone with the moxie to develop skills and learn content outside their discipline (as recommended by Alexandra Lord in chapter 12);
- someone who realizes they themselves are in charge of their career (as Cassuto and Van Wyck advocate in chapter 4);

- someone who finds loads of things interesting, not just in their scholarly field, and who would rather help *construct* the world than merely critique it (echoing Robert Weisbuch in chapter 2);
- someone whose work has "relevance" as well as prestige (adopting Michael McGandy's term from chapter 3);
- someone who proactively seeks out professional development resources available on campus even when they are hard to find (like Melissa Dalgleish did in chapter 8);
- someone who is able to articulate their skills and convince others that they can make a positive impact even in unfamiliar settings (as Augusta Rohrbach mentions in chapter 5);
- someone who connects with others everywhere they go, maintains those relationships, and is bold enough to ask for introductions (as recommended by Joseph Vukov in chapter 7);
- someone literate in the technologies relevant to their chosen industry or profession (as William Fenton describes in chapter 11);
- someone with the intellectual confidence to catapult themselves into strange new realms and believe that their general disciplinary skill set, with just a few bells and whistles added, would equip them to make good contributions to important projects (as Wilson and Aron's students learned in the "Many Professions of History" seminar described in chapter 9).

It has been very satisfying to read *The Reimagined PhD* and hear other voices celebrating some of the many facets of what I call *versatility*.

I also detected patterns in the turning points of the stories I published, particularly in the Hiring Success Story narratives, each which describes a specific PhD's first post-academic hire. Curious about the patterns, in 2017 I re-read them closely to see if I could identify what had been the key factors that got them these jobs. The total corpus consisted of 146 Hiring Success Stories, half from humanities and half from STEM.

The three factors that proved to be critical most often when a PhD got hired into that all-important first post-academic job were *extracurricular achievements, networking,* and *oral communication skills.*

Extracurricular achievements often resulted from coursework or self-directed study outside their discipline, and from volunteering on and off campus (service work).

Networking included knowing someone at the organization, and/or conducting informational interviews, which would "snowball" as each interviewee introduced the person to others, in some cases leading to the hiring manager for the position they ultimately attained.

Oral communication skills were usually displayed in research presentations and teaching demos, but also, strikingly, in extremely challenging interviews involving multiple interviewers, high pressure, and curve-ball questions—far beyond what academics normally imagine when thinking of interviews beyond the academy.

There were fewer differences between humanities and STEM hires than one might expect. Oral communication was a key factor more often for the humanists—naturally, since a higher proportion of them sought jobs that had education or communication as their main component. Secondly, the humanists and qualitative social scientists as a group had received much less social support in graduate school for their career explorations, and poorer advising, than those in STEM. STEM students also experienced these problems, to be sure, but more of the humanists did their career preparation work in secret, under stress, afraid to tell their advisers or anyone until the very end. Witness these two memorable quotes from two humanities or social science PhDs, both of whom happened to get hired by consulting firms:

> It should be noted that due to the stigma surrounding non-academic careers within my program, I did these activities without the knowledge of my dissertation advisor, which resulted in leading something of a double life during this year of job market preparation.[7] (Sociology PhD hired at a consulting firm)

> The entire time I was applying to McKinsey, I kept it secret from my professors and my fellow graduate students . . . my general sense was that there were more risks than benefits to being open about my job search. My professors had limited experience with non-academic employment, so there was very little they could have done to help me throughout the process . . . and I feared that "outing" myself too soon would have negative repercussions. This did, however, lead to a lonely experience, and without the support of my husband and family, I would have had a much worse time.[8] (Italian literature PhD hired at McKinsey)

But those were the only differences. Successful PhD hires turned on the same three factors most often for all disciplines: extracurricular achievements, networking, and oral communication skills.

These observations from my editor/publisher role lend specific, granular, grounded support to the urgent need for reform described in this volume and others before it. In most humanities doctoral programs today, transferable skills and knowledge must be developed furtively, on the sly, requiring extra emotional support from family and using time that would otherwise be spent on normal, healthy "life" activities like sleeping, exercising, socializing, and relaxing. Perhaps readers of this book already know that, but my unique perspective provides fresh confirmation.

Recommendation 1: Make Versatility Central

The PhD career-changers whose stories I published embody liberal arts and humanities values at the doctoral level. They are proactive, self-directed, omnivorous learners who follow their interests no matter where they might lead. Their sponge-like, enthusiastic acquisition of skills, relationships, and literacies outside their disciplines is what made them successful in making the leap.

Are all humanities PhDs like this? No. Are these authors' stories fully representative of how *most* humanities PhD careers go after graduation? No. Did some form of privilege help them? Probably.

But is this what we *want* doctoral students to be like? Yes. Are these people's career outcomes something we are proud of, something we want to encourage and materially support? Yes. Are these people making the power of the humanities more visible in the world and seeding humanities values wherever they go? Yes!

I submit to you that *versatility itself* should be seen as central to the humanities skill set. The ability to do many things competently, to move freely in all directions, to learn anything under the sun on an as-needed basis, is a superpower that humanities doctoral education can and should confer. Versatility should be what we *want* in PhD graduates, not just a happy side benefit for some. It should be a central desideratum of doctoral education, in the humanities and really in all of the arts and sciences. It is also what we need in order to simultaneously justify and reform doctoral education in the humanities.

In my reimagined humanities PhD program with versatility at the center, graduate school will be a period of supercharged, multivalent acquisition of diverse literacies, competencies, accomplishments, and experiences *alongside* subject matter expertise, research skills, and appropriate participation in disciplinary discourse. It should be a freewheeling, expansive, student-centered learning journey that is fun and a little bit wild. For some, it will be imbued with a keen awareness of world problems and the responsibility that I personally believe each humanities PhD has to somehow make things better. Graduates will emerge bristling with knowledge, skills, relationships, interests, and passions, ready to become reflective practitioners in any setting.[9] When they enter and succeed in those settings, the impact and value of the humanities will be magnified.

Isolation from the world cannot be a defining characteristic of this reimagined PhD. The world needs the most versatile thinkers we can possibly produce to help solve the pressing problems facing the human race. Humanities education is tremendously powerful. Its power comes from a unique synthesis of content knowledge, literacies, skills, and personal passions—and in my rather Deweyan opinion, its power is greatest when *applied* in specific contexts.

I can already hear the naysayers crying, "Instrumentalism! Gah!" We certainly do not want the learning outcomes of the humanities doctorate to be dictated by employers. Heck no. However, universities are employers too. If humanities PhD programs prepare students only for a certain job (a faculty job), then doctoral education is reduced to high-class vocational ed. Not very good vocational ed, either, considering how poorly most humanities doctoral programs actually train students for the faculty jobs of today. And even faculty jobs are changing. Vocational education is always already behind the times, training people for jobs that already exist while the world spins on, changing faster and faster.

The humanities are better than that. Broader than that. Deeper than that. While brute instrumentalism is certainly to be avoided, we should not automatically disparage anything that happens to be useful, for that disparagement undercuts the humanities just as much as brute instrumentalism does. It confines the scope and impact of our work to some abstract intellectual space floating above the world—seen by few, understood by fewer. John Dewey warned against using "ideals and sentiment" to cover over our brutalities.[10] To withhold respect for a humanities project because it is too useful, too applied, masks the brutalities of our current system.

Embracing versatility means embracing career diversity, for what graduates actually do with their versatility *is* the evidence that they are versatile. Career diversity is concrete, specific, measurable and improvable. For that reason, I argue that career diversity is the best place to start reforming doctoral education—in all the disciplines, but especially in the humanities. Career diversity is the wedge that if tapped with the right amount of force, can split the geode, revealing the hidden value of the humanities.

Observations While Wearing My Advocate Hat

Meanwhile, when interacting with decision makers in career centers and graduate schools in hope that they would subscribe (which some would call sales, but it was more than just sales), I saw patterns of a more structural sort. Many times, an institution that had initially declined my invitation to subscribe would reach out to me a year or two later and say, "OK, we're ready to subscribe." The turnarounds were striking, especially in cases where they had been very clear that they did not want or need my resource. What had changed, I wondered? A little digging revealed that sometimes it had been a single event like the retirement of a reluctant dean or director. Other times it had been a synergistic combination of two or more of the following: staff turnover, graduate student feedback, grant money, new positions being created (such as associate dean for Graduate Student Professional Development), new publications coming out on career diversity for PhDs, and conversations at national meetings (such as the

Graduate Career Consortium and the Council of Graduate Schools). The exact circumstances varied, and it generally took one to three years, but time and again, an institution that had not been ready before, suddenly was.

Another pattern was that sometimes the career center and the graduate school were both interested but didn't have the wherewithal separately and did not have a prior relationship with each other. Both units would balk. Then a year or two later, they would contact me to say they had decided to collaborate, sharing the costs and staff time required by the subscription (staff time was needed to build student awareness of the resource). And an unprecedented inter-unit partnership had been born. My online resource—the product I was "vending"—met a need so clear that a new working relationship had to be created between previously unconnected units.

My observations may seem quotidian—isn't all this just par for the course in sales?—but to me, it was not. I was fascinated to observe what it took, what had been the final ingredient that made each institution ready. I coined the term *institutional readiness* to denote *the moment when an institution finally becomes ready to increase its investment in career diversity for doctoral students.*

As mentioned earlier, a major reason why I created VPhD in the first place (and kept banging away for nearly a decade from my odd little niche as vendor-healer-crusader) had been to change academic culture. So, what is culture? How can you tell if it has been changed? Is it what people say to each other in the halls? Yes, partly. But it is also how resources are allocated—"habits, budgets, rules and incentives"[11]—that may seem quotidian but are not. Resource allocation is the most eloquent truth-teller there is about culture. It shows what is really valued at any institution. When one or more units decide to override prevailing fiscal and procedural norms for the sake of career diversity, that is real cultural change. I never got tired of it. It was beautiful to watch.

Recommendation 2: Encourage Collective Institutional Readiness

In my own past writings and presentations, I have provided suggestions for how humanities doctoral programs can be reimagined:

- Allow more time and provide more social support for self-directed professional enrichment, such as working or volunteering, taking courses outside the discipline, participating in clubs and committees, and enrolling in graduate certificate programs.
- Diversify the forms that humanities dissertations may take.
- Diversify the research methods considered appropriate for humanities inquiry, including quantitative and qualitative methods alongside traditional hermeneutic methods.

- Encourage *relevance* (per McGandy, in this volume) as well as rigor in research projects; do not avoid the applied, but rather seek it out, or at least let it in.
- Provide abundant professional development programming within and across departments that includes career paths beyond the academy.
- Specify PhD program outcomes and periodically evaluate program success.
- Regularly assess the career climate of PhD granting departments.

I still agree with all of those suggestions, and note that they harmonize with the more comprehensive vision described by Leonard Cassuto and Robert Weisbuch in *The New PhD* (2021). In their concluding chapter, "From Words to Actions," they endorse Jim Grossman's vision of the future history department and advocate for its adaptation to all disciplines. In that vision (paraphrased), the PhD-granting department of the future will

- orient incoming doctoral students thoroughly and transparently to all aspects of what they are about to experience;
- intentionally recruit a diverse cohort of doctoral students;
- broaden and diversify the curriculum and dissertation;
- publish full, transparent data on student satisfaction and PhD employment outcomes;
- encourage students and faculty to publish for a variety of public audiences;
- provide robust material and cultural support for career diversity;
- have faculty who are fully on board with career diversity.

Acknowledging that it is not straightforward to decide which of those priorities should be addressed first, they conclude "none of the above" and recommend starting with the incentive system instead, because the real problem is structural.[12]

I agree with that wholeheartedly. Incentives are indeed key, and are indeed currently determined by "the prestige economy that surrounds graduate education." Cassuto and Weisbuch propose an additional incentive, a more student-centered assessment vehicle that takes more variables into account than just research productivity:

Graduate schools need to be assessed by more student-centered measures. Prospective students need to know how well a program professionalizes its students, for example. How is the advising? The career counseling (for both professorial and nonprofessorial careers)? What kinds of support does the program offer students and for how long? What is the typical time to degree? These are just a few of the questions that prospective students increasingly want the answers to, and they're more important to students than how many citations the faculty earned for their publications.[13]

They propose a national website to gather this kind of information and rate (not rank) universities according to student-centered metrics, providing a "counterweight"[14] for the overly narrow research based metrics currently in use.

I love these ideas and agree that such a website would be very helpful. However, it concerns me that it may never be taken seriously by university presidents. It might be viewed as a doctoral version of Rate My Professor: interesting, but dismissible, and probably harder and more expensive than it looks to create.

It would be even better if the national organizations that rate and rank research universities, namely the National Research Council and the Carnegie Classification, were to be included in or even initiate a broad-based, collaborative national effort to reform doctoral education by reforming the way institutions are rated and ranked. Individual universities are reaching institutional readiness more and more often, but given the urgency of the moment, we have a special opportunity to achieve conscious, substantive, lasting reform, and that requires *collective* institutional readiness. Ratings and rankings are the keystone supporting the whole overarching incentive structure together—so it stands to reason that national organization participation is not only desirable but essential for sector-wide reform.

Since career diversity is in my view the best wedge issue to drive doctoral education reform, I further propose that the national organizations devise a new metric reflecting the extent to which research universities support career diversity for doctoral students. That metric should be based on

- the number, quality, and breadth of professional development resources provided to graduate students; and
- the institution's level of transparency about ALL PhD placements.

This new national career diversity metric could be publicly displayed alongside the ratings and rankings we have today. The pace of change would quicken as more and more university presidents decide to make career diversity a higher priority in order to increase their institution's career diversity score, and doctoral education would be on an upward spiral. If the kind of sector-wide transformation that is needed to save doctoral education is going to happen, it must include the ultimate gatekeepers, the overarching incentive system that motivates the entire academy. A web-based clearinghouse of student-centered information would be wonderful, but buy-in from the very top would be even better.

Helpful toward both visions might be an informal assessment instrument I devised in 2015[15] to measure career diversity at the departmental level, which I called the Career Climate Departmental Assessment. I made it simple and fun, like a scavenger hunt, to encourage its use. It consists of six multiple choice questions, each answer yielding a point value and the total points adding up to determine the department's overall "career climate" score. The questions ask to what extent the department

1 provides professional development resources and events focused on a range of careers,
2 promotes professional development resources and events on campus but outside the department,
3 promotes non-university-specific resources such as books and websites designed to help doctoral students explore careers beyond the academy,
4 knows where ALL of its PhD graduates got placed,
5 has systems in place for collecting and updating that information, and
6 makes that information easy to access.

This instrument can be used as-is by graduate students in their own departments, and the results uploaded to Cassuto and Weisbuch's proposed clearinghouse website, or it can be used as a starting place for the more official metric that I have rather fantastically proposed be developed by the national organizations. Any metric intended to quantify career diversity should be student-centered and should have the main attributes of my informal attempt: not too complicated, focused on the availability of resources and information, animated by a frank truth-telling spirit.

Meanwhile, each national organization that plays a role in doctoral education has a specific form of agency available to them right now. I call on all of them to decide that they have themselves reached institutional readiness and will now use their own unique positioning to begin the work of reimagining the humanities PhD—actively, thoughtfully, and collaboratively.

Grant makers that fund humanities research, such as the National Endowment for the Humanities, the Mellon Foundation, and others, should require a professional development component for all grant-funded studies involving graduate students or postdocs. The STEM fields provide a handy example. The National Science Foundation pioneered a "BEST" program in 2016 that instituted that requirement.[16] As a result of the BEST program, funding for professional development programming flowed into universities, and career resources were provided to *all* STEM students and postdocs, not just those involved with the funded projects. Funding in the humanities is tighter, but regardless, if all research grants required a professional development component, the professional development resources supported by grant monies would benefit all humanities doctoral students at the institution, not just the ones directly involved in the grants.

To develop specifications for what this programming should consist of, grant makers should consult the Graduate Career Consortium, an underutilized resource that has a wealth of expertise on exactly that subject. Graduate career counselors are more than just functionaries. They are subject matter experts on PhD career development. They are graduate career *educators* with rich knowledge and long experience in designing effective professional development programming.

Scholarly associations may not have magic wands,[17] but some have responded in a way that should be emulated by all. The Modern Language Association and American Historical Association in particular have created resources that recognize the real job market and that strongly support full-spectrum career preparation for graduate students. Other scholarly associations in the humanities should follow their lead. The American Chemical Society and the Association of American Geographers are among the leaders on the STEM side; their programs should also be mined for transferable ideas, because professional development for STEM PhD students is less different than humanists tend to think.

National policy and advocacy nonprofits that work to support, protect, and improve graduate education, such as the Council of Graduate Schools, the Association of American Universities, the Graduate Career Consortium, the National Postdoctoral Society, and other well-chosen stakeholders should collaborate to develop a joint statement of philosophy about career diversity as a desired outcome of doctoral education, and a national graduate career resource center for the use of graduate students and postdocs in all disciplines. This would supplement the resources made available by departments, scholarly associations, career centers, and graduate schools. Such a resource center would allow limited grant funding to be used as efficiently as possible. Mutual transparency and collaboration between these entities would do a world of good for graduate students and postdocs and build career diversity sector-wide.

Finally, I wish to call attention to another work-product of the Carnegie Foundation: Improvement Science, a program evaluation system that the Foundation created specifically for the purpose of assessing and improving the performance of educational institutions.[18] Since the Carnegie Foundation is so integral to the structure around the academy, why not go "all in" with Carnegie and use their program improvement methodology as well to help reform doctoral education? It's certainly a worthy starting place.

Whatever the exact process, it must begin now. Given the state of the world as we careen through the early twenty-first century—and the recent surge of energy in favor of doctoral education reform—the time is now to clean up the graduate school mess and reimagine a new PhD. We must go through a crucible of self-transformation if we are to survive. The best of what we do—the gold—will shine all the brighter once the dross is removed.

Notes

1 Leonard Cassuto, *The Graduate School Mess: What Caused It and How We Can Fix It* (Harvard University Press, 2015).

2 Paul N. Friga, "How to Fight Covid's Financial Crush." *Chronicle of Higher Education*, February 5, 2001.

3 David Attis, Managing Director of Research, the Education Advisory Board, telephone interview, June 5, 2020.

4 I no longer have any formal connection to Versatile PhD.

5 Plus other stuff too annoying to list such as negotiating terms with Purchasing departments, designing and re-designing the website, etc. In 2013, I hired a full-time employee (a humanities PhD of course!) who took over sales and retentions and eventually became director of operations.

6 ABDs are harder to find because very few of them actually say "ABD" on their LinkedIn profiles!

7 Geoff Bakken, "Hiring Success Story," Versatile PhD Premium Content (2016) 1, https://versatilephd.com/wp-content/blogs.dir/1/files/docs/vphd_public/2010/The-Versatile-PhD—About.pdf.

8 Nicole Robinson, "Hiring Success Story," Versatile PhD Premium Content (2016) 7, https://versatilephd.com/wp-content/blogs.dir/1/files/docs/vphd_public/2010/The-Versatile-PhD—About.pdf.

9 Donald A. Schon, *The Reflective Practitioner: How Professionals Think in Action* (TempleSmith, 1983).

10 See chapter 4, "Reshaping Ourselves and Our Societies," in Michael S. Roth, *Beyond the University: Why Liberal Education Matters* (Yale University Press, 2014).

11 Kenneth Prewitt, "Who Should Do What? Implications for Institutional and National Leaders," in *Envisioning the Future of Doctoral Education: Preparing Stewards of the Disciplines,* ed. Chris M. Golde and George E. Walker (Jossey-Bass, 2006), 23.

12 Leonard Cassuto and Robert Weisbuch, *The New PhD: How to Build a Better Graduate Education* (Johns Hopkins University Press, 2021), 323.

13 Cassuto and Weisbuch, *The New PhD,* 341.

14 Cassuto and Weisbuch, *The New PhD,* 342.

15 Paula Chambers, "Subject Matter Plus: Mentoring for Non-Academic Careers," in *The Mentoring Continuum: From Graduate School through Tenure,* ed. Glenn Wright (Syracuse University Press, 2015), 49-74.

16 National Institutes of Health, "Strengthening the Biomedical Research Workforce" (n.d.), https://commonfund.nih.gov/workforce.

17 James Grossman, "How Not to Confront the Jobs Crisis: Scholarly Associations Don't Have Magic Wands," *Chronicle of Higher Education*, May 2, 2019, https://www.chronicle.com/article/How-Not-to-Confront-the-Jobs/246231.

18 Carnegie Foundation for the Advancement of Teaching, "The Six Core Principles of Improvement" (n.d.), https://www.carnegiefoundation.org/our-ideas/six-core-principles-improvement/.

Appendix

● ● ● ● ● ● ● ● ● ● ● ● ● ● ● ● ● ● ● ●

Sample Syllabi for Adding
Graduate Seminars to
Curriculum

History 204B Winter Quarter 2017
The Many Professions of History
Wednesdays, 4–6:50 P.M.
Bunche 6265 (Department Reading Room)
Stephen Aron   Karen Wilson
saron@history.ucla.edu   kswilson@ucla.edu

COURSE DESCRIPTION: A professional development seminar with a practicum component, this course focuses primarily on exploring and demonstrating the ways in which the skills of historians are transferable to a variety of professions and exercised in diverse ways and roles. It requires students to engage in a collaborative project and be an active, reflective participant in producing an innovative experience of historical understanding. It asks students to engage with questions about the actual and possible roles and responsibilities of historians in 21st century society. It allows students to examine where have historians been, where are they now, where can they be, and where should they be as highly educated, actively engaged members of society.

As is typical, the seminar requires students to familiarize themselves with these subjects through critical readings and in-depth discussions. Atypically, the course requires students to engage in a collaborative applied research project designed to facilitate the acquisition and practice of a variety of skills useful in the numerous professions of historians. The project assignment intentionally aims to move students outside the carrel, classroom, and archive to diversify and expand their experiences with the practice of history. Student learning and reflection is facilitated through a combination of a customary seminar structure with practicum activities.

COURSE OBJECTIVES: As preparation for careers in the range of professions practiced by History PhDs, the course aims to:

1 facilitate student exploration and understanding of the many different professional applications of PhD training and skills;
2 help students acquire and/or improve skills in written and oral communications, collaboration, digital literacy, and quantitative literacy through practice and assessment;
3 improve students' intellectual confidence and self-presentation through practice and assessment.

EVALUATION: Grading for the course is letter grade or satisfactory/unsatisfactory. Assignments in the course will receive the following weights. For collaborative work, grades will be determined by student's individual contribution, by peer assessment, and by the overall quality of the final project.

Collaborative applied research project design and proof-of-concept paper	50%
Collaborative project presentation with visual/digital illustrations	25%
Course and project written reflections (blog posts)	25%

Students will be asked to assess their individual contributions as well as those of their team members to an assigned collaborative applied research project and presentation. Those assessments will inform (not determine) the final project grade, which will be collectively assigned (i.e., everyone gets the same project grade). The assessments and final project grade will be based on the following criteria:

- Were team roles, objectives, and timelines clearly articulated, tracked and documented? Did team members understand their roles, objectives, and timelines?
- Did the team deliver well-written, well-documented, and well-designed original audience-appropriate content? Did individual team members fulfill their assignments as expected?
- Did the team meet the project goals within the specified timeline?
- Were the deliverables acceptable to the project manager or potential outside collaborator/client?

Course Assignments

Active participation in all seminar meetings is required. There are some common required readings/viewings that will be part of class discussions.

Contributions to a Class Documentary/Mentoring Blog

Each student will be responsible for writing two 300–500 word blog posts for the course web site. These posts are aimed at professional peers and intended to (1) capture/document the experience of the course and project; and (2) offer mentoring advice to students who take the course in the future. Students will sign up for two dates on which to submit their posts during the quarter.

Each student will be responsible for editing/reviewing two blog posts by other students in the course. The point of the editorial review comments is to help the blog writer improve as a communicator. Students will sign up for two dates on which to review other students' posts during the quarter.

Collaborative Applied Research Project

Students will work in teams of 3 to 5 people to produce a design and proof-of-concept paper with a model contribution to the 1919 Project, a student-driven research and applied history enterprise (see below for more details about the project). The design will help shape the larger project and the model contributions will serve as prototypical elements as well as examples for future student contributors to emulate. Each team will have a pre-defined set of goals that it will be expected to meet by the end of the quarter. Students will be organized into project teams and receive their specific contribution assignments at the first class meeting.

Each project assignment will require collaboration, planning, time management, and interaction with a variety of people. Each team will deliver oral updates on work plans and accomplishments (periodically beginning **week 3**); a formal class presentation of its research and model designs (**week 4**); a written design concept, research summary, model description, and contribution draft (**week 8**), and a final customized live presentation on its design and contribution to an invited audience along with a final written design document (**week 10**). The projects are intended to aid students in developing diverse communications skills, collaboration skills, intellectual confidence, and, in some cases, technology-related and quantitative skills. Projects are structured to provide hands-on experience with real-world tasks that are increasingly required of historians.

The 1919 Project. The 1919 Project is a multi-faceted, course-base, long-term public history venture initiated by the History Department. Guided by faculty, undergraduate and graduate History students will work collaboratively to develop and sustain a set of activities, events, and resources to capture and convey the many histories of UCLA. Attentive to intellectual rigor and committed to making history useful to the UCLA community and the broader public, the 1919 Project has two goals: (1) to provide innovative experiential learning opportunities for students using the tools and methods of the discipline of history; and (2) to produce accessible, comprehensive, multilayered, engaging insights into the past that created today's UCLA. Participants in the 1919 Project will contribute to public talks and seminars, artifact-rich exhibitions, and podcasts featuring student research, among other public activities and outcomes. Further, a website and digital archive will be created as an on-going repository for student-produced historical narratives and analyses, video and audio recordings of events, crowd-sourced contributions of UCLA-related memories and documents, and other resources. The 1919 Project will continue beyond the university's centennial year, deepening its utility for future generations of students, scholars, and supporters of the university.

Required Books
Nina Simon, *The Art of Relevance* (Santa Cruz, Museum 2.0, 2016)
Patricia A. Pelfrey, *A Brief History of the University of California*, 2nd edition
(Berkeley: University of California Press, 2004)

Class Topics & Readings
Week 1—Introduction and Overview (January 11)

- Review of the course structure, objectives, assignments, and deliverables.
- Review of project options; organization of project teams; and explanation of assignment details.
- Sign up for blog entries and editing assignments.
- In-class activity: "Pitch Your [Personal] Project" and teamwork simulation.

Week 2—Historians as Independent Scholars (January 18)

- Discussion of the history of University of California and resources for researching UCLA historical topics.
- In-class activity: Walk through all project deliverables.

Guest: **Becky Nicolaides**, Independent Scholar

Required Readings before Class:
Patricia A. Pelfrey, *A Brief History of the University of California*, 2nd edition
  (Berkeley: University of California Press, 2004)
Shelley Bookspan, "Something Ventured, Many Things Gained: Reflections on Being
  a Historian-Entrepreneur," *The Public Historian*, Vol. 28, No. 1 (Winter 2006).
  http://www.jstor.org/stable/10.1525/tph.2006.28.1.67?seq=1#page_scan_tab
  _contents

Week 3—Historians as Creators (January 25)

- Discussion of different audiences and different media for communicating history and historical insights.
- Team progress reports.
- In-class activity: Teams brainstorm how the 1919 Project could be
  done as a television program and develop 3-minute pitch to deliver
  to guest speaker.
- In-class viewing with guest speaker: WDYTYA episodes.

Guest: **Mellissa Betts**, Producer, "Who Do You Think You Are?" docu-
mentary television series

Required Readings/Viewings before Class:
"What If Your High School History Teacher Had Been Totally Wasted? Behind the
  Scenes of Comedy Central's Hilarious New Show, 'Drunk History,'" *Mother Jones*,
  July 3, 2013. http://m.motherjones.com/media/2013/07/comedy-central-drunk
  -history-will-ferrell-funny-die-jeremy-konner-derek-waters
Drunk History webisodes—http://www.cc.com/shows/drunk-history

Week 4—Historians as Innovators (February 1)

- Discussion of new and emerging forms of historical research,
  analysis, teaching, curation, publishing, and public engagement.
- Project team presentations: Formal outline of project plan, roles,
  objectives, and process by each team (~15 minutes each).

Guest (via Skype): **Rachel Deblinger**, Director, Digital Scholarship Commons, UCSC Library

Required Reading/Viewings before Class:
Todd Presner, "Welcome to the 20-Year Dissertation," *The Chronicle of Higher
  Learning*, November 25, 2013. http://www.chronicle.com/article/Welcome-to-the
  -20-Year/143223
Molly Osberg, The Assassin's Creed Curriculum: Can Video Games Teach Us
  History? http://www.theverge.com/2014/9/18/6132933/the-assassins-creed
  -curriculum-can-video-games-teach-us-history

Website: Mapping the Republic of Letters http://republicofletters.stanford.edu/
Website: MicroPasts http://micropasts.org/
Website: 15 Minute History http://15minutehistory.org/

Week 5—Historians as Museum Professionals (February 8)

- Discussion of historians engaged in the practice of history in museums and the role of scholarship in society and historians with the public.
- Team progress reports.
- In-class activity: Using the Simon book as a guide, groups (not project teams) propose a specific exhibition or educational activity based on a historical topic related to UCLA and oriented to an imagined visitor/participant drawn from a random list of possibilities (e.g., first grader, tween, undergrad, retiree, person with intellectual challenges, potential funder, etc.).

Guest: **Carolyn Brucken**, Curator, Western Women's History, Autry National Center

Required Readings before Class:
Nina Simon, *The Art of Relevance* (Santa Cruz, Museum 2.0, 2016)

Week 6—Historians as Advisors, Opinion Shapers and Policy-makers (February 15)

NOTE: This class will meet only from 4–5:15 P.M. as students are expected to attend the "Why History Matters" program on February 16, featuring the current and past mayors of Los Angeles.

- Discussion of historians in the arenas of government service, public policy, and politics.
- In-class activity: Class brainstorm on topics and questions to raise with the mayors the next evening.

Required Readings before Class:
Rick Perlstein, "What Gay Studies Taught the Court," *Washington Post*, July 13, 2003. https://www.washingtonpost.com/archive/opinions/2003/07/13/what-gay -studies-taught-the-court/d8e3988c-dfa7-498c-a281-15d2b043a3a0/?utm_term =.e322c7c82da4
Neeta Krishna, "A Think Tank History: A View from India," On Think Tanks, August 6, 2014. https://onthinktanks.org/articles/a-think-tank-history-a-view -from-india/
David Armitage, "Why Politicians Need Historians," *The Guardian*, October 7, 2014.

http://www.theguardian.com/education/2014/oct/07/why-politicians-need
-historians
Office of Mayor of Los Angeles and brief history. https://en.wikipedia.org/wiki
/Mayor_of_Los_Angeles

Week 7—Historians as Leaders (February 22)

- Discussion of historians engaged in leading organizations, altering institutions, and challenging conventions.
- Team progress reports.
- In-class activity: Class brainstorm about naming/renaming Ronald Reagan UCLA Medical Center—how historical case could be made to retain or rename; how consensus could be built for either position, how either position could be communicated to campus community and broader public.

Guest: **Rosalind Remer**, Vice Provost and Lenfest Executive Director, Center for Cultural Partnerships, Drexel University

Required Reading before Class:
Michael H. Schill. OU's Dunn and Deady Halls—Next Steps *(Note: Read the letter and all of the related documents referenced and linked to it).* https://president .uoregon.edu/content/deady-and-dunn-halls-next-steps
Kenneth R. Weiss, "UCLA to Name Medical Center for Ronald Reagan," *Los Angeles Times*, April 20, 2000, http://articles.latimes.com/2000/apr/20/news /mn-21584

Week 8—Historians as Communicators (March 1)

DUE FROM EACH TEAM: Written draft project concept, research summary, and model project contribution.

- In-class activity: Short team presentations of draft concept and model contribution.
- In-class activity: Workshop on presentation design and visual communications.

Guest: **Patrick Frederickson**, designer

Required Readings before Class:
John Theibault, Stephen Robertson, Laura Zucconi et al, "Part 5. See What I Mean? Visual, Spatial, and Game-Based History," in *Writing History in the Digital Age*, Kristen Nawrotzki; Jack Dougherty, eds. (Digital Culture Books, 2013). http:// quod.lib.umich.edu/d/dh/12230987.0001.001/1:8/—writing-history-in-the-digital -age?g=dculture;rgn=div1;view=fulltext;xc=1

Week 9—Cutting Edge History: Practicing History in the Future (March 8)

- Discussion of how will historians practice history in 5–10–20 years in the future? What needs to change in how historians are trained? What is your future in history? How will you achieve it?
- In-class activity: Rehearsal and critique of formal presentations of project design concept and model project contribution.

Guest: none

Required Readings before Class:
William Cronon, "Storytelling," *The American Historical Review* (2013) 118 (1): 1–19. http://ahr.oxfordjournals.org/content/118/1/1.full.pdf+html
Peter Novick, *That Noble Dream: The "Objectivity Question" and the American Historical Profession*, pp. 510–521—**excerpt on class web site under Week 9.**

Week 10—Final Project Presentations to Invited Guests (March 15)

DUE FROM EACH TEAM: Written final project concept, research summary, and model project contribution.

Acknowledgments

First and foremost, we would like to thank our many contributors who made this volume possible. The first idea for this volume began in 2016, as a volume of published conference papers from *Crossroads: The Future of Graduate History Education* at Drew University. Lenny Cassuto first encouraged us to take the idea a step further and build on the spirit of the conference with an edited volume designed to speak to the realities of modern graduate education. In addition to his contributions to the volume itself, his experience and mentorship have been invaluable to all of us. His work in the field has been an inspiration.

Robert Townsend was also hugely influential in crafting both *Crossroads* and *The Reimagined PhD*. In addition to Lenny, Rob was another keynote speaker at *Crossroads*, who also generously contributed to this volume. His thoughtful conversations with him at annual conferences and general enthusiasm for the academic profession were inspirational not only to the volume, but to our individual professional development. Both Lenny and Rob are a testament to the fact that mentors can be found outside of your department and outside of your institution.

We'd also like to thank the many people who made *Crossroads* possible. As students in Drew University's PhD program, Leanne and Jordan were inspired to put together a conference that would highlight features of Drew University's History and Culture PhD program. Jonathan Rose, founding director of graduate studies for the program, had written two publications on the History and Culture program. These publications on the PhD program's launch and its progress served as the inspiration for creating *Crossroads*. His mentorship and guidance encouraged Jordan and Leanne to think about the issues modern graduate students face and to not just create a small symposium, but to put together an event that would bring together scholars from the United States and beyond. The effort to launch such a project took a tremendous amount of support. Thank you to Robert Ready, former dean of the Caspersen School of Graduate Studies, C. Wyatt Evans, former program director of the History & Culture program, and Corinn McBride, former director of graduate admissions at Drew University, for supporting and funding *Crossroads*. Most importantly, thank you to our colleagues and friends who helped facilitate and participated in the conference—especially, Brian Shetler, Daniel Michalak, Becca Miller, Michael Hitchcock Burns, and Rebecca Van Horn. We'd also like to thank our numerous presenters and participants who made the event possible, as well as the American Historical Association and Jim Grossman whose organization of a plenary session on their then new Career Diversity initiative helped make the conference a success.

Transitioning from the conference to a consolidated, edited volume was its own feat. During those long months of soliciting contributions, putting together proposals, collecting and editing work, we were fortunate to have a large support system. Thank you to Chris Taylor, former dean of the Caspersen School of Graduate Studies and College of Liberal Arts at Drew University, Edward Baring, former program director of history and culture, as well as John Witherington, former executive director of graduate admissions at Drew University, for your enthusiasm and support. We're pleased that *Crossroads* and this conference began as a combination of forces between faculty, staff, and students.

During the completion of the volume, Leanne and James transitioned to staff positions at Princeton University. We would like to thank the many faculty and staff who encouraged and supported us as we wrapped up this project, most notably Kristy Novak, Judy Hansen, Amy Pszczolkowski, and Eva Kubu.

Last but not least, we want to thank our families, without whom this would not have been possible. We are grateful for their encouragement to pursue graduate education and, finally, careers in education. Their support made this volume possible.

Bibliography

Alliance for Networking Visual Culture. "About Scalar." n.d. https://scalar.me/anvc
/scalar/.

Alvarado, Rafael, and Paul Humphries. "Big Data, Thick Mediation, and Representa-
tional Opacity." *New Literary History* 48 (2017): 729–749.

American Association of University Professors. "Data Snapshot: Contingent Faculty
in US Higher Ed." n.d. https://www.aaup.org/news/data-snapshot-contingent
-faculty-us-higher-ed#.XXlzIihKgdU.

American Historical Association. "AHA Career Contacts." n.d. https://www
.historians.org/jobs-and-professional-development/career-diversity-for-historians
/career-diversity-resources/aha-career-contacts.

———. "The Career Diversity Five Skills." 2016. https://www.historians.org/jobs-and
-professional-development/career-resources/five-skills.

———. "Career Diversity for Historians." n.d. https://www.historians.org/jobs-and
-professional-development/career-diversity-for-historians.

American Philosophical Society Library. "Americanization: Then and Now." n.d.
https://diglib.amphilsoc.org/labs/americanization/index.html.

Aron, Stephen, and Karen Wilson. "The Many Professions of History (UCLA)."
American Historical Association, n.d. https://www.historians.org/jobs-and
-professional-development/career-diversity-for-historians/career-diversity-resources
/career-diversity-faculty-resources/the-many-professions-of-history-(ucla).

"The Art of Employment: How Liberal Arts Graduates Can Improve Their Labor
Market Prospects." Burning Glass Technologies, 2013. https://www.burning-glass
.com/research-project/liberal-arts/.

Association of Public and Land-Grant Universities. "Public University Values." n.d.
https://www.aplu.org/projects-and-initiatives/college-costs-tuition-and-financial
-aid/publicvalues/publicvalues-resources/q3/employment-and-earnings.pdf.

Barboza, Luendreo. "You're a First-Generation Graduate Student—How Do You
Succeed?" *Cooper Square Review*, March 8, 2018. http://coopersquarereview.org
/post/youre-a-first-generation-graduate-student-how-do-you-succeed/.

Basalla, Susan, and Maggie Debelius. *"So What Are You Going to Do with That?"
Finding Careers Outside Academia*. 3rd ed. University of Chicago Press, 2014.

Bender, Thomas. "Expanding the Domain of History." In *Envisioning the Future of Doctoral Education: Preparing Stewards of the Discipline—Carnegie Essays on the Doctorate*, edited by Chris M. Golde and George E. Walker, 295–310. Jossey-Bass, 2006.

Berg, Maggie, and Barbara K. Seeber. *The Slow Professor: Challenging the Culture of Speed in the Academy*. Reprint ed. University of Toronto Press, 2017.

Beyond the Professoriate. "Where Will You Take Your PhD?" n.d. https://beyondprof.com/.

Bledstein, Burton. *The Culture of Professionalism: The Middle Class and the Development of Higher Education in America*. Norton, 1965.

Bloom, Jennifer L., Amanda E. Propst Cuevas, James Warren Hall, and Christopher V. Evans. "Graduate Students' Perceptions of Outstanding Graduate Advisor Characteristics." *NACADA Journal* 27, no. 2 (September 1, 2007): 28–35. https://doi.org/10.12930/0271-9517-27.2.28.

Bok, Derek. *Higher Education in America*. Princeton University Press, 2013.

Booth, Alison. "Digital Future of Graduate Study in the Humanities (Roundtable Remarks)." 2019.

Campbell, Ryan C., Danny D. Reible, Roman Taraban, and Jeong-Hee Kim. "Fostering Reflective Engineers: Outcomes of an Arts- and Humanities-Infused Graduate Course." In *2018 World Engineering Education Forum—Global Engineering Deans Council (WEEF-GEDC)*, 1–6. IEEE, 2018. https://doi.org/10.1109/WEEF-GEDC.2018.8629714.

Canadian Association for Graduate Studies. "Graduate Professional Development Program." n.d. http://www.ca.cags.ca/gdps/index.php.

"Career Opportunities Institute: University of Virginia." *Public Historian* 3, no. 3 (1981): 137–138. https://doi.org/10.2307/3377745.

Career Services, Queen's University. "Grad Maps." n.d. https://careers.queensu.ca/gradmaps.

Carey, Kevin. "The Bleak Job Landscape of Adjunctopia for PhDs." *New York Times*, March 6, 2020. https://www.nytimes.com/2020/03/05/upshot/academic-job-crisis-phd.html.

Carnegie Foundation for the Advancement of Teaching. "The Six Core Principles of Improvement." n.d. https://www.carnegiefoundation.org/our-ideas/six-core-principles-improvement/.

Cassuto, Leonard. "Can You Train Your Ph.D.s for Diverse Careers When You Don't Have One?" *Chronicle of Higher Education*, August 22, 2018. https://www.chronicle.com/article/Can-You-Train-Your-PhDs-for/244323.

———. *The Graduate School Mess: What Caused It and How We Can Fix It*. Harvard University Press, 2015.

———. "The Overlooked Lesson of the Ronell-Reitman Case." *Chronicle of Higher Education*, September 16, 2018. https://www.chronicle.com/article/The-Overlooked-Lesson-of-the/244508.

Cassuto, Leonard, and Robert Weisbuch. *The New PhD: How to Build a Better Graduate Education*. Johns Hopkins University Press, 2021.

Chace, William M. *One Hundred Semesters: My Adventures as Student, Professor, and University President, and What I Learned along the Way*. Reprint ed. Princeton University Press, 2006.

Chambers, Paula. "Making the Leap: Key Factors That Get PhDs Hired into Non-faculty Jobs." North Carolina Graduate Deans, October 26, 2017.

———. "Subject Matter Plus: Mentoring for Nonacademic Careers." In *The Mentoring Continuum: From Graduate School through Tenure*, edited by Glenn Wright. Syracuse University Press, 2015.

Clark, William. *Academic Charisma and the Origins of the Research University*. Reprint ed. University of Chicago Press, 2007.

CLIR. "CLIR Postdoctoral Fellowship Program." n.d. https://www.clir.org/initiatives -partnerships/postdoc/.

CommentPress. "Welcome to CommentPress." n.d. https://futureofthebook.org /commentpress/.

Committee on Science, Engineering, and Public Policy. *Reshaping the Graduate Education of Scientists and Engineers*. National Academies Press, 1995.

Connected Academics, n.d. https://connect.mla.hcommons.org/.

Consortium of Canadian Graduate Student Professional Development Administrators. n.d. https://ccgspda.wixsite.com/grad-pd.

Council of Graduate Schools. "Pathways through Graduate School and into Careers." 2012. http://pathwaysreport.org/.

Courant, Paul N., and Terri Geitgey. "Preliminary Examination of 'Free Riding' in US Monograph Publication." *Journal of Electronic Publishing* 19, no. 1 (Summer 2016). https://doi.org/10.3998/3336451.0019.101.

Crain's Chicago Business. "A New Nonprofit Helps Match Donors with Causes." February 28, 2019. https://www.chicagobusiness.com/nonprofits-philanthropy /new-nonprofit-helps-match-donors-causes.

Damrosch, David. "Vectors of Change." In *Envisioning the Future of Doctoral Education: Preparing Stewards of the Discipline*, edited by Chris M. Golde and George E. Walker. Jossey-Bass, 2006.

Denecke, Daniel, Keonna Feaster, and Katherine Stone. "Professional Development: Shaping Effective Programs for STEM Graduate Students." Council of Graduate Schools, 2017. https://cgsnet.org/ckfinder/userfiles/files/CGS_ProfDev _STEMGrads16_web.pdf.

Des Jardin, Molly. "Teaching 'East Asian DH.'" 2019. http://dx.doi.org/10.17613/xcs8 -7x30.

Dewey, John. *Democracy and Education: Introduction to the Philosophy of Education*. Macmillan, 1916.

Digital Humanities Now. n.d. http://digitalhumanitiesnow.org/.

Digital Paxton. "Digital Paxton: Digital Collection, Critical Edition, and Teaching Platform." n.d. http://digitalpaxton.org/works/digital-paxton/index.

"Discovering Our Roots: The PhD Lineage Contest Winners." *APS News Online*, n.d., March 1999 edition, sec. The Back Page. https://www.lorentz.leidenuniv.nl/history /explosion/APS_back_page.html.

Dunbar, John Raine. *The Paxton Papers*. M. Nijhoff, 1957.

Dunn, Sydni. "Why So Many Academics Quit and Tell." *ChronicleVitae*, December 12, 2013. https://chroniclevitae.com/news/216-why-so-many-academics-quit-and-tell.

Eakin, Emily. "Professor Scarry Has a Theory." *New York Times Magazine*, November 19, 2000. https://archive.nytimes.com/www.nytimes.com/library/magazine /home/20001119mag-scarry.html.

Edge, Jessica, and Daniel Munro. "Inside and Outside the Academy: Valuing and Preparing PhDs for Careers." Conference Board of Canada, November 24, 2015. https://www.conferenceboard.ca/(X(1)S(worzlymvnfqnfropi1z5ztvc))/e-library /abstract.aspx?did=7564&AspxAutoDetectCookieSupport=1.

Ehrenberg, Ronald G., and Charlotte V. Kuh. *Doctoral Education and the Faculty of the Future*. Cornell University Press, 2008.

Ehrenberg, Ronald G., Harriet Zuckerman, Jeffrey A. Groen, and Sharon M. Brucker. *Educating Scholars: Doctoral Education in the Humanities*. Princeton University Press, 2009.

Emerson, Ralph Waldo. "The American Scholar (1837)." In *Selected Writings*, edited by Stephen E. Whicher. Houghton Mifflin, 1957.

"Faculty Diversity." n.d. https://www.facultydiversity.org/.

Faculty of Graduate Studies, York University. "Degree Requirements | Current Students | English | Faculty of Graduate Studies | York University | English." n.d. http://english.gradstudies.yorku.ca/current-students/degree-requirements/.

———. "Graduate & Postdoctoral Professional Skills (GPPS)." n.d. http://gradstudies.yorku.ca/current-students/enhancing-your-experience/graduate-postdoctoral-professional-skills/#squelch-taas-tab-content-0-0.

Fallon, Sam. "The Rise of the Pedantic Professor." *Chronicle of Higher Education*, March 1, 2019. https://www.chronicle.com/article/The-Rise-of-the-Pedantic/245808?cid=cr&utm_source=cr&utm_medium=en&elqTrackId=60196e66569c4f408ce4f8b152facc86&elq=427facbf3df345769ded4ab02c33776c&elqaid=22469&elqat=1&elqCampaignId=11084.

Fenton, William. "Guide to Diaries Held at the American Philosophical Society." American Philosophical Society, n.d. https://search.amphilsoc.org/diaries/search.

———. "The Rising Stars of the Digital Humanities." *Inside Higher Ed*, August 2, 2017. https://www.insidehighered.com/digital-learning/article/2017/08/02/rising-stars-digital-humanities.

Field, Kelly. "A Professor 'Who Looks Like Them.'" *Chronicle of Higher Education*, July 2, 2017. http://www.chronicle.com/article/A-Professor-Who-Looks-Like/240475.

Fink, John, and Davis Jenkins. "Shifting Sectors: How a Commonly Used Federal Datapoint Undercounts over a Million Community College Students." *Mixed Methods Blog*, n.d. https://ccrc.tc.columbia.edu/easyblog/shifting-sectors-community-colleges-undercounting.html.

Fischer, Karin. "It's a New Assault on the University." *Chronicle of Higher Education*, February 18, 2019. https://www.chronicle.com/interactives/Trend19-Intrusion-Main.

"For the Greater Good: Boosting the Value of Industry Partnerships." Educational Advisory Board, 2017. https://attachment.eab.com/wp-content/uploads/2019/07/For_Greater_Good_URF_Finals.pdf#page=21.

Fournier, Auriel. "Family Ties and Grad School 'Why's.'" *Inside Higher Ed. GradHacker*, December 10, 2013. https://www.insidehighered.com/blogs/gradhacker/family-ties-and-grad-school-whys.

Gallup Clifton Strengths. "StrengthsFinder 2.0." n.d. https://www.gallupstrengthscenter.com/home/en-us/strengthsfinder?utm_source=strengthsfinder&utm_campaign=coming_soon&utm_medium=redirect.

Geiger, Roger L., et al. *A New Deal for the Humanities: Liberal Arts and the Future of Public Higher Education*. Edited by Gordon Hutner and Feisal G. Mohamed. Rutgers University Press, 2015.

Gillespie, Nick. "Who's Afraid of the MLA?" *Reason*, December 27, 2005. https://reason.com/2005/12/27/whos-afraid-of-the-mla/.

Gold, Matthew K., and Lauren F. Klein, eds. *Debates in the Digital Humanities 2019*. University of Minnesota Press, 2019.

Golde, Chris M., and Timothy M. Dore. "At Cross Purposes: What the Experiences of Doctoral Students Reveal about Doctoral Education." Pew Charitable Trusts, 2001. www.phd-survey.org.

Goldrick-Rab, Sara. *Paying the Price: College Costs, Financial Aid, and the Betrayal of the American Dream*. University of Chicago Press, 2017.

Graduate Career Consortium. "Home—Graduate Career Consortium." n.d. https://gradcareerconsortium.org/.

Grafton, Anthony T., and Jim Grossman. "No More Plan B." *Chronicle of Higher Education*, October 9, 2011. https://www.chronicle.com/article/No-More-Plan-B /129293.

———. "No More Plan B: A Very Modest Proposal for Graduate Programs in History." *Perspectives on History*, October 2011. https://www.historians.org /publications-and-directories/perspectives-on-history/october-2011/no-more -plan-b.

Grant, David. *The Social Profit Handbook: The Essential Guide to Setting Goals, Assessing Outcomes, and Achieving Success for Mission-Driven Organizations*. Chelsea Green, 2015.

Greenleaf, Robert K. "The Servant as Leader." 1970. http://www.ediguys.net/Robert _K_Greenleaf_The_Servant_as_Leader.pdf.

Grossman, James. "Hierarchy and Needs." *Perspectives on History*, September 1, 2018. https://www.historians.org/publications-and-directories/perspectives-on-history /september-2018/hierarchy-and-needs-how-to-dislodge-outdated-notions-of -advising.

———. "How Not to Confront the Jobs Crisis." *Chronicle of Higher Education*, May 2, 2019. https://www.chronicle.com/article/how-not-to-confront-the-jobs-crisis/.

———. "Imagining Ph.D. Orientation in 2022." *Chronicle of Higher Education*, August 28, 2017. https://www.chronicle.com/article/Imagining-PhD-Orientation -in/240995.

Hackman, J. Richard. "What Is This Thing Called Leadership?" In *Handbook of Leadership Theory and Practice*, edited by Nitin Nohria and Rakesh Khurana, 107–118. Harvard Business Review Press, 2010.

Humanities Indicators. "The State of the Humanities in Four-Year Colleges and Universities." American Academy of Arts and Sciences, 2020. https://www.amacad .org/sites/default/files/media/document/2020-05/hds3_the_state_of_the _humanities_in_colleges_and_universities.pdf.

ImaginePhD. "Welcome." n.d. https://www.imaginephd.com/.

Inside Higher Ed Careers. n.d. https://careers.insidehighered.com/.

Institutional Research & Decision Support, Stanford University. "PhD Jobs." n.d. https://irds.stanford.edu/phd-jobs.

James, William. "The PhD Octopus." *Harvard Monthly*, March 1903.

Jaschik, Scott. "The Ph.D. Skill Mismatch." *Inside Higher Ed*, January 5, 2018. https://www.insidehighered.com/news/2018/01/05/study-shows-academic-job -searches-languages-value-alt-ac-skills?utm_source=Inside+Higher+Ed&utm _campaign=db1d03ed99-DNU20180105&utm_medium=email&utm_term=0 _1fcbc04421-db1d03ed99-198627041&mc_cid=db1d03ed99&mc_eid =8446eda839.

Kennedy, John F. "Remarks at Amherst College." 1963. http://arts.gov/about/kennedy.

Koenigs, Thomas. "Fictionality Risen: Early America, the Common Core Curriculum, and How We Argue about Fiction Today." Edited by Osucha Batker and

Augusta Rohrbach. *American Literature* 89, no. 2 (June 1, 2017): 225–253. https://doi.org/10.1215/00029831-3861493.

Kramnick, Jonathan. "What We Hire in Now: English by the Grim Numbers." *Chronicle of Higher Education*, December 9, 2018. https://www.chronicle.com/article/What-We-Hire-in-Now-English/245255.

Kriegel, Robert J., and David Brandt. *Sacred Cows Make the Best Burgers: Paradigm-Busting Strategies for Developing Change-Ready People and Organizations*. Grand Central, 1996.

Kuo, Maggie, and Jia You. "Explore the Skills That Can Open Career Doors after Your Doctoral Training." *Science*, November 27, 2017. https://www.sciencemag.org/careers/2017/11/explore-skills-can-open-career-doors-after-your-doctoral-training.

K–12 Blueprint. "Maker & STEM." May 13, 2014. https://www.k12blueprint.com/toolkits/maker-stem.

Laurence, David. "Demand for New Faculty Members, 1995–2016." *MLA Profession*, Winter 2019. https://profession.mla.org/demand-for-new-faculty-members-1995-2016/.

Leshner, Alan, and Layne Scherer, eds. *Revitalizing Graduate STEM Education for the 21st Century*. National Academies Press, 2018.

Library Company of Philadelphia. "Fellows Commons." n.d. https://librarycompany.org/academic-programs/fellowscommons/.

———. "Redrawing History: Indigenous Perspectives on Colonial America." n.d. https://librarycompany.org/redrawing-history/.

———. "Seminars." n.d. https://librarycompany.org/seminars/.

March, Peter. "Broader Impacts Review Criterion—Dear Colleague Letter." National Science Foundation, n.d. https://www.nsf.gov/pubs/2007/nsf07046/nsf07046.jsp.

Marx, John, and Mark Garrett Cooper. *Media U: How the Need to Win Audiences Has Shaped Higher Education*. Columbia University Press, 2018.

McGuirl, Barbara, and Gordon L. Olson. "Business History Has a Future." *Public Historian* 3, no. 3 (July 1, 1981): 153–159. https://doi.org/10.2307/3377752.

Mcubed. "Mcubed 3.0 Essentials." n.d. https://mcubed.umich.edu/mcubed-essentials.

Menand, Louis. *The Marketplace of Ideas: Reform and Resistance in the American University*. Norton, 2010.

Mendelson, Edward. "Old Saul and Young Saul." *New York Review*, September 26, 2013. https://www.nybooks.com/articles/2013/09/26/old-saul-and-young-saul-bellow/.

Modern Language Association. "Job List." n.d. https://www.mla.org/Resources/Career/Job-List.

———. "Report of the MLA Task Force on Doctoral Study in Modern Language and Literature." May 2014. https://www.mla.org/Resources/Research/Surveys-Reports-and-Other-Documents/Staffing-Salaries-and-Other-Professional-Issues/Report-of-the-Task-Force-on-Doctoral-Study-in-Modern-Language-and-Literature-2014.

———. "Report of the MLA Task Force on Ethical Conduct in Graduate Education." Delegate Assembly Meeting, January 2020. https://www.mla.org/content/download/115847/2439024/J20-Item-8e-Report-from-the-Task-Force-on-Ethical-Conduct-in-Graduate-Education.pdf.

Moody, Josh. "How Many Universities Are in the U.S. and Why That Number Is Changing | Best Colleges | US News." *U.S. News & World Report*, February 15, 2019. https://www.usnews.com/education/best-colleges/articles/2019-02-15/how-many-universities-are-in-the-us-and-why-that-number-is-changing.

Morgan, Paige C. "Requested Skills & Expertise, DH/DS Library Positions, 2010–2018. Mouse over for More Info, or Sort by Skills or Years. Created for DLF Forum 2018." Tableau Software, October 15, 2018. https://public.tableau.com/views/Requestedsk illsexpertiseDHDSlibrarypositions2010-2018/RequestedskillsandexpertiseDHDS frontfacinglibrarypositions2010-2018?:embed=y&:display_count=yes&:origin =viz_share_link.

Morgan, Paige C., and Helene Williams. "When Does a New Role Cease to Be New? Situating the Work of Library-Based Digital Humanities/Scholarship Support Positions." 2018. https://scholarlyrepository.miami.edu/librarypapers/4/.

My IDP Science Careers. n.d. http://myidp.sciencecareers.org/.

NACE Staff. "Paid Interns/Co-Ops See Greater Offer Rates and Salary Offers Than Their Unpaid Classmates." National Association of Colleges and Employees, March 23, 2016. https://www.naceweb.org/job-market/internships/paid-interns-co -ops-see-greater-offer-rates-and-salary-offers-than-their-unpaid-classmates/.

National Institute of Health. "Strengthening the Biomedical Research Workforce." n.d. https://commonfund.nih.gov/workforce.

Neatline. n.d. https://neatline.org/.

Nowviskie, Bethany. "On the Origin of 'Hack' and 'Yack.'" *Bethany Nowviskie*, January 8, 2014. http://nowviskie.org/2014/on-the-origin-of-hack-and-yack/.

Nyquist, Jody D., and Bettina J. Woodford. "Re-envisioning the Ph.D.: What Concerns Do We Have?" Pew Charitable Trusts, 2000. https://depts.washington .edu/envision/resources/ConcernsBrief.pdf.

Office of Communications. "'60 Minutes' Features Princeton's Transformative Efforts to Increase Socioeconomic Diversity." Princeton University, April 29, 2018. https://www.princeton.edu/news/2018/04/29/60-minutes-features-princetons -transformative-efforts-increase-socioeconomic.

O'Hehir, Andrew. "When a Woman Is Accused of Sexual Misconduct: The Strange Case of Avital Ronell." *Salon*, August 18, 2018. https://www.salon.com/2018/08/18 /when-a-woman-is-accused-of-sexual-misconduct-the-strange-case-of-avital-ronell/.

Okahana, Hironao, and Enyu Zhou. *Graduate Enrollment and Degrees: 2007 to 2017.* Council of Graduate Schools, 2018.

Omeka. n.d. https://omeka.org/.

Peaker, Alicia, and Katie Shives. "From First-Gen College Student to First-Gen Grad Student." *Inside Higher Ed. GradHacker*, December 12, 2013. https://www .insidehighered.com/blogs/gradhacker/first-gen-college-student-first-gen-grad -student.

Pennamon, Tiffany. "HSI Pathways Program Aims to Increase Hispanic Representation in the Professoriate." *Diverse: Issues in Higher Education*, February 25, 2019. https://diverseeducation.com/article/139471/.

Pettit, Emma. "What the Numbers Can Tell Us about Humanities Ph.D. Careers." *Chronicle of Higher Education*, January 6, 2019. https://www.chronicle.com/article /What-the-Numbers-Can-Tell-Us/245417.

Pho, Helen. "Career Tips for First-Generation Grad Students." *Inside Higher Ed*, October 8, 2018. https://www.insidehighered.com/advice/2018/10/08/career -advice-first-generation-grad-students-opinion.

Pitt, Rachael. "Australian Employers' Expectations and Perceptions of PhD Graduates in the Workplace." In *Proceedings of the 2012 Quality in Postgraduate Research Conference*, edited by Margaret Kiley, 233–234. http://www.qpr.edu.au /Proceedings/QPR_Proceedings_2012.pdf.

Pitt, Rachael, and Inger Mewburn. "Academic Superheroes? A Critical Analysis of Academic Job Descriptions." *Journal of Higher Education Policy and Management* 38, no. 1 (January 26, 2016): 88–101. https://doi.org/10.1080/1360080X.2015.1126896.

Posselt, Julie R. *Inside Graduate Admissions: Merit, Diversity, and Faculty Gatekeeping.* Harvard University Press, 2016.

Prewitt, Kenneth. "Who Should Do What." In *Envisioning the Future of Doctoral Education: Preparing Stewards of the Discipline,* edited by Chris M. Golde and George E. Walker. Jossey-Bass, 2006.

Princeton University. "Prospective Graduate Students Get a Peek Inside Princeton Ph.D. Programs." October 10, 2018. https://www.princeton.edu/news/2018/10/10/prospective-graduate-students-get-peek-inside-princeton-phd-programs.

The Professor Is In. "The Professor Is In | Getting You through Graduate School, the Job Market and Tenure. . . ." n.d. http://theprofessorisin.com/.

Rackham Graduate School, University of Michigan. "Rackham Program in Public Scholarship." n.d. https://rackham.umich.edu/professional-development/program-in-public-scholarship/.

Rogers, Katina. "Outside the Pipeline: From Anecdote to Data." n.d. https://katinarogers.com/2012/11/05/outside-the-pipeline-from-anecdote-to-data/.

Rohrbach, Augusta. "LinkedIn Post Announcing Survey." March 5, 2019.

———. "Realism 2.0." In *The Oxford Handbook to American Literary Realism,* edited by Keith Newlin. Oxford University Press, 2019.

———. *Thinking Outside the Book.* University of Massachusetts Press, 2014.

Rose, Marilyn. "Graduate Student Professional Development: A Survey with Recommendations." Canadian Association for Graduate Studies and Social Sciences and Humanities Research Council of Canada, September 2012. http://www.cags.ca/documents/publications/working/Report%20on%20Graduate%20Student%20Professional%20Development%20%20-%20A%20survey%20with%20recommendations%20FINAL%20Eng.OCT%202012.pdf.

Roth, Michael S. "Reshaping Ourselves and Our Societies." In *Beyond the University: Why Liberal Education Matters.* Yale University Press, 2014.

Schneider, Nathan. "A Literary Scholar's Voice in the Wilderness." *Chronicle of Higher Education,* February 17, 2014. https://www.chronicle.com/article/A-Literary-Scholars-Voice-in/144733.

Schon, Donald A. *The Reflective Practitioner: How Professionals Think in Action.* TempleSmith, 1983.

Schonfeld, Robert C. "A Taxonomy of University Presses Today." *Scholarly Kitchen,* October 13, 2016. https://scholarlykitchen.sspnet.org/2016/10/13/a-taxonomy-of-university-presses-today/.

School of Graduate Studies, University of Toronto. "10,000 PhDs Project." n.d. https://www.sgs.utoronto.ca/about/10000-phds-project-overview/.

Seltzer, Beth. "One Hundred Job Ads from the Humanities Ecosystem—Profession." *MLA Profession,* Fall 2018. https://profession.mla.org/one-hundred-job-ads-from-the-humanities-ecosystem/.

Shit Academics Say (@AcademicsSay). "I Don't Always Get Emotional. But When I Do I Call It Affect." Twitter, March 25, 2015. https://twitter.com/academicssay/status/580693264904359936?lang=en.

———. "Just Wondering if You Had Time to Grab a Coffee to Discuss How Busy We All Are." Twitter, February 21, 2019. https://twitter.com/AcademicsSay/status/1098647081965768707.

Shore, Bruce M. *The Graduate Advisor Handbook: A Student-Centered Approach.* University of Chicago Press, 2014.

Stearns, Peter N., and Joel A. Tarr. "Curriculum in Applied History: Toward the Future." *Public Historian* 9, no. 3 (1987): 111–125. https://doi.org/10.2307/3377191.

Stein, Arlene, and Jessie Daniels. *Going Public: A Guide for Social Scientists.* University of Chicago Press, 2017.

Stewart, Debra. Paper presented at the Western Association of Graduate Schools, Fargo, ND, April 2014.

"Survey Response to Question 10 Submitted to Augusta Rohrbach." n.d.

Thomas, Lindsay. "'The Irrational Sense of Having Done One's Job Well': Professionalization, Graduate Education, and DH." Chicago, 2019.

Tompkins, Jane, and Gerald Graff. "Can We Talk?" In *Professions: Conversations on the Future of Literary and Cultural Studies,* edited by Donald E. Hall. University of Illinois Press, 2001.

Townsend, Robert B., and Julia Brookins. "The Troubled Academic Job Market for History." *Perspectives on History,* February 5, 2016. https://www.historians.org/publications-and-directories/perspectives-on-history/february-2016/the-troubled-academic-job-market-for-history.

Underwood, Ted. "The Stone and the Shell." n.d. https://tedunderwood.com/.

University of British Columbia. "PhD Outcome Tracking." n.d. http://outcomes.grad.ubc.ca/explore.html.

University of California, Berkeley Graduate Division. "Professional Development Guide." n.d. https://grad.berkeley.edu/professional-development/guide/.

University of Toronto. "Biochemistry, University of Toronto—BCH 2024H." n.d. http://biochemistry.utoronto.ca/courses/bch2024h-professional-development-2/.

University of Washington–Tacoma. "Jeff Cohen—We Are First Generation." https://www.tacoma.uw.edu/node/46396.

———. "We Are First Generation." https://www.tacoma.uw.edu/news/we-are-first-generation.

US Aid. "What We Do." February 16, 2018. https://www.usaid.gov/what-we-do.

UW Graduate School, University of Washington. "David Eaton, Graduate School Dean." http://grad.uw.edu/student-alumni-profiles/dean-eaton/.

———. "First-Generation Graduate Students." http://grad.uw.edu/for-students-and-post-docs/core-programs/first-generation-graduate-students/.

———. "What a Good Mentor Does." https://grad.uw.edu/for-students-and-post-docs/core-programs/mentoring/mentoring-guides-for-students/what-a-good-mentor-does/.

Van Wyck, James M. "Academia Is Not a Container." *Inside Higher Ed,* November 2, 2020. https://www.insidehighered.com/advice/2020/11/02/academia-must-reconsider-its-binary-thinking-and-be-open-new-metaphors-lead-new.

———. "How Graduate Advisers Can Bolster Their Career Guidance." *Inside Higher Ed,* June 11, 2018. https://www.insidehighered.com/advice/2018/06/11/ways-advisers-can-better-inform-phd-students-careers-today-opinion.

Versatile PhD. "The Versatile PhD: Helping Graduate Students and PhDs Envision, Prepare for, and Excel in Non-Academic Careers since 1999." https://versatilephd.com/.

Veysey, Laurence R. *The Emergence of the American University.* University of Chicago Press, 1965.

Waggoner, Jess. "Graduate Study for First Generation Students." *Inside Higher Ed.*

GradHacker, December 8, 2013. https://www.insidehighered.com/blogs
/gradhacker/graduate-study-first-generation-students.

Walker, George E., Chris M. Golde, Laura Jones, Andrea Conklin Bueschel, and Pat
Hutchings. *The Formation of Scholars: Rethinking Doctoral Education for the
Twenty-First Century.* Jossey-Bass, 2008.

Weisbuch, Robert, and Leonard Cassuto. "Reforming Doctoral Education, 1990 to
2015, Recent Initiatives and Future Prospects." Andrew W. Mellon Foundation,
June 2, 2016. https://mellon.org/media/filer_public/35/32/3532f16c-20c4-4213-805d
-356f85251a98/report-on-doctoral-education-reform_june-2016.pdf.

"Welcome to IGERT.Org." n.d. http://www.igert.org/.

Wilson, Woodrow, and Arthur S. Link. "Princeton for the National Service (1902)."
In *The Papers of Woodrow Wilson*, vol. 16. Princeton University Press, 1972.

Wright, Glenn, ed. "Subject Matter Plus: Mentoring for Nonacademic Careers." In
The Mentoring Continuum: From Graduate School through Tenure. Syracuse
University Press, 2015.

Wulff, Donald H., and Ann E. Austin. *Paths to the Professoriate: Strategies for
Enriching the Preparation of Future Faculty.* Jossey-Bass, 2004.

Notes on Contributors

STEPHEN ARON
President and CEO, Autry Museum of the American West, and professor emeritus of history, UCLA

A past president of the Western History Association and elected member of the Society of American Historians, Stephen Aron's most recent book, *The American West: A Very Short Introduction*, was published in 2015. Prior to taking the helm at the Autry Museum in 2021, Aron spent twenty-five years on the faculty at UCLA, including a stint as chair of the History Department. While chair, he worked closely with Karen Wilson in spearheading the American Historical Association's Career Diversity for Historians Pilot Program at UCLA, which was funded by the Andrew W. Mellon Foundation.

VERNITA BURRELL
Associate professor of English, East Los Angeles Community College

Vernita Burrell earned her bachelor's degree from Hunter College, as well as a master's degree from Loyola Marymount University and a PhD in English from Fordham University. Her dissertation, "The Ambiguities of Abolition: Pro- and Anti-Slavery Writings, 1757–1824," focuses on the nuances and complexities about slavery and abolition that go beyond the conventional binary pro- and anti-slavery arguments within eighteenth-century slavery discourse. Her primary interests have always been connected to teaching, and she has experience teaching at a range of institutions. Her academic training is informed by her deep experience and appreciation for musical theater—she had a successful ten-year run as an actress doing summer stock, tours, and musicals across the United States.

LEONARD CASSUTO
Professor of English and American studies, Fordham University

Leonard Cassuto has been described as "America's graduate advisor." He is the author of numerous books and articles, including *The Graduate School Mess: What Caused It and How We Can Fix It* (2015), and writes a widely read column ("The Graduate Advisor") for the *Chronicle of Higher Education*. His most recent book, coauthored with Robert Weisbuch (who also contributes to this volume) is *The New PhD: How to Build a Better Graduate Education* (2021).

PAULA CHAMBERS
Founder, Versatile PhD

Paula Chambers has spent nearly two decades advocating for career diversity for humanities PhDs, first as a graduate student, then as a nonacademically employed PhD, and finally as the founder and original CEO of Versatile PhD. In 1999, while dissertating in rhetoric and composition at Ohio State, she founded WRK4US ("work for us"), the first online community for humanities PhD students interested in nonacademic careers. In 2010, she transformed that community into Versatile PhD, a web-based nonacademic career resource for humanities PhDs, funded by university subscriptions. By popular demand, Versatile PhD began serving STEM disciplines as well in 2013, and attracted a high percentage of the top 100 research universities as subscribers. She has published in several edited collections on PhD career development and presented to graduate students, faculty and administrators at many research universities all over the United States. She sold Versatile PhD in 2018, but continues to write, speak and care about doctoral education.

MELISSA DALGLEISH
Research training center coordinator, Peter Gilgan Centre for Research and Learning

Melissa Dalgleish is the research training center coordinator at the Hospital for Sick Children (SickKids) in Toronto, Canada, where she works in the Peter Gilgan Centre for Research and Learning. She provides researchers-in-training with the skills and expertise they need to succeed during their degrees and fellowships, as well as in academic, industry, government, and nonprofit careers. Her workshops and events cover everything from mRNAi analysis to creating an effective LinkedIn profile, and her trainees have gone on to become influencers in every sector. Prior to joining SickKids, she worked in the Faculty of Graduate Studies at York University, where she managed graduate and postdoctoral research funding competitions and launched the Graduate Professional Skills Program, which offers academic and career development opportunities to over 6,000 master's and PhD students. She is a regular contributor to the *Chronicle of Higher Education* and *Inside Higher Ed.*

WILL FENTON

Director, Research and Public Programs, Library Company of Philadelphia

Will Fenton is the director of Research and Public Programs at the Library Company of Philadelphia and the editor of *Ghost River: The Fall and Rise of the Conestoga* (2019). He earned his PhD from Fordham University in August 2018 (English Department). Fenton specializes in early American literature and the digital humanities, for which he has received support from the American Philosophical Society; Haverford College Quaker and Special Collections; Humanities, Arts, Science, and Technology Alliance and Collaboratory; Library Company of Philadelphia; Modern Language Association; New York Public Library; NYC Digital Humanities; and Omohundro Institute of Early American History & Culture. His writings have appeared in academic journals (*American Quarterly, Common-Place,* and *ESQ*); academic blogs (Eighteenth-Century Common, MLA Connected Academics, Omohundro Uncommon Sense, and the Organization of American Historians); and public platforms (*Philadelphia Inquirer, Slate,* and *Inside Higher Ed*).

LEANNE M. HORINKO

Graduate program assistant, Princeton University

Leanne M. Horinko is the graduate program assistant in the History Department at Princeton University. She supports the graduate programs in history of science and history in a range of areas including prospective student's initial visit to campus, organizing dissertation defenses, and the departments' dossier service and departmental professional development. Prior to joining Princeton's history department, she worked for eight years in graduate admissions, where her professional portfolio included the day-to-day strategic planning of graduate school enrollment in addition to the research and development of new graduate programs. In 2016 she co-organized the *Crossroads: The Future of Graduate History Education* conference at Drew University. Her professional publications have appeared in *The Canadian Review of American Studies* as well as on *Inside Higher Ed*'s *GradHacker* column, the Organization for American Historians' blog, *Process: A Blog for American History*. She received her MA in history from Drew University. She has also worked with Authorship in Modern American Textbooks (AMAT), a digital humanities project.

ALEXANDRA M. LORD

Chair and curator, Division of Medicine and Science, National Museum of American History

Alexandra M. Lord received her AB from Vassar College and PhD from the University of Wisconsin, Madison. She is the chair of the Medicine and Science Division at the National Museum of American History. Previously, she was the branch chief for the National Historic Landmarks Program of the National Park Service and a historian for the U.S. Public Service. She began writing and speaking about her experiences leaving academia after leaving a tenure-track position. Her work has appeared in places ranging from the *Chronicle of Higher Education* to the *Washington Post* to scholarly journals. In 2010, her book, *Condom Nation: The U.S. Government's Sex Education Campaign from World War I to the Internet*, received the British Medical Association's prize for its best popular book on medicine.

MICHAEL J. MCGANDY

Senior editor and editorial director of Three Hills, Cornell University Press

Michael J. McGandy is senior editor and editorial director of the Three Hills imprint at Cornell University Press. Previously he worked at Rowman & Littlefield, W. W. Norton, and Gale Group. He is also the author of *The Active Life: Miller's Metaphysics of Democracy* (2005), and coeditor of *The Task of Criticism: Essays on Philosophy, and Community* (2005) as well as of *Commonplace Commitments: Thinking through the Legacy of Joseph P. Fell* (2016). His essays and book reviews have appeared in *Transactions* of the Charles S. Piece Society and the *Journal of Speculative Philosophy*. He holds a PhD in philosophy from Fordham University.

JORDAN M. REED

Upper school history teacher, Morristown-Beard School

Jordan M. Reed earned a PhD in history and culture at Drew University, where he was a Caspersen School fellow. His academic research focuses on the authorship of American history textbooks in the twentieth century, particularly the books that emerged in the aftermath of the Second World War. With Leanne Horinko, he co-organized *Crossroads: The Future of Graduate History Education*, a national conference held at Drew University in 2016, which inspired this volume. His scholarship has been published in *The History Teacher* and *Book History*, among other outlets. Currently, he teaches history and writing at Morristown-Beard School in Morristown, New Jersey.

AUGUSTA ROHRBACH

Senior director of Strategic Initiatives, Tufts University

After earning a PhD in English from Columbia University, Augusta Rohrbach taught at Harvard, Brown, and Washington State University. She served as editor-in-chief of *ESQ: A Journal of the American Renaissance* from 2005 to 2014. She has held a variety of posts within and beyond the academy, including resident humanist at the Fletcher Maynard Academy. She is currently the senior director of Strategic Initiatives at Tufts University.

Her publications include *Thinking Outside the Book: Knowledge Production and New Media* (2014); *Truth Stranger Than Fiction: Race, Realism and the U.S. Literary Marketplace* (2002); and "Authorship" in *Digital Pedagogy in the Humanities: Concepts, Models, and Experiments* (forthcoming).

ROBERT TOWNSEND

Director, Washington, DC, office of the American Academy of Arts and Sciences and codirector of Humanities Indicators

Robert Townsend served in a variety of roles at the American Historical for twenty-three years, before he began overseeing the work of the American Academy of Arts and Sciences' Washington office. As the director of the Humanities Indicators Initiative, he oversees one of the most widely circulated data-driven projects on the humanities. His articles—such as "How Are History PhD Programs Responding to the Job Crisis," "The Many Careers of History PhDs," and "Use Data to Make a Strong Case for the Humanities"— have appeared in venues such as *Perspectives on History* and the *Chronicle of Higher Education*. He is also the author of *History's Babel: Scholarship, Professionalization, and the Historical Enterprise in the United States, 1880–1940* (2013).

JAMES M. VAN WYCK

Assistant dean for professional development, Princeton University

James M. Van Wyck is an assistant dean for professional development in the Office of the Dean of the Graduate School at Princeton University. As a member of the GradFUTURES team, he serves as the primary liaison to the humanities and social science graduate programs at Princeton and manages graduate student professional development programs, strategic communications, the GradFUTURES Fellows program, including the University Administrative Fellows Program, and the Community College Teaching Initiative. Prior to Princeton, he worked for Robert Weisbuch and Associates (RWA), where he served as a senior research fellow and associate. He was also a multiyear postdoctoral fellow at Fordham University, where he taught literature, public speaking, composition, and upper-level electives including "Leading and Leadership."

JOSEPH VUKOV

Assistant professor and graduate program director, Loyola University Chicago

Joseph Vukov is assistant professor and graduate program director in the Philosophy Department at Loyola University Chicago. His writing on graduate school and higher education has appeared in the *Chronicle of Higher Education* and *Vitae*.

ROBERT WEISBUCH

Former president of the Woodrow Wilson National Fellowship Foundation and Drew University

Robert Weisbuch has a long history as an advocate for normalizing non-academic careers since his time at the Woodrow Wilson National Fellowship Foundation where he led two initiatives, The Humanities at Work and, with Earl Lewis, The Responsive PhD. Literature on the latter and another pamphlet, "Diversity and the Doctorate," are available on the Foundation website. In 2016, he coauthored "Reforming Doctoral Education, 1990 to 2015: Recent Initiatives and Future Prospects" with Leonard Cassuto for the Andrew M. Mellon Foundation, and that report became the seed for their coauthored study, *The New PhD: How to Build a Better Graduate Education* (2021). His essays on serving as a college president and on other topics in higher education have appeared in the *Chronicle of Higher Education* and *Inside Higher Ed*

KAREN S. WILSON

Graduate career officer, UCLA History Department

Karen S. Wilson works closely with the American Historical Association's Career Diversity for Historians Pilot Program at UCLA, funded by the Andrew W. Mellon Foundation. Her position puts her in partnerships with faculty and graduate students to create career paths.

Index

ABD (All But Dissertation), 43, 126, 177, 189n6
academia, outside, 56, 58–67, 68n6, 96, 162–163
academic administration: career, 43–44, 169, 173; outside academia and, 68n6; skills, 107; with systemic change in graduate education, 10
academic publishing: author platform and, 25, 26, 39n5; costs, 27, 40n20; crisis and, 40n13; influence economy and, 25, 29–32, 35–38; prestige regime in, 24–29, 32–35; state of, 39n7; trends in, 26–27, 31; university presses and, 25–26, 27–29
acting, for professional connections, 52, 98
action, call to: administrators, 156–157; digital humanities career, 156–157; faculty, 155; students, 153–154
action, collective: action to, 176–189; as advocate, 183–184; with collective institutional readiness, 184–189; as editor/publisher, 178–181; versatility and, 182–183
actionable, networking as, 90
administrative work: humanities PhDs in, 8; skills, 158n6; teaching and, 39n4
administrators, call to action, 156–157
admissions: graduate programs and, 81–83; internships, 17
adviser-advisee relationships: challenges of new model for, 45–48; generational

determinism with, 42; leadership and, 48–52, 76; practices and attitudes, xvii, 43–45; teaching within, 44–45, 48
African Americans: literary form and realism, 60; slave narratives, 60–61
Alliance for Networking Visual Culture, 150
Alumni Relations Office, 20
Alvarado, Rafael, 66–67
ambiguity, with graduate education and change, 55–56
American Academy, 6
American Alliance of Museums, 167
American Anthropological Association, 165
American Association of University Professors, 158n5
American Chemical Society, 188
American Council of Learned Societies, 61, 164
American Geophysical Union, 165
American Historical Association (AHA), 19, 41n30, 61, 120, 131n3; Career Contacts, 169; career diversity and, 8, 22n1, 39n8, 165; Career Diversity Initiative, 22n1, 121; role of, 188
American Philosophical Association, 165
American Philosophical Society, 151
American Quarterly, 157
"American Scholar, The" (Emerson), 21
Andrew W. Mellon Foundation, 18, 22n1, 82, 147

217

96; outside STEM, 89; as resource, 129; team players and, 90. *See also* networking
collegiality, 168, 174
colonial biases, 152
Columbia University, 14, 141n1
communication: oral skills, 172, 181; scholarly, 34, 107, 147, 148; written skills, 171–172
community, orientations and, 83–86
community college: Community College Research Center, 141n1; East Los Angeles Community College, 139; role of, 85; as safe haven, 140; teaching at, xviii, 15–16, 133–135, 136, 137, 169
Community College Research Center, Columbia University, 141n1
compatible skills, 159n24
conferences: planning before arrival, 93–94; professional connections and, 92–94
Cooper, Mark Garrett, 69n20
corporate work, 163
COSEPUP report, 12
costs: academic publishing, 27, 40n20; with digital humanities career and salary range, 147; Ithaka cost study, 40n20
Council of Graduate Schools, 9, 107, 176, 184, 188
Council on Foundations, 167
COVID-19 pandemic, xiii, 5, 22, 27, 141, 176
crises: in academic job market, 120; financial, 5; jobs, 6; museums and existential, 61; public health, 27; scholarly publishing and, 40n13
cross disciplines, professional connections, 96–97
culture: Alliance for Networking Visual Culture, 150; disrupted through familiarity and forced collaboration, 126–128
curriculum vitae (CV), xix, 32, 36, 84, 97, 174. *See also* resumes

Damrosch, David, 14
DAM (digital asset management) systems, 150
data: Integrated Postsecondary Education Data System, 141n1; transparency with departmental outcomes, 135; visualization, 148

Debates in the Digital Humanities (Gold), 142, 153–154
Debelius, Maggie, 101, 113
degree-granting institutions, in higher education, 40n12
deliverable products, 170
Des Jardin, Molly, 155
development internships, 17
Dewey, John, 21, 183
diary research guide, 151, 158n16
Dickinson, Emily, 22
digital asset management (DAM) systems, 150
digital humanities (DH): Boston Digital Humanities, 68n3; collaboration and, 156; in job advertisements, 158n6; skills requested in job advertisements, 148
digital humanities (DH) career: administrators and, 156–157; calls to action, 153–157; faculty and, 155; from fellowship to employment, 149–153; GLAM alternative and, 147–149; graduate students and, 142–143, 153–154; job market, 144–147; job postings, 145; methodology, 143–144; salary range, 147
Digital Humanities Now (DHNOW), 143–144
Digital Library Federation (DLF) 2018 Forum, 148
Digital Paxton, 151–152, 157
digital scholarship, 142, 145, 148, 151, 157n3, 167
digital skills, 145
digital technologies, 55
digital tools, 64, 68n18, 154
Dirks, Nicholas B., 56, 62
disciplinary journals, 165
discussion forum, STEM, 177
diversity, 51; pedagogy and, 53. *See also* career diversity
doctoral degrees (PhDs): awarded in humanities, 7; career tracks for, 24, 119–120; lifetime earnings with, 78; occupational distribution of, 4; as professional degree, 11; skills, 59–60, 64–65; STEM, 7, 8, 179, 188; training for, 62–64, 78–79, 82–83. *See also* graduate education; humanities PhDs
Doktorvater (doctor-father), 46